GRAHAM
HENRY
The X Factor

Proudly supported by

GRAHAM HENRY
The X Factor

With Bob Howitt

Queen Anne Press

Acknowledgements

I would like to acknowledge John Graham, Alan Faull and the members of the Auckland Grammar School 1st XV's of 1975 - 1980. The Auckland University Rugby Club and the players of the senior team from 1981 - 1986. Rex Davy, John Graham, Mac McCallion, George Duncan, Paul Wilson, Graham Paterson, Jim Blair and members of the Auckland and Auckland Blues rugby teams from 1987 - 1998. The staff and students of Kelston Boys High School. The Welsh Rugby Union, David Pickering, Trevor James, Steve Black, Lyn Howells, Allen Lewis and the members of the Welsh Team. Without their support, dedication, skill, and friendship, none of the enclosed would have been possible. Finally, a big thank you to author Bob Howitt, David Jones, and publisher Bill Honeybone and the team at Celebrity Books for encouraging me to undertake the project.

©1999 Copyright: Graham Henry

Queen Anne Press
is a division of
Lennard Associates Limited
Mackerye End, Harpenden
Herts AL5 5DR

First published in 1999 by:
Celebrity Books, New Zealand.

ISBN 1-85291-623-0

Layout/design by Benefitz Graphics Ltd, Takapuna, Auckland.
Typeset by Benefitz Graphics Ltd.
Cover Art by Dallas Bennett.
Printed and Bound in Wales by WBC Book Manufacturers, Bridgend

Contents

Foreword 7

1 Anyone for cricket?.. 11

2 Step aside, Maurice.. 35

3 Hitting the zone 57

4 So long Zinny, farewell Fitzy 79

5 Weighing up the offers 95

6 'I'm off to Wales!' 115

7 Come in, the Redeemer 123

8 A woman's perspective 143

9 Come on, Cymru! 153

10 Finding the winning edge 179

11 Anatomy of a rugby team 195

12 And so to the World Cup.............................. 215

Dedication

To Raewyn whose personal sacrifice, understanding
and support far exceeds my highest expectations.
To Matthew, Catherine and Andrew for being positive young
people who accepted and supported my dedication to rugby.
To my parents Allen and Ann for their
unconditional love and support over 53 years.

Foreword

GRAHAM HENRY HAS ALWAYS been single-mindedly focussed. I taught him history in the sixth form at Christchurch Boys' High School. During one history lesson close to a University Entrance accrediting examination, I had been successfully side-tracked by less eager scholars to discuss the weekend test match.

Henry, a fanatical schoolboy first XV and first XI player, interrupted me in full flight, saying, "Sir, I want to get accredited this year, could we please stick to the subject?" I reluctantly returned to the machinations of Otto von Bismark!

Henry was accredited in history that year. I have known him well since and his progress has been marked by a similar focus, determination and success.

Graham Henry has been a restless, driven soul, never fully satisfied with his lot and that became one of his personal strengths. He has not been prepared to just let things happen, rather he set himself targets, went for them and having reached them, set himself new challenges.

Some, in his early days, thought the young man was flying too high. He went to university and gained a Physical Education Diploma and began his teaching career, soon finding progress in education restricted by lack of a degree qualification.

Typically, he set about getting this while working full time at Auckland Grammar School and by extra-mural study at Massey University. This was an enormously challenging workload for him and, moreover, his full-time job did not suffer because of the extra demands on his personal time.

A degree ensured his promotion and his eventual leadership of a major boys' secondary school in Auckland. He simply saw this progress through the ranks to the top as his due - he had worked for it and had no doubts about his ability to handle the job.

At the same time as he was climbing the professional education ladder - and he was a fine schoolmaster and a successful principal - he began to develop remarkable skills as a rugby coach.

In the early 1980s, he produced some of the best first fifteens in Auckland Grammar School's long rugby tradition. Typically, as he achieved unbeaten years and Auckland secondary school championships, he sought more challenging coaching roles. That restless, driven streak again.

"I'm getting bored, DJ," was a statement that always meant he was about to move on from whatever current role he had mastered. He looked towards coaching a provincial team and learned that an outstanding schoolboy coach in Auckland could not aspire to provincial coaching without serving a successful apprenticeship on the club rugby scene.

Henry, who had played senior rugby for Auckland University, coached that club to a Gallaher Shield win. First mission accomplished.

This success led in quick succession to the Auckland Colts, Auckland B and then the prestigious A team. His remarkable success with the A team is well documented, but typically again Henry had to move on. During these years he was an amateur coach while still running his secondary school.

The challenges of schoolmastering were diminishing in Henry's eyes and the advent of the professional rugby coach was, for him, a masterpiece of timing. He became a full-time professional rugby coach and, because of his reputation, commanded a remuneration which dwarfed his miserly public servant's salary. His successes in NPC and Super 12 championships predictably spurred him to seek the real challenge. "I'm getting bored again, DJ." He was also aware that professional coaches do not always have a lengthy career.

Henry indicated to the NZRFU he was interested in coaching the All Blacks, the final goal in his driven progress. To this point, he had successfully met all his self-imposed targets. This final prize eludes him. Can we say he has failed? Or have others failed to see in him those special qualities that have led to him succeeding spectacularly with every significant team he has coached?

The driven nature of the man, combined with an almost ruthless determination to achieve his goals, did not always endear him to less perceptive rugby administrators. He was often unnecessarily dismissive of them and this counted against him.

However, his whole focus as a coach was on his team and the management group that he built around himself. From these men, players and managers, he earned a respect which developed into a healthy loyalty. This is one of his special qualities as a coach.

As his teams grew in confidence and success, so did the bonds between Henry, his players and their managers grow. He is a fearless and very able selector, being on the one hand prepared to drop stars when they are not performing and on the other able to spot a raw talent which he can develop into his team's pattern.

He is that rare phenomenon amongst rugby coaches who can dissect, analyse and intellectualise the game rather than rely on a superficial, blood and guts, emotional approach.

He spends hours viewing tapes, looking at patterns, seeking small but crucial innovations which will give his team the edge. He is clear on his team's pattern and tactics, based on his thinking, arguing and talking about rugby and his assessment of his own team's strengths and the ability and weaknesses of his opponents.

He then has the uncanny knack of coaching his players as to how each game should be played. Each week's training is based exclusively on the next weekend's opponents. Trainings are planned and focussed and each player understands the team's patterns and where he fits into it. His team talks on the day of a match quietly, firmly and convincingly focus on the previous week's preparation and tactics.

Guts, pride, physical commitment are assumed by Henry as given in a rugby player. He demands that the players apply their skill, their concentration, their knowledge of the game, coached and imparted week by week, to the match ahead. He urges his players to seek personal excellence in their positions and to constantly look for quality team performance.

Graham Henry coaches a rugby team. He does not just train it and that is what makes him so special. Moreover, in spite of his pursuit for excellence in his players he gives them space and time to themselves, which keeps them fresh and keen to perform. He has a passion for rugby and that intense personal determination that has marked his development as arguably the most able coach in the game today.

Graham Henry's restless relationship with job satisfaction, which has characterised his progress through life, inevitably meant that once he believed he was good enough to coach an international side he expected that such would be his due.

As the top practising New Zealand coach, the All Black job was his obvious target. The NZRFU did not see it this way. It was intimated he should wait his turn. Typically impatient (and probably bored again), Henry sadly but understandably accepted the Welsh position, one fraught with potential disaster for a professional coach.

His record suggests he will continue to be successful and Wales will prosper. Before he retires he should be given the final recognition of an ambitious, remarkably successful New Zealand coach – the job of coaching the All Blacks. That would appropriately recognise Graham Henry's record and talent.

D. J. (John) Graham, CBE
May 1999

Chapter 1

Anyone for cricket?

A teacher needs to find the trigger inside each student that will release his or her best work. Some students need to be pushed, others need space. Some need every detail explained, others work better on instinct.

Tara van Derveer, women's basketball coach,
Stanford University

I GUESS THE GRAHAM HENRY STORY, the Graham Henry sporting story, that is, starts with a cricket theme. Not that I wasn't passionate about rugby from my earliest days, growing up in a family where my parents were totally supportive. I mean, I played in the Christchurch Boys' High School first fifteen and followed the All Blacks so avidly I could quote you every test score from the late 1950s and early 1960s.

No, cricket became my consuming passion for a while because of a lucky break I received in my first year out of college. You see, John Ward broke a finger. John Ward of South Canterbury. John Ward, who was the best wicketkeeper in New Zealand by a mile at the time.

But you can't keep wickets with a broken finger. Mac Anderson, the Canterbury selector, knew that. He obviously needed a replacement and for some obscure reason he selected Graham Henry, an enthusiastic young fellow who'd performed energetically with the gloves for the highly successful Christchurch Boys' High School first eleven, a team that featured several individuals who would make their mark nationally – Dayle Hadlee, David Trist, Cran Bull, Alan Hounsell and Robert Anderson.

Robert Anderson was the son of Mac and his presence in the first eleven probably accounted for the Canterbury coach looking in on our team more than he might otherwise have done. Which is obviously where he spotted me bounding around behind the stumps. I'd actually come into the first eleven as a fourth former, getting my break when exam commitments rendered several more senior individuals unavailable.

If we thought *our* team was garlanded with talented cricketers, when we played our annual game against Auckland Grammar School we encountered Mark Burgess, Hedley Howarth, Ross Dykes, Terry Jarvis, John Millener, Rex Hooton and the incomparable Grahame Thorne. They were a marvellous team. We were certainly the two strongest cricket colleges in the country and we had some classic encounters.

Anyway, there I was one year out of college suddenly being rushed into the Canterbury team as wicketkeeper. It would have been a daunting experience in any circumstances but that year it so happened that Canterbury's bowling attack was spearheaded by Gary Bartlett, arguably the quickest bowler in the world at the time, backed up by Dick Motz and Bruce Taylor, also hostile and also New Zealand representatives.

It was what you might describe as a fearsome learning experience! Bartlett was sensationally quick and fired a lot of short deliveries down the leg side. I have never been so sore in my life, diving all over the place to retrieve his thunderbolts. I recall on one occasion being knocked flat by a ball which struck me in the chest. Bartlett showed no compassion. "Get up, you little prick, and take the next one!" he barked at me.

In those days the new ball was taken when the opposition posted 200 runs. I remember one Plunket Shield encounter in which Central Districts was fighting desperately to avoid outright defeat. The Central tailenders, interested only in survival and not in scoring runs, had stalled on 170.

Brian Hastings, our captain, decided to become proactive, ordering me to let 30 byes through in a hurry so we could claim the new ball. It didn't do anything for my reputation as a wicketkeeper, suddenly having 30 byes posted against me, but it did allow the skip to reactivate Bartlett with a bright new cherry. I'd like to record that we finished them off and claimed outright points but Murray Chapple and Dave Kinsella hung in doggedly, defying us until stumps.

They were exciting times. I was young and reckless and thrilled to be involved. It's still a bit of a mystery how I got there for I was desperately short on club experience, let alone representative experience, when first selected. I'm sure no one ranks me among the great Canterbury wicketkeepers, but I survived, gloved most of the catches that came my way, effected the occasional stumping and it can probably be said I justified Mac Anderson's faith in me. It was an experience I would recall on occasions when I became an influential representative selector myself. Should I risk an untried young player I consider has the potential to succeed? Why not? Someone took a huge gamble on me 30 years ago and we all survived.

My cricketing career didn't blossom in the manner of so many of those around me, probably, I suspect, because I always felt I had more potential than I was ever able to justify. Although I got to represent Otago while studying at Otago University, I never managed to displace Barry Milburn, another wicketkeeper who would represent his country. I was utilised as an opening batsman but never scored enough runs to justify a continued existence in the team.

Rugby would eventually come to dominate my life but for a long time cricket shared equal status. Indeed, with a little more encouragement when I was teaching in Christchurch in the 1970s, I might have given more to cricket as a coach.

Because Christchurch Boys' High was a school built on tradition, seniority counted ahead of ability when it came to the appointment of coaches. When I indicated my interest in taking a team, the master in charge of the sport offered me the under-14 sevens. That is, the seventh-best team of players aged under 14 which, as you can imagine, was a seriously long way down the pecking order.

Being an upstart, I said no, I wouldn't waste my time. Whereupon the cricket master and I engaged in an animated discussion. He insisted that because I was the newest teacher in the school, I had to start at the bottom. I reminded him that I had played at representative level which I believed gave me an important qualification that most, if not all, of the other coaches lacked. As a result of our discussion, I finished up coaching the under-14 firsts!

I was enormously fortunate that my parents, Allen and Ann, were so supportive in my formative years. They would have preferred that I was a better student less obsessed with sport but they nevertheless gave me every encouragement. My only brother, Brian, 19 months my senior, was a far more diligent scholar than I. He finished up as head accountant of the National Bank and these days works as an accountant with the Labour Department.

My parents, people of strong, sound principles, never purchased anything unless they could afford it. And they repeatedly stressed the value of a complete education. Sport, they often reminded me, would never provide me with a living. We often have a giggle about that these days! Aged 84 and 83, they still live in Christchurch, in Matai St, only 200 metres from Boys' High, the school that their sons attended.

My early years were in Auckland with my father in the RNZAF, based at Hobsonville. He flew Catalinas and Sunderlands around the Pacific Islands until failing sight meant he lost his pilot's licence. After that, the family moved back to Christchurch where he operated a busy service station in Riccarton Road. Commitments on Saturday mornings meant he was seldom available to deliver Brian and I to our sporting venues and therefore seldom saw us play. But most Saturday afternoons in winter, he'd take Brian and I, and my mother's father, along to Lancaster Park to watch the feature senior club game of the week.

If my sporting career flourished the first year out of Christchurch Boys' High, academically I was a disaster. I took all the wrong advice when I enrolled at university, deciding to pursue an arts degree … in the subjects I was weakest at. What I really wanted to do was have a go at a physical education degree but I let other people convince me that there was no future in phys-ed, that I'd get bored in my thirties.

While I was succeeding as a sportsman, playing cricket for

Canterbury and senior rugby for Old Boys, academically I was a write-off. It was a goofy experiment that failed; I didn't pass a paper, unlike Brian, who was powering ahead towards his B.Com degree and a stirling career in the bank. The third member of the family, Carol, seven years my junior, was a talented musician, who won several provincial awards with her piano playing. She married a construction engineer, Trevor Kempton, and now lives in Dunedin with three children. In recent years she has attended Teachers College and now teaches children with learning handicaps.

If the bank was right for Brian, obviously it was a good place for Graham. Right? Wrong! After six months I was bored out of my tree. I was no closer to knowing what my true vocation was but I most definitely knew it wasn't functioning as a teller and would-be accountant/manager at the National Bank.

My next employment was with Firestone, the tyre people, as a serviceman working heaps of shift work. For the first time since leaving Boys' High, I actually knew what I was doing. This wasn't a career move. This was a stepping stone towards the next important stage of my life. It paid huge money, money that would allow me to move south to Dunedin and enrol at Otago University in pursuit of the physical education degree I knew was my calling.

What a transformation. Instead of forcing myself to concentrate on classical literature or whatever, I found myself completely immersed in my studies. This was me. This was what Graham Henry had been put on this planet for. I was always a lover of sport and from a surprisingly young age I had urges to coach. So working towards a degree in physical education was perfect for me, because the coaching of sports teams was a natural extension of those studies.

That the degree involved such subjects as exercise physiology, sports psychology, nutrition, motivation and fitness training prepared me ideally for the rugby coaching that would soon enough become such a major part of my existence and, eventually, take over my whole life.

I always felt, although it's not something I have ever bragged about, that my physical education degree gave me a huge advantage over the average rugby coach who might have trained in marketing, economics, medicine or whatever.

After the futility of my studies at Canterbury University, it was enormously gratifying to graduate in Dunedin. Indeed, I can state that I have never failed a paper since that terrible year in Christchurch. It was part of the great learning curve which we must all experience. Although it was thoroughly depressing at the time, I believe I was a better person for enduring it. What it taught me was that you should never let other people make the important decisions for you. Heed their advice by all means but make your own decisions, basing them on your own knowledge and instincts.

So much of my training and preparation of rugby teams relates back to those delightful days in Dunedin. I'd always been interested in the scientific side of sport and therefore related strongly to my studies on the conditioning of sports teams. In this now-professional rugby age, it's essential to relate to young people, people on the move. Though some critics back in New Zealand felt my relationship with my players was not always perfect, I believe one of my strengths as a coach was my ability to manage people in groups. Organising a rugby team is really an extension of your training as a teacher of education. The organisation of training sessions equals flow and intensity which equals how you play on a Saturday. My background in education was invaluable when I became a serious rugby coach.

Once graduated, I returned to Christchurch to attend Teachers College. Now here's a topic on which I have really strong views. This being essentially a rugby book, I won't digress too far, but I believe trainee teachers should operate as apprentices in schools rather than have to endure endless classes at Teachers College. Some professional development is necessary but with a vastly reduced workload. Aspiring teachers should be at the coal-face, with the kids. The Government is wasting a huge amount of money, in my opinion, keeping them at Teachers College.

While coaching would deliver me my greatest rewards in rugby, I have many fond memories of my days as a player. All Black selectors were never interested in me. And if the representative coaches of Otago, Canterbury and Auckland, the three unions in which I played at senior club level as a first-five, thought I exuded rare talent, they disguised their enthusiasm well. I played for Union and University in Dunedin, High School Old Boys in Christchurch and University in Auckland.

The four seasons I had with High School Old Boys after my

return to Christchurch were thoroughly enjoyable. They were a comparatively weak side when I linked up with them in 1970. With no obvious captain in the squad, I was the man for one of those seasons. We developed a marvellous team spirit and played good quality rugby with an average assortment of players. We had no individual stars and precious few representatives but we were always at the top end of the competition and narrowly lost the final to Christchurch, in the rain, one year.

Our coach for two of those seasons (1971 and 1972) was John Graham, a distinguished All Black loose forward of the 1960s who had been my history and social studies teacher at Christchurch Boys' High. He would come to have a major influence on my destiny.

When John Graham quit Christchurch (having moved across to Linwood High School as the head of the history and social studies) at the beginning of 1973 to take up the appointment of headmaster at Auckland Grammar School, he asked me whether I would be interested in heading north myself should a suitable position become available. I must have replied in the affirmative because a few months later he telephoned to offer me a post teaching physical education. I jumped at the offer and by the beginning of the third term in 1973 was settled in Auckland. It would take another too-good-to-refuse offer a quarter of a century later before I would abandon the Queen City.

A question I'm often asked is where and when I first coached a rugby team. The answer is no show stopper. It was while I was involved with the High School Old Boys club. Another guy and I decided to prepare a colts team for an end-of-season competition. I didn't see it as the start of anything big. In fact, I can't even remember how successful we were. I was in my mid-twenties at the time, utterly enthusiastic and wholly consumed by sport. Just being involved was satisfaction enough.

Prior to that while teaching at Boys' High, I had helped out with midweek kids' teams. Not really as a coach. More as an organiser, as teachers were in those days. Junior schools rugby was pretty low-key in Christchurch at the time. It was organised for Wednesday afternoon and not that well accepted. The greater rugby emphasis was on Saturday morning when many of the same kids turned out for their clubs. It wasn't at all like Auckland where all school grades operated on Saturday mornings.

It was refreshing to come under the John Graham umbrella. An outstanding headmaster, he set high standards for the staff and the students and was ever ready to recognise and promote talent. In the Christchurch setting, you had to wait until someone died before an opening occurred. At Auckland Grammar, if John Graham felt you had ability, he gave you the opportunity to express it.

The 1974 rugby season, during which I turned 28, is one I recall with great fondness. It ranks right up there with some of those vintage years of the nineties when NPC successes and Super 12 triumphs were being strung together.

And it was all so unexpected. Having paid my membership to the University club at Merton Road, I turned up expecting to play socially. That was until the first-five in the senior team broke his leg. When they starting looked around for a replacement, there weren't that many of us with experience in the position. Step forward, Graham Henry.

We fielded the oldest backline in the world. It featured three Peters brothers (of which Winston, not for his rugby exploits, became the most famous), Dave Palmer (who would die in the Erebus air crash) and Gary Weinberg, who'd each played at representative level, Grahame Thorne, who in his inimitable fashion was still, at 28, commanding headlines, Peter Collis and myself.

Our pack included such seasoned performers as Denis Thorn, Greg Denholm, Dave Syms, Mac Fatialofa and Ken Baguley. Our coach was Bob Graham, John's brother. After starting the season with no expectations whatsoever we sneaked through the back door to win.

Such things as play-offs didn't exist in those days. The team that finished with the most championship points claimed the Gallaher Shield. We obviously weren't expected to succeed because we were allocated Eden Park No 2 for our final fixture. We won while Suburbs, co-leader going into that final weekend, was toppled by Ponsonby in the main encounter. When the dust settled, it was to the realisation that University had claimed the title. It was a marvellous year and afforded an excellent introduction to Auckland society.

NEW ZEALAND HERALD
24 August 1974

The Auckland Rugby Union's hopes for a thrill-packed last-second decision on the Gallaher Shield quietly ebbed away at Eden Park on Saturday.

Only 200 people watched University deal to Manukau on the back ground while Suburbs saw its championship hopes blown away by Ponsonby. Had Suburbs won, there would have been a midweek play-off at Eden Park.

It was an affecting moment as University marched across to the No 1 field to get the trophy, the players hoisting captain Dave Syms on to their shoulders in celebration.

The winning of the Gallaher Shield was only part of the rugby delight I experienced that year. Nev McMillan, Grammar's history master who won acclaim in later years as a statistician and author of such renowned works as *Men in Black* and *The Encyclopedia of New Zealand Rugby*, and I were appointed to coach the Auckland Grammar 3A side.

It wasn't long before Nev and I realised we possessed uncommon talent in the side, particularly along the backline which I was fortunate enough to be responsible for. At first-five was Nicky Allen, who would represent his country (with distinction) at the age of 22, in the midfield was John Collinson, who would play a lot of games for Auckland, and at fullback and on one wing were two of quickest sprinters in New Zealand, Gary Henley-Smith and Peter Beguley. In 1975 at the senior nationals, they would finish first and second in the 100 metres dash.

With talent like that in the backline, it wasn't too challenging for Nev and me to formulate a game plan. At every opportunity we moved the ball to the wingers, who spent most of the season running away scoring tries. We won the competition undefeated.

I suppose I could have overwhelmed myself with modesty at the 3A team's stunning success. "Aw-shucks," I could have proffered to John Graham, "we just had so much talent, anybody could have coached that team to win the championship." But that wasn't how I approached him. After one epoch-making year in Auckland, I was ready for bigger challenges. I told him I wanted to coach the first fifteen!

It should be explained here that while the 3A team had performed heroics, the first fifteen had experienced a rather dismal time in 1974, losing several of its traditional fixtures and going down to New Plymouth Boys' High by a large score.

John Graham was a former All Black and therefore accustomed to success. I knew him to be a winner and I knew he wouldn't be happy with a losing first fifteen because rugby is vitally important to schools like Auckland Grammar and forms an integral part of the school.

There wasn't a lot of discussion at the time. But when 1975 rolled around, Derek Stubbs, the head of physics who had prepared the first fifteen the previous year, and myself were named joint coaches. We were to form a happy and successful partnership. Indeed, through '75 and '76 the team was unbeaten.

I must confess that even in those days I had an ambition to coach Auckland and the All Blacks. It was just a seed in the back of my mind. You have to be an idiot to believe in your twenties that you will go on to become a representative coach, or better. But there's nothing wrong with ambition. If you're a talented player, you should aim to become an All Black. If you're a successful coach, you should set equally challenging goals.

Anyway, back in '75, long before anyone identified Graham Henry as a potential Auckland (and Welsh) coach, I was fortunate to be able to call on several of the pupils who'd helped make the 3A team great the previous season, notably Allen, a player with all the attacking gifts in the world, Collinson, the flying winger Beguley and fullback Henley-Smith.

The '76 team was captained by John Drake who would anchor the All Black World Cup-winning scrum 11 years later. John was a guy for whom I had a lot of respect – a straight shooter who was an excellent coach of the scrum. I used him many times to set the platform early season with the Colts, Auckland and the Blues. When coaching, he was a man of few words... but most of them were gems.

One player who didn't make the starting fifteen in 1976 because, in his own words, he was "fat and lazy" and didn't possess any burning desire to play rugby at the time, was Gary Whetton. Gary and his twin brother Alan wouldn't feature regularly in the first fifteen until 1977 as seventh formers. However, the team did include

John Mills, another who would go on to represent his country. Ironically, Mills and John Buchan, who came into the first XV the next year, operated as loose forwards at school. Both would win their All Black spurs as hookers.

The school provided the perfect environment for preparing a rugby team. The kids were always on tap and we'd train at 3.30pm. They were intelligent, keen, talented and wanted to play. A coach couldn't ask for more.

I guess I was a lateral thinker even in those early days. I was prepared to introduce concepts that hadn't been attempted before. One was setting a flat backline, with both five-eighths and the centre virtually standing still and expediting the ball to the speedy blokes on the outside. Bearing in mind that Henley-Smith had established a New Zealand sprint record of 10.4s and that Beguley was almost as fast, you can imagine how many runaway tries we scored.

Peter Beguley isn't a name that will feature on anyone's list of great New Zealand rugby players, yet he was the best winger I ever coached. A player of rare skill with blistering pace, he could step anyone. He was big, with an in/out swerve – the outstanding individual in a team of huge talent. But unfortunately, he was forced to abandon physical sport after sustaining a stress fracture in the back.

By comparison with the two seasons that preceded it, 1977 wasn't a notable year at Auckland Grammar. Notwithstanding the presence of the Whetton brothers in the scrum, the team performed modestly. Fourth was our lot. And yet 1977 is a year vividly etched in my memory – for two reasons.

The first was that I coached rugby that winter while on crutches. I'd snapped my Achilles tendon playing cricket and spent seemingly endless months in a plaster cast. It all happened because I'd approached John Graham telling him I had too much on my plate, trying to coach the first cricket eleven as well as rugby. He released me from my cricket commitments, whereupon I volunteered my services to the Cornwall club, who found a place in their senior line-up for me along with such distinguished representative performers as Graham Vivian, Rodney Redmond, Dave Anderson, John Kasper and Arch Taylor.

I was enjoying the season immensely, until I tried to glance a ball to leg from Gary Troup in a match against Papatoetoe and went down in a screaming heap, my Achilles blown.

The other reason 1977 comes so easily to mind is because of the emergence of a most remarkable player. Late in 1976, one of the boys in the hostel suggested I go down to the bottom ground at Grammar and check out a third former playing for the sixth grade side who was apparently raising a few eyebrows. I found this fellow kicking goals from the sideline out of the mud. He could run and chip-kick. In fact, there didn't seem to be anything he couldn't do. He was absolutely brilliant. I inquired his name. Grant Fox, they told me.

So late in 1977 when we took the Auckland Grammar first fifteen on a tour of Fiji, we included a few young guys. Grant Fox, then a fourth former, was among them.

GRANT FOX
The team for the tour of Fiji was announced at school assembly. One of the names read out was Fox. I was more curious than anything because there were two guys named Fox playing rugby, myself and Andy, a sixth former. After assembly, we approached Graham Henry to determine which one of us had been selected. To my astonishment, because I had not the foggiest idea anyone had even been looking my way, it was me.

We played a match against the Fijian outer islands in which every member of the opposition fronted up in bare feet. So we played in bare feet as well. It didn't stop young Fox, who was troubled by a sore hamstring, from kicking a penalty goal from halfway.

He was obviously a footballer of extraordinary talent, causing me to select him at first-five for our "test" against Combined Suva Schools. Although effectively operating on one leg, he performed beautifully and was in essence the difference between the two teams. Afterwards, though, he was in considerable pain. And not just because of an ugly brawl that erupted and caused the match to be abandoned 10 minutes early. Young Fox was carrying a serious injury.

Upon our return, Grant and I went to see a sports medicine

expert who was horrified at the extent of the injury. Our star fourth former had torn the muscle tendon off the bone. In the opinion of the specialist, Fox would never play rugby again. It wasn't the diagnosis either Fox or I wanted. So I then referred him to Graeme Hayhow, an Auckland physiotherapist who'd worked closely with sports teams. He conceded that it was a serious injury but believed he could put it right.

On Hayhow's instructions, we set up a pulley at the hostel and throughout the summer Grant religiously worked away strengthening the muscle. The fact he went on to accumulate more than 4000 points in a celebrated first-class career demonstrates how diligently he applied himself to the recovery process. But then again, when it came to sport, Foxy applied himself diligently to everything he attempted.

Foxy spent the next three years as the kingpin of the first fifteen. We effectively lived together because he boarded at the hostel of which I was the master. We spent endless hours talking sport, mostly rugby and mostly tactics. Foxy was Foxy, hugely competitive, frighteningly so.

GRANT FOX
I related to Graham right from the start because we had the same analytical approach to rugby. He was a meticulous planner and researcher who as a coach believed in playing to your team's strengths and away from the opposition's. That exactly equalled my philosophy. This was the side of the game I enjoyed and together we spent a lot of time plotting strategies.

At training, we'd usually start with a touch contest between the forwards and the backs with me refereeing. They invariably became blood matches and I'd get abused from both sides. I recall on one occasion making a mistake, whereupon Foxy walked off. That's how competitive he was. He was a marvellous student, in all senses. He had a map of the field in his mind and could visualise any given situation. He was years ahead of his time in running the game. I can only describe him as extraordinary.

In Foxy's final year, Auckland Grammar was the New Zealand representative at the Pan Pacific Youth tournament in Taiwan, of all places. We confronted some huge teams – Tonga, Western Samoa and Australia. Without Foxy, we could have been in trouble but he guided us through every game and in the final, against Tonga, scored all the points including a try, which was unusual for him.

Much of the philosophy I would apply when I became coach of Auckland some 15 years on was formulated in those years at Auckland Grammar, a good bit of it in animated, after-hours discussions with Foxy.

One thing I was guilty of in those days, which I've since exorcised from my personality, I'm pleased to report, was the abuse of players. Because I always wanted my teams to win, I would abuse the players fearfully in practice situations. I said things to schoolboys then I wouldn't dare say to experienced international players now. Society has changed, for the better, thank goodness. And so has Graham Henry!

As I developed as a coach, I came to appreciate that it is important to be innovative. You've got to think outside the square and not just use everybody else's ideas. Auckland Grammar won a lot of games back in the seventies because we were original.

ALLAN FAULL
Auckland Grammar first XV manager
Under Graham's guidance the first fifteen won 41 matches on the trot. When you were coached by Graham, you were coached. Every player knew what he had to do. There were diagrams and blackboards, which the kids soaked up. They loved him. During games, Graham never stalked the sideline shouting like some coaches. He stood, usually behind the goalposts, quietly observing. He was a brilliant reader of play and with a few instructions at halftime he could change the whole complexion of a game.

Graham could see a player and know exactly which position suited him. He spotted Martin Crowe playing soccer, recognised his natural talents and introduced him into the first fifteen as a winger. Martin finished up as the top tryscorer.

I recall one year we had a diminutive, if big-hearted, player at centre, Rhys Humphries. Things were fine until we came up against St Paul's College which had a giant in the No 15 jersey, James Buutveld, a New Zealand schools representative. I decided we would operate a one-out defensive system. It's common now but we may have been the first in New Zealand to apply it. My guys were thoroughly bemused when I first explained it, but I knew Buutveld would run over the top of us if we played an orthodox backline defence. Against St Paul's we used the one-out defence, with Humphries concentrating on Buutveld, who was completely thrown by what we were doing.

We won that game but unfortunately in a match later in the year against Sacred Heart, their young fullback Kieran Crowley (another All Black in the making) kicked several important penalty goals which halted our winning sequence, allowing St Paul's to share the championship with us.

One year, we were lacking in sizable locks and used Craig Reid and Rangi Moeka, neither of whom weighed more than eleven and a half stone. If they were going to survive in the Auckland schools competition, they needed hardening. So we practised with our tight five against the eight forwards from the second fifteen, working on lineouts, rucks and mauls. Then we packed between 30 and 40 scrums, five against eight, till our guys were crying. It toughened them up.

Our right winger in 1980 was a strapping lad called Martin Crowe who would go on to become a cricketing celebrity. He was our leading tryscorer, not because of dancing feet or electrifying pace, although he was talented. No, he benefited more than anyone I can think of from Foxy's genius. Foxy devised all these clever moves down the right-hand blindside which invariably left Martin with an unopposed run to the goalline. He was a champion finisher, although half the time all he had to do was catch the ball and fall over the line.

They were stimulating times back then. It was nothing to have 10,000 spectators ringing the field for our annual clash with King's College. King's was always competitive, as was Sacred Heart, while the school that was coming through was Kelston Boys' High, a college I would have a lot to do with in later years. In 1977, Kelston interrupted our winning sequence, taking out the championship .

I coached Auckland Grammar on my own from 1978 to 1980.

Thanks to Foxy's major input, we won the championship every year, completing the '79 and '80 seasons undefeated.

MURRAY DEAKER
Radio sports talkback host
I used to travel down from Orewa, where I was living, to watch the Auckland Grammar first fifteen play because what they were doing, inspired by Graham, was revolutionary. He was the best schoolboy coach I ever saw in my life. Schools rugby had traditionally been played between the two 22s, but Graham had developed patterns and strategies that were stunningly effective. He experimented with a flat backline, pretty radical stuff at schoolboy level, and he had his players training without a ball to establish defensive patterns.

Whenever the Grammar first fifteen positioned itself on attack, it invariably scored. That would become a hallmark of the Auckland teams under Henry in the nineties. His teams consistently won by big scores, playing a classic brand of rugby.

Even then, I believed a team should train the way it intended to play. We rehearsed fundamentals and moves until we had them perfect, always with attitude. Those Grammar sides of the seventies played football of outstanding quality. They produced rugby of which any team would have been proud, be it at school, club, representative or international level.

Some of the guys had a bit of trouble with motivation after they left college and started playing in the third grade. Having operated regularly with thousands of adoring school fans on the sideline, with endless hakas booming out, they found the lack of intensity deflating. It was all right for Foxy – he went straight into the University seniors. But a lot of boys, I know, found playing third grade a bit of a downer and many of them were actually lost to rugby.

ALLAN FAULL
Graham was really a professional back in the days he coached Auckland Grammar. He out-thought teams. One school put out a newsletter with suggestions on how to beat

AGS, which was in the middle of its great winning streak. It said, "They've got brains but we've got brawn." That's exactly how Graham would have perceived it himself. He outsmarted opponents. It didn't matter if his team conceded height and weight – he'd work on achieving quick ruck ball to get his wings racing away.

I remember him saying he wanted to coach the All Blacks. He was in his thirties at the time. He asked me to try and arrange for him to win a coaching appointment at a higher level. I'm not sure I had any influence but he eventually became coach of the New Zealand schools team.

Besides being uncommonly gifted at analysing opponents and preparing tactics, he was committed to winning and hated losing. If AGS was to play in Wellington, he wouldn't accept travel by bus or train – he'd insist his team flew to the venue. Because his teams always produced the goods, no one ever objected.

He'd get up in the middle of the night to check if it was raining, in case he had to change his tactical plan. When there was a game coming up, Graham only ever thought rugby. He related brilliantly to kids and was excellent as a classroom teacher. People did things because they respected him. He came round and helped me paint my house once, and I hadn't even asked him.

Graham was to the rugby players at Grammar what John Graham was to the staff. Under them, you were automatically motivated. Neither wasted praise on individuals for achieving what they were expected to do. "Well done" is as much as you'd get out of John Graham for winning the championship and Graham was rather like that. Although he personally expected success, he never burdened his players with such expectations, only ever telling them to do their best. Mind you, he never sent them on to the field without a strategy to ensure they would win!

Perhaps because of his age, people tended to underestimate Graham. The Grammar Old Boys club made a monumental mistake in 1981 when he offered them his services as a senior coach. They said he'd have to serve his apprenticeship with the fifth grade. Graham promptly went off and coached University. More than that, he took Grant Fox and a whole host of his first fifteen players with him.

After six years with the first fifteen, I was ready for a fresh challenge. John Graham was, as always, tremendously supportive. He appreciated that I had aspirations to coach at a higher level and let me go. I approached Grammar first but was told I'd have to start with the fifth grade side. They seemed to think I was too young to handle the seniors. So I offered myself to University and in 1981 took over as coach of the University seniors – not without some opposition. The club had been experiencing a rather lean time. In fact, the Gallaher Shield hadn't found its way to the Merton Rd clubrooms since 1974, when I had worn the No 10 jersey in the veterans backline.

I'm not sure what I expected when I took on the University job. Because of my long association with college pupils who were so malleable and basically did what you demanded of them, I'd forgotten that university students and graduates tended to operate from their own agendas. At the first training run, only six players turned up. I got on the phone after that and sought to conjure up a degree of urgency. But I came to recognise that I was dealing with laidback individuals. I was probably a bit too serious for the university culture and tradition. I mean, I was dealing with people like Greg Denholm who, on a matter of principle, had turned down an All Black jersey twice and who around capping time turned up for a match in a dinner suit, having come straight from the ball!

I was a young buck expecting, and wanting, all the players to be serious. They were an eclectic bunch for most of whom rugby was an entertaining pastime but certainly not their major preoccupation.

Takapuna smashed us by more than 30 points in our second game. My expectations weren't excessive that season, but hell! Then we lost again. I was beginning to wonder why I'd ever abandoned the Auckland Grammar first fifteen. But from a rubbishy, disorganised start, we banded into a competent team, turned the tables on Takapuna in the championship round and came through to finish second.

GRANT FOX

It was my intention to return to Te Puke and get involved in the family kiwifruit business after I left Auckland Grammar, but Graham pressured me to stay and play rugby for University. It was against my father's wishes but I guess we'd all have to say it was a smart decision. Those were the days when representative players still made up to a dozen appearances a year for their club. Sadly, that's dwindled away to almost nothing.

Between seasons, I worked on recruiting players to fill a few important gaps and we gradually developed into an accomplished team, to the point where we almost won the championship in 1983 and did take it out the following year. We actually played better rugby the year we missed out. But Foxy, of all people, turned in a shocker against Ponsonby. He couldn't kick a goal to save himself and broke down in the dressing room afterwards. I told him not to worry about it. Foxy, being Foxy, obviously did and the next season he killed Ponies with his play and his kicking.

NEW ZEALAND HERALD
12 August 1984

The bitter memory of condemnation for over-robust rugby was laid to rest on Saturday when University put together a disciplined team effort to beat Ponsonby 19-3 to win the Auckland club championship.

When the chips were down, the University team from hooker to fullback were models of angelic innocence. Rugby was the name of the game and so well did University play that Ponsonby was a beaten side from the first minutes.

Amid the celebrations coach Graham Henry, who inspired his team to 20 wins from 21 games, was entitled to his moment of glory. But Henry calmly put the credit back on the players.

The side had been subjected to some pretty cruel criticism, he said. "Now I hope the players will be given some credit. It is a really good side with a lot of gifted talent. It was not easy out there – it took a good team to carry it off."

In the years I worked with University a lot of players went on to higher honours. Foxy was the most notable but Nicky Allen, John Drake and David Kirk also won international recognition while John McDermott, John Collinson, Glenn Young, Mark Gray, Glenn Twentyman, Grant Dickson, Mata'afa Keenan, Tim Burcher, Bryce Bevan, Richard Fry and Tua Saseve all wore the blue and white of Auckland.

A young fellow who came through from third grade in 1983 as a fresh-faced 19-year-old was Sean Fitzpatrick. When he fronted up for pre-season training he regarded himself as a prop. I took a good look at him and suggested he could struggle in that position. I thought he was better equipped to play hooker. He was a bit apprehensive at first but the conversion was completed during a pre-season trip to Australia. Turned out to be not bad advice, I thought!

A lot of the things we were doing, Auckland adopted. Same moves with the same names. Of course, a lot of that was Foxy's influence. No one prepared for a game quite like Foxy. Even at school, he would diligently compile lists of moves and photocopy them for every player in the squad. He and Tim Burcher were operating together at club and representative level and obviously a lot of moves revolved around them.

GRANT FOX

Graham was in some ways autocratic but he was also a good listener. If a whole group of players was opposed to something, he'd take notice. But that was rare because he planned so intricately. Once he identified a particular strength in the opposition, or it might be one particular tryscoring move, he wouldn't let up until he'd worked out a way of nullifying it.

Auckland in the early eighties was coached by John Hart, who had brought his business standards to rugby administration with great effect. I first got to know John in the relaxed and ever-convivial atmosphere of the New Zealand Barbarians clubrooms in Cricket Avenue, only a Grant Fox drop-kick from the main oval at Eden Park. I'd encountered him previously when I was coaching Auckland Grammar School. He used to pop in occasionally to see if there were any emerging stars (and there always were).

But it was over a quiet beer or two each week, usually on a Saturday night, that we engaged in what I always regarded as stimulating discussions. I could talk rugby tactics for hours, and still can. I wouldn't know whether Harty found our chats rewarding or not. Maybe he regarded me as a threat – I don't know. But I certainly took plenty out of those sessions.

If you're a serious coach, you need people to bounce your ideas off. In later years I would use Rex Davy, the Auckland manager. Back in the early eighties I used to bounce theories off Hart. Ever the extrovert, he had pretty clearly defined views on most issues. I didn't always agree with his philosophies, and nor should I, but I respected him hugely because he was the founder of the professional environment that had embraced Auckland rugby and would make the blue and whites supreme for a decade and a half. As a coach, you need people you can talk the game to, people who will tell you if you're not right.

John Graham was another who often shared in those discussion groups at the Baabaas clubrooms. I remember one pet topic was whether Foxy as a first-five should stand still or run on to the ball. I was dogmatic that he should distribute the ball while stationary. Harty had the contrary view while John Graham, ever the philosopher, usually had two bob each way. I conceded later that Hart was right and I was wrong about static first-fives.

Hart had a wider view of coaching in those days whereas I was a tactical, technical coach not involved in the game's greater issues. I tended to coach, say well done chaps and go home. I was beginning to appreciate that there was a culture embracing the game I needed to hook into.

MURRAY DEAKER

Graham developed a reputation as being standoffish, which couldn't have been further from the truth. He's always been a player's coach who loved dissecting the game.

There are a lot of similarities between Graham and Laurie Mains. Neither likes centre stage and both are completely passionate about the game. They're both pretty stubborn, too.

Graham is a person who's made the most of his talents,

absolutely. Having graduated from Otago University as a phys-edder, he completed a B.Ed in maths as an extra-mural student at Massey University while committing himself to coaching – that's how dedicated he was.

As if I didn't have enough on my plate with running the University seniors, operating as deputy headmaster at Kelston Boys' High (having transferred there from Auckland Grammar in 1982) and trying to be a worthwhile husband and father, for some reason I agreed to take on the coaching of the New Zealand secondary schools team in 1983. I probably saw it as an important stepping stone.

While I enjoyed my association with the schools team, it was plain I had over-committed myself. By the time I returned from a two-month tour of the UK in early 1985, I was exhausted. I had no sooner completed that assignment than I was involved in the University senior team's trainings for the new season. Around that point, I nearly fell off the rails.

The schools' trip was a great experience because we got to play at all the great stadiums – Murrayfield, Cardiff Arms Park, Lansdowne Road and Twickenham. In light of developments 15 years later, it was ironical that the only loss should be to the Welsh.

We had a team flush with talented footballers – Daryl Halligan, Jon Preston, Matthew Cooper, Stephen Bachop, Rhys Ellison, Duane Monkley, Robin Brooke and Steve Gordon amongst them – but we came a gutser in Cardiff because after hammering the Scots, the guys thought they were the bee's knees.

We didn't pay enough attention to the weather, being convinced we could run the ball all over the park and exhaust the Welsh as we had the Scots. But it started to rain and our expansive game turned to cardboard. We lost 12-9. It was a good learning curve for everyone. Although we had quality loose forwards and two excellent locks, we struggled at times in the scrum, finding the British teams played a more physical game and were always confrontational at scrum time.

In 1986, I applied for the principal's job at Palmerston North Boys' High, having a gut feeling I would get it. It was a single-sex school with an outstanding sporting and academic record and I saw it as a plum job. But Dave Syms won the appointment, thank

God. At the time, I was gutted, but if I'd moved to Palmerston North I probably wouldn't have coached. Who knows what I might be doing now!

Later that year, after John Hart had been promoted to the All Black selection panel, I decided to have a go at the Auckland coach's job. There were two other contenders – Maurice Trapp (involving Bryan Williams as his assistant) and Barry Herring, the long-time coach of the Auckland B team.

At the time, the ARU management committee comprised 27 delegates who all had a vote. After the first ballot, there were nine votes for Herring, nine for Trapp and nine for Henry. The chairman, Malcolm Dick, instructed the delegates to reconsider the three candidates and vote again. After the second ballot, there were nine votes for Herring, nine for Trapp and nine for Henry. The stalemate of all stalemates. "Well," chairman Dick advised the gathering, "we're not leaving here till we make an appointment. Someone is going to have to change his vote." A discussion ensued after which it was apparent at least one delegate was prepared to reconsider. After the third ballot, Maurice Trapp was declared the new selector-coach of Auckland.

Again, fate was kind to me. In hindsight, I don't believe I was ready to take on mighty Auckland at that point, although I would certainly have given it my best shot. I consider I was better qualified when I won the appointment four years later. Maurice Trapp and Beegee were certainly the correct appointees at the time. They carried on from where John Hart had left off and Auckland fans were treated to another four years of sparkling rugby and almost endless success. Incredibly, the Ranfurly Shield, which was in the trophy cabinet when they arrived, would still be there five years later. Some bloke called Henry would eventually lose it

Although a couple of appointments had gone against me, I was successful with two others. At Kelston Boys' High, I was installed as headmaster following the death of Jim Paton and my new coaching role was with the Auckland Colts.

The Colts were a stimulating challenge, a bit like coaching the Auckland Grammar first fifteen. There were heaps of talented players around jumping out of their skins. Our philosophy became that whatever the Auckland A team could do, we could do better. If they ran up 60 points, we'd hit 70.

In the time I had the Colts, we played 40 matches and won 39. Mind you, we should have been successful, when you consider the talent I had at my disposal, being able to call on players like Matthew Ridge, Inga Tuigamala, Craig Innes, Pat Lam, Eroni Clarke, Olo Brown, Craig Dowd, Robin Brooke and Mark Carter. In one game we demolished a useful Waikato Colts team by 112 points to four.

We played exciting, enjoyable rugby. Sometimes as a coach you get bogged down with winning, without worrying about the processes that got you there. The trophy becomes all important, the only objective, and you realise you've sacrificed the quality of performance in your desperation to proclaim yourself number one.

With the Colts, that never applied. We had a wholly refreshing approach, committing ourselves to attacking rugby. Our yardstick was the Auckland A team. Under Trapp and Williams at the time, they were playing attacking rugby of marvellous quality, consistently running up large scores. They were our motivational force. Whatever they did, we were determined to go one better. And on a lot of occasions we did!

My involvement with those extremely talented Colts teams helped prepare me for the Auckland challenge when it was finally offered to me in 1992. After a decade of greatness, Auckland was in danger of sliding off the top of the mound. But by introducing many of the players I'd worked with in the Colts we were able to prevent that happening. Auckland would stay mighty.

Chapter 2

Step aside, Maurice

Who knows what force gnaws at us, telling us that our accomplishments, no matter how sensational, are not enough, that we need to do more?

Arthur Ashe, Days of Grace

IF YOU'RE AMBITIOUS, there's always a danger of becoming over-zealous and indulging in actions which you'll later regret. I've always been ambitious and as the nineties rolled around, I must confess I pursued some strategies about which I now feel embarrassed.

It was very simple in my mind: I wanted to coach the Auckland rugby team, a goal I had harboured for a long time. With some 15 years' coaching behind me, most of it successful, I believed I had something to offer at top representative level. I wanted to go all the way.

In 1990, I declared my hand by standing against Maurice Trapp and Bryan Williams. Considering their team of the previous season had won 19 matches out of 19, claimed the South Pacific championship and the NPC, beaten the Wallabies and retained the Ranfurly Shield, I was obviously perceived as a supreme optimist at best.

But I was registering my intent. I had been winning impressive reviews for the quality of rugby the Auckland Colts were playing and it was important, I believed, to let Auckland's administrators know that when Maurice Trapp stepped aside, I was the logical successor.

Unfortunately, I didn't leave it at that. In my opinion, Auckland, by 1991, although still enormously successful – it lost one game in 16, to Otago at the House of Pain, a result that cost it the NPC title – was going downhill. The team urgently needed a new voice and a new direction before the problems compounded and the team toppled off its pedestal.

I could see worrying signs but I didn't know whether Auckland's administrators were aware of them. So I decided to offer some assistance, about which I now feel pretty coy. I prepared copious reports and comments which I submitted to the decision-makers at the ARU. The message I was determined to deliver was that the Auckland team urgently needed a new direction, a feeling I expressed in bold terms.

The Auckland team of the late eighties had been outstanding, probably the best team in the world, including international sides. It had played sublime rugby. By the early nineties, however, standards had slipped. It was still a highly successful side but was no longer operating with the awesome physical power and skill as previously.

Many of the top players' standards were also not as they had been. The game they were playing lacked the "edge". The team had become more forward orientated and at times was labelled boring, which was a little harsh because it was still by far the best team in New Zealand. What was happening was that the older forwards were controlling the pattern more and more. I believed the team needed a fresh direction from a coaching viewpoint and some new faces. There were young, talented players available who had come through the colts team I had coached, individuals like Eroni Clarke and Craig Dowd.

I know my attitude hurt Maurice and Beegee and I am embarrassed and far from proud now about what I did. When I was preparing to move to Wales in mid-1998 I came across copies of the letters I'd sent to the union. They didn't make pretty reading. I said to my wife Raewyn, "Look at this – can you believe I was so desperate and ambitious to win that appointment?" It's a skeleton that's going to remain in my cupboard.

Although Maurice Trapp chose not to stand for coach in 1992, my appointment was anything but automatic, with more than a few of ARU committee supporting the perennial challenger for the position, Tank Herring. I'd struggled to get a senior coaching position back in 1981 and it was the same with the ARU. The cynical side of me saw politics intruding. They weren't assessing me on the strength of my record, which stood up alongside anyone's; they were more concerned about me, Graham Henry. I was a schoolteacher from Canterbury. Was that the sort of person Auckland wanted coaching its representative team? I know there were several administrators who regarded me with suspicion. Some didn't change their view, either, for a long time.

I was relieved to get the job. Such appointments usually only come along every three or four years, so to have missed out then would have been devastating. Who knows how I would have reacted?

The first essential was to build a formidable management team. In effecting this, I looked for strong characters, people who were well qualified and who, when necessary, were movers and shakers. I didn't want a cluster of yes-men around me.

For assistant coach, I chose John Graham, a man I'd first encountered when I was a pupil at Christchurch Boys' High School. He had a profile as an ex-All Black captain and boasted vast experience, having previously being involved with Auckland during Eric Boggs' time as coach. Above all, he was a person you could trust totally – he had no hidden agendas. He was totally supportive of me and the team. Also, he was someone who spoke his mind, ever prepared to debate rugby technique and tactics, being excellent for bouncing ideas off. We had some marvellous discussions at times, and we didn't always agree. But he knew that once I made my decision, whether he agreed with it or not, that was it, after which he was always totally supportive. John also had a hard edge, necessary for the development of a successful rugby team. Words cannot express my appreciation of the support he gave me in my early years of coaching Auckland.

The manager I wanted was Rex Davy, who ran a real estate company in west Auckland. I'd got to know him during the Development team's tour of Argentina in 1989 when he was assistant to John Carter. I was impressed with Rex's ability to relate to people, regardless of their station. Always humble and pleasant, he got along with managers, liaison officers, bus drivers, corporate people and players. He even got on with Canterbury people! I loved the guy.

Environment is everything in a rugby team. If you haven't got that, there's no way the players will operate up to their potential. Rex helped create that environment with good balance. He knew when to be strict and he knew when to ease the pressure by shouting a few raspberry drinks (although sometimes he forgot to tell the coach when he'd had enough raspberry drinks!) Because he was a keen student of the game, I could talk rugby with him and used him as an important sounding board. He was never a yes-man. Above all else, he was a good mate. We still keep in touch and he still offers suggestions on how I could improve my coaching!

Who else for trainer but Jim Blair, who'd been involved with Auckland teams since the early 1980s and who had revolutionised rugby conditioning in New Zealand. Jim was a hell of a good judge of an athlete, possessing an almost sixth sense that would tell him whether an athlete was right or not. He was also an astute judge of an athlete's personality, stemming from his extensive experience. He was the guru.

We spent a lot of time setting up grids. He was a master at developing exercises to develop a particular skill. In these, he demonstrated a lot of originality. He also possessed a great voice, developed from his days of working as a PT instructor in the armed forces. When Jim barked, the guys jumped. He was thus motivational as well as instructional as a trainer. Over time, he was the number one conditioning coach in New Zealand by some distance.

Obviously the first year was going to be my most difficult because I could see the team required a major overhaul. Several players who had been outstanding contributors to the Auckland (and All Black) cause were fast approaching the twilight zone and would need replacing, sooner rather than later. In a man-management sense, that was going to be the most difficult part. The team, more than the personalities involved, came first. If I didn't start culling, the team would go under. High-profile heroes needed to be dropped, and only one person could do that – the new coach.

Before I had to concern myself with such traumatic issues, I tried to stall Craig Innes' defection to league. I was holidaying in the Bay of Islands during the summer when the rumours of Craig's departure reached me. At the time, of course, he was fresh out of New Zealand's none-too-successful World Cup campaign in the UK. I knew Craig well, having selected him as a schoolboy for the Auckland Colts, and I managed to track him down by phone. When he confirmed he was switching to league, I tried to entice him back to rugby and the fine Auckland team I would be coaching. But this was three years before rugby went professional and what show did I have, offering him cold pies and sandwiches against the $NZ300,000 or whatever the Leeds League Club was going to pay him?

When it came to shaping the team for the 1992 season, there were a number of established All Blacks who I didn't see featuring in my top line-up – Alan Whetton, who was being overtaken as a blindsider by Michael Jones; Steve McDowell, now challenged by Craig Dowd; Bernie McCahill, under pressure from both Eroni Clarke and Waisake Sotutu; and Terry Wright, the speedster who was under threat from the more bruising Inga Tuigamala.

They were all marvellous sportsmen for whom I had huge respect, as players and people. But I had to make changes so the Auckland team would regenerate. Breaking the news to them was difficult. It was a task I never found easy. As it turned out, the four survived in the squad and made a modest number of appearances during the season.

Auckland had taken out some insurance for the future by sending a Development team to Argentina in 1990. Actually, the truth is that it was my initiative and I got to coach the team. Auckland had been at the top for a long time but it was important to have fresh blood coming through.

We played five matches in Argentina against strong provinces and won them all. Peter Fatialofa, beyond the development phase of his career but a great asset to Auckland rugby, was taken along to provide leadership and guidance. What a sparkling array of talent the side possessed. Consider these names, in the light of subsequent events: Olo Brown, Craig Dowd, Robin Brooke, Mark Carter, Pat Lam, Eric Rush, Ant Strachan, Jason Hewett, Eroni Clarke, Shane Howarth, Frank Bunce, To'o Vaega and John Ngauamo. Eleven of those 13 became All Blacks and Lam also went on to captain Samoa.

Craig Dowd was only the number four prop on that tour behind

Peter Fats, Olo and Graham Dowd. But he was only 20 and we were up against some seriously powerful props in a country where scrummaging had become an art form.

Pat Lam was captain, and he and I achieved an excellent relationship. He was a superb young leader with the ability to take my ideas on to the field and implement them. Otherwise, it's all a waste of time. It's bloody important that the captain understands his coach and heeds his instructions. My philosophy has always been to push the ball wide and in South America, where they were thirsting for physical contact, the passport to victory was through the backs. I certainly didn't want the ball to linger in the set pieces and Pat understood that. I'm sure if we'd played formal, traditional rugby, we would have lost three of the five games. Tucuman was the strongest of the teams we opposed and fancied its chances but it couldn't handle our high-speed, high-risk, ball-in-hand approach. It was a game none of our opponents was prepared to play.

I always prepared the teams I selected to be creative and enjoy their rugby, to take on the opposition at express pace. Every team I've ever been involved with has enjoyed playing rugby that way. The guys appreciate having the opportunity to do exciting things, to extend their skills and their thought processes. Such rugby is only possible, of course, after a lot of rehearsing.

The teams that I coached always had a wealth of moves to call on – some would say too many. Foxy was a factor here. In our days together at Auckland Grammar we'd spent endless hours discussing tactics and plotting manoeuvres. Foxy never participated in a competition game without methodically preparing a sheet of moves which he would distribute among all the players. It was a practice I continued.

Preparation is all important if you want to succeed as a sports coach. One of the major reasons Auckland and, later, the Auckland Blues were successful was because, as the coach, I did my homework. It was burdensome before the advent of professionalism because I had to dovetail rugby coaching with my role as the principal of Kelston Boys' High, which often meant studying videos and preparing training schedules through till two o'clock in the morning.

Obviously Auckland and the Blues were reasonably talented sides to start with, but if you didn't do your homework, you didn't win. That meant preparing specific schedules for every game.

Well... that's perhaps an exaggeration. Obviously in a season of up to 25 games you'd drive your players mad if you came up with in-depth analyses of the opposition every time.

There are obviously fixtures you know you can win with a minimum of preparation. You ease off a bit with them and target the important matches. The classic example, which I'll deal with more intimately later, was Auckland's Ranfurly Shield challenge against Canterbury in 1995, a game not too many pundits thought we could win.

I studied probably six videos of Canterbury's games, after which I was confident I knew what they would do from any set piece. Armed with that information, my players nullified them so comprehensively, we won the game by 35 points to nil, the widest winning margin ever achieved by a challenging Ranfurly Shield team.

Analysis of your opposition in the modern game is critical. I do it before every game but the amount of information I pass on to the troops varies. I pick their mood before I decide how much to shovel on to them.

The Development team tour of Argentina was invaluable for me, providing an important insight into the players of the future. It provided me with fresh challenges, having to prepare strategies to combat a style of play you would rarely encounter back home. Not the least benefit of touring overseas, particularly to countries with language barriers, is that it really pulls the team together. We were a really tight unit by the time we returned to New Zealand.

Getting into the 1992 season, my first with Auckland, wasn't easy. Laurie Mains had just taken over the All Blacks and, concerned with the fitness levels of many of those who'd participated in ill-fated World Cup campaign, he'd sacked Jim Blair as trainer and taken on Martin Toomey, who had ordered the country's leading players to start pounding the roads to improve their aerobic levels. That was fine for Laurie, who was building towards an international campaign that started in late April, but it didn't help the Auckland coach whose first assignment was a Super 6 tournament kicking off in March. I had to start working with a team of runners. Though Laurie's training was counter-productive for us, I must say he certainly sharpened up the All Blacks and they were a hell of a lot fitter than previously. The guys themselves acknowledge that and I know they had an enormous amount of respect for him. He had a job to do – it's just that it didn't help us, that's all.

The Super 6, or South Pacific Championship as it was known, didn't have the status or colour of the Super 12 series which, when introduced in 1996, instantly became the glamour provincial rugby tournament in the world.

The Super 6 certainly had merit because it pitted Queensland, New South Wales and Fiji against Auckland, Wellington and Canterbury in a competition, at a time when traditionally rugby was low-key. And it attracted good crowds. But for Auckland, laden with All Blacks, it fell at an awkward time. Too many players had a conflict of interest, from sevens to international commitments. The All Blacks were seldom in the right state of mind which was frustrating for the coach. You couldn't expect them to start peaking in March when they had tests, Ranfurly Shield defences and the NPC challenge ahead. And don't forget, we're still talking the glorious days of amateurism. Professionalism was still a long way off.

The '92 season was a challenging one for me. I set out to coach from the front where I've always coached from. Gary Whetton, who I retained as captain – even though he was being axed from the All Blacks – had previously exercised a lot of control but he was depowered by me. He still had authority on the field but he wielded less influence in the day-to-day running of the team. This was not a reflection on Gary's ability. It was simply my style. I had to coach from the front and I always will.

We had our moments that year, retaining the Ranfurly Shield and putting 62 points on Ireland. In fact, in my six and half years with Auckland, I don't think we ever lost to a touring side. In 1993, we defeated the British Lions in a thriller at Eden Park. On that topic, I hope Lions tours are retained because it would be most unfortunate if teams like Auckland never had the opportunity to play them again.

What Auckland didn't achieve in 1992 was success in the NPC. It was the year in which play-offs were introduced, something none of us had experienced. The week before the semi-finals Auckland survived a storming Ranfurly Shield challenge from North Harbour. We were in trouble, seven points down at halftime, but a monumental performance from the pack in the second half and some masterly play by Grant Fox got us home in front of a full house and in a near test match atmosphere at Eden Park.

The guys put so much into that defence – near the end of a long season in which the All Blacks had played five domestic tests and toured Australia and South Africa – they lost their focus in that final week. There were distractions. Early in the week it was uncertain whether our semi-final would be staged on the Saturday or the Sunday and some of the players were hostile at the prospect of playing on a Sunday; in fact, they were going to refuse to play. As it turned out, we got our Saturday game, but it showed how easily you can lose focus, and Waikato blew us away, a rare setback on Eden Park.

It was a sobering reverse, although we would bounce back and win four NPCs on the trot after that. But it was a loss, an important loss. And I hate losing. For me, losses are like a death in the family. Saturday night is bad enough, and drinking only seems to make things worse. But on Sunday mornings, I always feel as though the sky has fallen in, especially with my psyche.

While the loss to Waikato was a disappointment for all the obvious reasons, personally it was a frustration because I knew there were individuals in the Auckland Rugby Union who were always searching for an excuse to replace me. I always felt my position was under some pressure until, in 1995, we so comprehensively outplayed Canterbury in the shield challenge that there was nothing left to criticise.

While it was great to be the holder of the Ranfurly Shield, it proved to be something of a millstone. I'd inherited it from Maurice Trapp who had taken it over from John Hart. When I hit the scene in 1992, the shield had been in Auckland for an incredible seven seasons.

I soon sensed that public interest in the shield had diminished. They say familiarity breeds contempt and Aucklanders had simply become blasé about the trophy. The hype that was traditionally associated with the famous old "log" no longer existed in the Queen City. We had to hype ourselves.

John Hart had created a culture within the Auckland team back in the eighties designed to make Auckland the best team in the world. That culture was often referred to and it was what got us through week after week, because shield hype certainly wasn't doing it. The trophy provided a huge motivation for the opposition but for the Auckland guys each challenge – with only a handful of exceptions – became just another day at the office.

It was inevitable that at some stage Auckland would fall over and the trophy would move on. It was just a shame I was holding the reins when it happened, against Waikato in 1993. Actually, Waikato was well prepared and Ian Foster played out of his skin at first-five. The Mooloos were one team, one of the few teams, who weren't daunted by playing on Eden Park.

I hesitate to say it was a relief to have the shield move on because, as you know, I hate losing, but the trophy was unquestionably going to do more for Waikato (and ultimately New Zealand) rugby than having it survive for a tenth season in Auckland.

Not that I was in such a magnanimous state of mind immediately the shield departed after 62 successive defences. I felt it was the end of the world when I woke the next morning. My son Andrew had been playing for Cornwall and it was the club's prizegiving. I said to my wife Raewyn that I couldn't possibly turn up there because they'd give me hell! She thought otherwise, thank goodness. It was the best possible thing I could have done. There were 300 people present and it was obvious the Ranfurly Shield had a low priority. It made me realise the world was still going on, that no one was going to shoot me.

The Monday morning assembly at Kelston Boys' High was a hoot. The pupils there are delightfully black and white, unlike their counterparts at Auckland Grammar School who are pretty conservative and wouldn't say boo. As I approached the stage that morning, a chant of "Mooloo, Mooloo!" broke out, which made me smile. I bled all over the stage, told the kids what it was like to lose the shield after 62 challenges and nine years. But I really don't think anyone apart from Graham Henry was too concerned. The sun kept coming up that next week.

The following Saturday the guys went out and smashed King Country by 97 points to three, which is still a record score for the NPC first division. From there we disposed of North Harbour and Otago to win the championship. In what would be his final appearances for Auckland, Foxy was brilliant. If we hadn't won the NPC, I might have been history. I hadn't received a lot of positive media at that stage and there were administrators only too eager to see me replaced.

I would win and lose the Ranfurly Shield more times than anyone. Waikato would take it twice (in 1993 and 1997) and Taranaki once (in 1996) while we had the satisfaction of winning it back from Canterbury (in 1995) and Waikato (in 1996).

It was symptomatic of the shield malaise that existed in Auckland that when we arrived back home from Hamilton after our successful challenge at the beginning of October '96, there were five people to meet our bus. Not five thousand, not five hundred, just five! When Canterbury or Waikato or Taranaki win it, there are thousands thronging the airport or in the city centre to trumpet their heroes home. We clapped each other off the bus in '96. I had the distinct impression a lot of Auckland fans didn't want us to bring the trophy home, that they felt it was doing more for rugby elsewhere. I sometimes felt it would be nice to be coaching in another province where people were thirsting for success and trophies. Just imagine what the shield would mean to Otago, say, where they haven't seen it since 1957.

Auckland's glorious shield era was recognised by the Auckland Rugby Union at a dinner held during the summer. Every player who had participated in the 61 defences of the shield from 1985 to 1993 received an invitation and the wives and partners were involved also. It a marvellous celebration. There were two speakers – John Hart, who'd won it, and Maurice Trapp, who'd kept it. Graham Henry, who'd lost it, wasn't required to come forward which upset a few people in my court. Not me, I'd have to say. I'm sure it wasn't done deliberately. I think my supporters were probably overly sensitive.

The ultimate for the coach of any sporting team is to achieve success while maintaining a favourable public image which comes from having the media on your side. Through those early seasons with Auckland, I would have to concede that my relationship with the media was less than perfect. I'm not naturally a grumpy bastard or arrogant or unfriendly. But that's how I was perceived, I know.

I concede it was probably my fault. Besides coaching the Auckland rugby team, I was holding down a huge job at Kelston, a school with a roll of 1250 and a staff of 100. It was a far more responsible position than coaching a rugby team. On the home front, Raewyn was teaching at Baradene College and coaching netball at school and club level while the children were demanding, as children are. Matthew and Catherine were at secondary school and Andrew at primary school. Therefore, I was hellishly busy. Without insulating myself, I could never have done both jobs.

Maurice Trapp, my predecessor, had been self-employed

which, I'm sure, allowed him to organise his week very methodically, whereas I was regularly rushing between Eden Park and Kelston and trying to work in some quality time with my family, after which I'd work through to one or two o'clock every night to keep on top of everything to ensure I did both jobs properly.

Since the advent of professional rugby, I'm more relaxed and a positive media person. I have so much more time to give to the players. Back in those early days with Auckland, I didn't have time to go through the niceties. And that's why I was seen as not being media-friendly.

The fact was, I couldn't afford to have a stuff-up because there wasn't time to correct it. Which is why I kept such a tight rein on myself. The media invariably react favourably to sports officials they share an association with, who are gregarious, available and who keep them informed. I was understandably branded media-unfriendly because my work schedule didn't really allow me to be any of those things, not consistently anyway.

Once the press start to get a snitcher on you, they can turn really nasty. This bloke Graham Henry had dared to drop a whole bunch of the media's favourite All Blacks. Furthermore, he was callous about how he informed them. In his first year, Auckland, mighty Auckland, didn't even win the NPC. And in his second year… horror of horrors… he lost the Ranfurly Shield. How can he possibly remain in the job?

Unlike the Sunday papers, which are always likely to come up with a shock-horror story on anyone or anything involved in rugby, the *New Zealand Herald,* which has been publishing daily for almost as long as Auckland has been in existence, treads a more temperate path, certainly on its sports pages. It's extremely rare for the paper to criticise a coach, unless his team is performing abysmally. Mine was winning pretty consistently.

So you can imagine my concern when in 1994 a journalist I regarded as a trusty friend tipped me off that the *Herald* was preparing a feature for its weekend edition that was, in part, uncomplimentary to the coach of the Auckland rugby team. Interestingly, the paper hadn't involved its senior rugby correspondent Wynne Gray, nor any of its daily sports writers. The article was put together by Peter Calder, who aired all the gripes about me that were doing the rounds. It mentioned the dropping of established All Blacks and my apparent lack of sensitivity. I was branded abrasive. It could have been worse, but it didn't do a hell of a lot for my reputation as a person. It was the sort of negative article that could have been written about any one of a host of rugby coaches around New Zealand in the still-amateur days, as they struggled like hell to balance the employment that brought in the income with the coaching that was their labour of love.

PETER CALDER
NZ Herald
Henry says the hardest part of making [tough] decisions is that "you've got to upset people you have the highest regard for, but that's my job and I accept it." It's an oblique acknowledgement that Henry's left more than a few bruised egos in his wake as he's climbed to the top of Auckland rugby. On-the-record comments are hard to come by when it comes to his past and some make it plain they belong to the school of thought that if you can't think of something nice to say about somebody, you say nothing.

It's acknowledged by plenty of players that Terry Wright and Bernie McCahill have yet to be told, face to face and man to man, that they've been dropped from the side.

Few dispute his [Henry's] knowledge of the game; few defend his personal style, which they find abrasive and often dismissive.
Also
In Henry's first year, the A team failed to make the finals of the NPC. Last year [1993] it rectified that, beating Otago for the top title, but went into the championship having lost the Ranfurly Shield to Waikato. It was an unprepossessing start to Henry's spell as coach and seasoned observers suggest he will have to produce better results this year if he wants to hold on to the job when it comes up for grabs in November.

Around that time the Sunday papers were also pretty negative. I was mindful of the image being projected but there wasn't much I could do about it then. As I said, I was insulating myself to ensure I coped with my joint roles as headmaster and coach. Being up till 2am night after night analysing videos doesn't leave you much time for the social niceties that might help you seduce a few rugby correspondents. I did it the way I had to do it. Success was paramount. If the Auckland team hadn't been successful, I was the only person accountable. There could be no buck-passing. As a coach, the last thing you want is to be relieved of your position.

Image didn't matter a hoot at Kelston Boys' High. I wasn't being judged there on a week by week basis. Instead of a squad of 25 rugby players, I was responsible for 100 teachers who in turn had 1250 pupils to look after and I was determined no one was going to say I wasn't doing the job well.

I probably became a better principal because of my demanding schedule. It forced me to delegate authority, which is what you should do anyway. As a consequence, the people under me developed strongly. Steve Cole is now headmaster at St Paul's College in Hamilton, Jim Dale is headmaster of Westlake Boys' High and, when I finally resigned in 1996 to become a full-time rugby coach, Steve Watt, a pretty useful rugby player himself in his day, took over at Kelston.

I know the school had a lot of pride that I was coach of Auckland. In a way, it enhanced the school. Looking back, while sometimes I wonder how I managed to juggle both appointments, I don't believe I could have handled the situation differently. The only thing that suffered was my public image and I could live with that. The Auckland rugby team won four consecutive NPC titles and claimed the Ranfurly Shield back from Canterbury in a memorable performance, while Kelston made its mark academically and in sport. One year, the school had two students in the top 10 in New Zealand in Bursary while on the sports fields Kelston became national champions in rugby, soccer, basketball and touch. It was, without question, one of the top schools in the country and there was a real pride in its achievements. I have the fondest memories of the school. The staff collectively were an outstanding group of professionals, all supportive of each other. The spirit among the staff at Kelston was legendary.

My time as Auckland rugby coach spanned two distinct eras – the still-amateur days from 1992 through 1995 followed by the swift, dramatic transformation to professionalism which, of course, ushered in the Super 12 competition which would, overnight, become the most significant provincial rugby event in the world.

There were any amount of highlights in those early years,

including the thrilling victory over the 1993 British Lions at Eden Park. Our All Blacks – eight of them – were coming off the test at Lancaster Park and had to be handled carefully which made for a difficult build-up. It was a hell of a gutsy performance because during the match we lost our fullback Shane Howarth, meaning Waisake Sotutu, a specialist threequarter, had to drop back to an unfamiliar position while we introduced Craig Adams at centre, a greenhorn whose only outing for Auckland had been against Buller.

The Lions were a quality side with a lot of character. Under Gavin Hastings' leadership, they led 18-11 at halftime. Our guys were able to up the tempo in the second half and four penalty goals by Foxy, giving him six for the match, allowed us to claim a most satisfying victory by 23 points to 18.

A month earlier we had taken on Transvaal at Ellis Park in Johannesburg in the final of the Super 10, the forerunner of the Super 12. The two competitions had almost nothing in common, apart from pitting many of the leading provincial teams of South Africa, Australia and New Zealand against each other.

The mighty Super 12, which would benefit each participating player by some $45,000, would be administered by the NZRFU and would become every New Zealand rugby person's total focus from February to late May. The Super 10 wasn't half as super. The players didn't make a bean out of it. It was organised by the participating teams and because only Auckland, Otago, Waikato and North Harbour (the top four teams from the previous season's NPC) were involved from New Zealand, there was a lukewarm support and interest from the rest of the country. Until we reached the final, that is. Then suddenly, miraculously, everyone seemed to be cheering for Auckland. Which was understandable, I suppose, because it was New Zealand against South Africa and in rugby, there's no more spirited contest.

Without searching for excuses, the odds were almost impossibly stacked against us. In light of the status of Super 12 now, it seems almost unbelievable that the NZRFU would schedule its All Black trials six days before the Super 10 final. They weren't to know a New Zealand team would have to travel to Johannesburg, of course, but it demonstrates the modest status accorded the tournament at the time.

Thirteen Auckland players were involved in the trials staged at the Rotorua Stadium on a Sunday. It meant we didn't arrive in

South Africa until the Tuesday morning whereupon we had to take a connecting flight down to Durban where we quartered ourselves until the Friday.

Hardly surprisingly in the circumstances, therefore, that we faded in the final quarter after establishing a 17-10 advantage, although really we blew it. Twice winger Terry Wright, a top guy and a quick, highly-skilled winger, was put in the clear with only the fullback to beat but each time he was stopped. I felt he was the man for the occasion, having proven himself such a great finisher, but that performance showed that at the age of 30, he'd lost the competitive edge. He didn't play for Auckland again.

He wasn't the only international winger I dropped that season. The other was Inga Tuigamala who lost his focus in an NPC match at Carisbrook, allowing Jeff Wilson to score a matchwinning try for Otago. I replaced him on the wing with Waisake Sotutu for the remaining matches. As it turned out, it precipitated his move towards league.

Inga could be a devastating attacker but was prone to lapses of concentration on defence. His blunder allowed Otago to slip past us in the dying minutes for a 25-21 victory which, naturally, nearly brought the roof down at the House of Pain. The Otago fans loved Goldie's heroics, but I wasn't amused. I wasn't used to losing and it brassed me off going down because it was a game in which we'd done enough to win.

Whenever Auckland lost, I always conducted a post-mortem at which I would put everything on the table. There was never any camouflage. If Auckland was defeated by a better team – and such occasions were rare – I accepted that, but usually the cause was mistakes by ourselves. It was important to identify those and ensure they didn't happen again.

It was unfortunate that Inga switched to league, although from a personal standpoint it was probably the best thing he could have done. Certainly, his domestic circumstances in Auckland weren't great when he was playing rugby. He was trying to support the whole family. I tried to talk him out of going to league, but as with Craig Innes, in those amateur days, the very best that could be offered – through the All Black Club – was employment. And that didn't measure up against the telephone figures those guys were being offered to play league. Inga going to league was obviously the right decision for him and what an outstanding sportsman he has become. I recently watched him play for Newcastle against Richmond in an important English premier club rugby game and he was the difference between the two sides, scoring two tries from from centre and one from the wing. I've been enormously impressed with how he has matured. He's so sensible in what he's done. Although he's helping raise a family, he's now studying for the future – he's a very impressive young man.

Poor old North Otago, one of the battlers of the third division, copped the backlash four days after our loss to Otago. Auckland had for some seasons taken the Ranfurly Shield on tour and on this historic occasion had agreed to put it at stake in Oamaru. It was a famous first for a town which, through its two outstanding boys' boarding schools, Waitaki and St Kevin's, had consistently churned out high quality rugby players. Unfortunately, North Otago, with insufficient employment to retain many of its scholars, had never achieved any notable success itself.

For a town with a population of 12,000, it was astonishing that 6000 should turn out for the shield challenge, a record – which still stands – at Centennial Park. Before we headed out of the town the next day, North Otago's beaming chairman Tony Spivey assured us that the takings from the game would sustain the union for the next three seasons. That gave us all a fuzzy feeling as we journeyed on to Christchurch for our next appointment.

It would have been in North Otago's interests for us to have walloped Otago handsomely and to have arrived in Oamaru in a feel-good mood. Instead, the grumpy coach Henry was still hurting from events at Carisbrook – and took it out on the players. The result, which became a statistician's delight, was a victory by 139 points to five. And it should be recorded that after five minutes the crowd were ecstatic as North Otago led by five points to nil!

No one enjoyed the experience more than John Kirwan who scored eight tries. Shane Howarth prospered too, scoring 36 points, including four tries.

An interesting postscript to the Oamaru encounter is to consider the whereabouts of 12 of the 17 Auckland players used that afternoon in 1993: Shane Howarth is now the Welsh fullback, John Kirwan is a player-coach in Japan, Inga Tuigamala spreads his talent between Newcastle and Samoa, Waisake Sotutu now operates in Japan, Lee Stensness has taken up a contract in France, Jason Hewett plays in England, Zinzan Brooke is player-coach of

Harlequins in England, Pat Lam has played for Newcastle, Northampton and Samoa, Daniel Manu represents New South Wales and Australia, Jason Chandler has been playing with L'Aquila in Italy, Kevin Nepia is operating in France and Ross Nesdale is the back-up hooker for Ireland. If that isn't enough, the coach draws his pay packet from the Welsh Rugby Union, too!

The only ones who didn't succumb to overseas offers were Grant Fox (who retired at the end of that year), Robin Brooke, Olo Brown, Eroni Clarke and Craig Adams.

Always striving to be innovative, I decided to introduce a second fitness adviser at the commencement of the 1994 season, John Davie, who'd worked with the Dallas Cowboys and promised to introduce "explosiveness" into the Auckland game. It was never my intention to replace Jim Blair, who'd been faithfully dispensing his special brand of fitness preparation on behalf of Auckland for a decade. However, Jim misunderstood my motives and, being the dogged Scot he is, declined to be involved.

It was simply my intention to shift all the bums along on the bench to make room for another, for someone who would add extra dimension to our training. It was a storm in a teacup. I'd wanted Jim to remain in control, with Davie assisting, but Jim didn't see it that way. It cannot be said that Davie's methods were hugely successful and after a few weeks he was released. The whole episode had the effect of sharpening up Jim, who'd lost a bit of his sting after 10 years in the role.

The 1994 season was especially satisfying because to win the NPC we had to overcome Otago at Carisbrook and North Harbour – which had been enjoying its most productive year – at Onewa Domain. In those days, the play-off venues were simply the opposite of where you'd played the qualifying games. We'd hosted Otago and North Harbour at Eden Park, so it meant we'd be on the road for the semi-final. Such was the competitive nature of our team, as you would expect of a side led by Zinny, that they relished this additional challenge. I remember Zinny saying, "When we win the title this year, no one will be able to belittle the achievement through us having a home advantage." And we did win, in style against Otago but only after a rather ugly, spiteful confrontation with North Harbour.

Otago has the most feared scrum in New Zealand rugby now

but five years ago it struggled to contain Auckland's awesome front row of Sean Fitzpatrick, Olo Brown and Craig Dowd (although in those particular play-offs Kevin Nepia deputised for Dowd, who was carrying an injury).

Gordon Hunter was coaching Otago then and had the blue and golds playing adventurous, sevens-style rugby. It was important to maintain concentration for 80 minutes because if you gave them half a chance, guys like Jeff Wilson, John Timu, Marc Ellis and Paul Cooke could tear you apart. However, we always felt Otago was vulnerable at first-five where Stephen Bachop, although a very talented player, was not the bravest when it came to tackling. It sounds harsh, but it was an area we always targeted. Physically, he wasn't equipped to deal with barnstorming loosies like Zinny.

The guys were chuffed at winning so handsomely at Carisbrook. Obviously any semi-final victory is a thrill, but they don't call Carisbrook "the House of Pain" for nothing. Otago had beaten the Springboks earlier in the season and had a home record in the NPC probably second only to Auckland's on Eden Park. It's a marvellous play to play because the atmosphere is so conducive to producing skilled, attacking rugby. My teams always enjoyed their visits to Dunedin. It was a marvellous place to play.

Unfortunately, the '94 grand final at Harbour's humble headquarters in Takapuna a week later wasn't such a treasured occasion. The unpleasantness that manifested itself on what should have been a grand celebration of rugby could be traced to a number of factors. For a start, it was brother against brother and such confrontations always have the potential to flare up. Also, there existed a degree of animosity between the two unions, Aucklanders often perceiving their North Harbour counterparts as a bunch of upstarts, imposters almost. There wasn't the same respect for North Harbour rugby as for Otago, say. On top of that, there were a number of inflammatory posters belittling Auckland displayed prominently around the city. The one outside Onewa Domain, positioned so our players couldn't miss it, declared: "Nike… our boots are made for walking in, and they're going to walk all over Auckland."

I encountered Harbour coach Brad Meurant shortly before kick-off and we wished each other well. There was no suggestion the game would degenerate into the ill-tempered, ugly spectacle it did. Although, as always seemed to apply at Onewa Domain, it was blowing a gale which wasn't conducive to free-flowing rugby. This was the greatest moment in Harbour's brief history and plainly the players were over-stoked but, having said that, it takes two to tango and our guys weren't innocent.

Although a couple of players were sent off – Eric Rush for Harbour and Robin Brooke for us – I personally didn't consider the game too bad. Niggly certainly, unattractive definitely. But after the early confrontations, I felt it settled down into a good, old-fashioned, uncompromising game of rugby. I didn't think much of it afterwards and that night I went out and socialised quite happily. Next morning, all hell broke loose. We (both teams, that is) were accused of bringing the game into disrepute, we were shocking role models. Everyone, from the coaches down, deserved to be suspended and several were, as it turned out, from citings made by the NZRFU. It was a major issue on the Paul Holmes show on television that evening. Obviously, there wasn't much else happening in the world that weekend!

Personally, I prefer to remember the occasion for the magnificent performance from our forwards in the second half. We were in big trouble at halftime, behind on the scoreboard and required to operate for the next 40 minutes into the teeth of a gale.

If there was one person you wanted on your side that afternoon, it was Sean Fitzpatrick. When things got tough, Fitzy got going. He thrived on challenges and he recognised the enormity of the task confronting us that afternoon. He loved those key games; in fact, he lived for them.

He had achieved a magnificent rapport with his fellow front rowers, on that occasion Olo Brown and Kevin Nepia, and functioned mightily in tandem with his captain, Zinny. There's no question that throughout the nineties, until that wonky knee forced his retirement, Fitzpatrick was the best scrummager in the world. When you removed him from a pack, you downgraded it drastically. It was more than coincidence that two of Auckland's three tries at Onewa were scored by Olo Brown and Fitzy; Fitzy's five-pointer coming from relentless pressure that resulted in Harbour's first-five Warren Burton dropping a pass almost on his goalline.

For the All Blacks, Fitzy was the commander and Zinny his faithful lieutenant but the roles were reversed with Auckland and the Blues. In both instances, their leadership qualities were major factors in their teams' stunning successes.

Fitzy never said a lot in the Auckland environment which is a testament to the man because he wasn't prepared to usurp Zinny's authority. Quite often, particularly on major occasions, I would suggest it appropriate for him to say a few words. When he did speak, people sat up and took notice. If he'd spoken too often, it would have lessened the impact.

At training, his contribution was huge, especially in the scrums. And on important match days, he was a colossus, as in that final at Onewa Domain that afternoon in October 1994. It wasn't pretty rugby, but it was entirely appropriate in the circumstances – powerful scrummaging, rolling mauls, total commitment. And Fitzy was the man making it happen.

Auckland's leading tryscorer in '94 – in fact, he also headed the NPC aggregate that season – was Waisake Sotutu, a player who deserved to be an All Black. Most of his games were on the wing although he played his first representative games at centre (outside Eroni Clarke), deputised occasionally at fullback – where admittedly he was a little shaky – and rounded out a distinguished career at second-five. I came in for some criticism for using him in midfield in 1997, but there weren't many options. Carlos Spencer was injured and I was using Lee Stensness at first-five and Jeremy Stanley at centre. It was Waisake or me at second-five! He was one of the most skilful players I coached and a great team man.

The 1995 season, the last we experienced with rugby as an amateur game, was a challenging one for provincial representative coaches like myself because of the demands upon our international players. For example, Auckland had to travel to South Africa and play Free State in a Super 10 fixture without our star All Blacks, who were involved in a summer training camp under Laurie Mains, who was preparing them for the World Cup. It was a bit of joke at the time, playing at altitude in 35 degree temperatures without guys like Sean Fitzpatrick, Olo Brown, Zinzan Brooke, Robin Brooke and Carlos Spencer. In the circumstances, we did well to hold Free State to 15-21. I was delighted when the Super 12 was introduced because the Super 10 had meant so little to us.

The '95 season was a bizarre mix for me as a coach. It was highlighted by the 35-0 Ranfurly Shield win over Canterbury but Auckland – and I'm responsible here, I can't pass the buck – slipped into a mode where winning became more important than the process by which it was achieved. At times, we forgot to enjoy the occasion and playing became a chore.

It wasn't helped, of course, by the All Blacks having the World Cup as a major focus in mid-year followed by the the tour of France and Italy at season's end. Unfortunately, the touring party for France and Italy was announced before the NPC had concluded, which I never believed was a smart thing to do. Too many of the guys were thinking about the tour before they'd finished their rugby business back home.

After we'd defeated North Harbour 60-26 (reversing the result of our round-robin game at Takapuna six weeks earlier) we played the NPC final against Otago at Eden Park. I wasn't happy because I didn't feel the guys were mentally right. They'd won too easily in the semi-final and had that forthcoming tour on their minds.

In a sense, it was like the All Blacks at the World Cup. Beating England so comprehensively in the semi-final had relaxed them whereas the Springboks, who were incredibly lucky to get past France, were on edge. Forgetting about the food poisoning issue, which certainly wouldn't have helped, you had two different psyches.

We won that '95 final courtesy of a penalty try awarded by Colin Hawke. It outraged the Otago fans, and, in fact, the rest of New Zealand, and wasn't the way we wanted to win the championship. That penalty try, and all the publicity that surrounded it, would come back to haunt me as a coach. In the 1998 Super 12 final against the Canterbury Crusaders, there was a stronger case for a penalty try being awarded than had confronted Colin Hawke, I believe. But Paddy O'Brien stubbornly kept resetting scrums. Subconsciously, I'm sure he remembered the controversy that surrounded Colin's decision. Paddy never awarded the penalty try I believed was well justified, thus allowing the Crusaders to stay in the game. To their great credit, they hit back and eventually won through a last-minute try by James Kerr. I think most people would accept that a penalty try in that third quarter would have given the game to the Blues.

Chapter 3

Hitting the zone

Every great achievement was a dream before someone of vision turned it into a reality.

Henry Kissinger

WE USED TO REFER to it as being In The Zone. Others might describe it simply as being on a roll. It's that perfect union rugby players spasmodically achieve when sensational things happen, almost by instinct. They buzz. And when they are In The Zone, anything's possible. The score can rocket ahead in multiples of seven. Proud opponents can be left thoroughly demoralised.

The Auckland and Auckland Blues teams with which I was involved from 1992 to 1998 slipped into The Zone just enough times to make all the planning, all the scheming, all the soggy nights at training, all the criticism, all the heartburn worthwhile. In a sense, it's why we coach... when you can sit back and observe dazzling things happening, when your team is operating with sheer precision.

Auckland hit The Zone against North Otago in that 139-point performance at Oamaru in 1993, although admittedly that was against one of the game's minnows. Probably the finest example was when the Blues slipped into overdrive in a Super 12 game against the Western Stormers at Eden Park in 1998. Everything turned to gold that day. We finished up scoring 11 tries against a highly-regarded opponent. The Blues also found The Zone in the Super 12 play-off games against Northern Transvaal and Natal in 1996.

Teams engage The Zone only when their attitude is 100 per cent. As a coach, your greatest concern is that players are not mentally attuned when they take the field. If they are, you've done your job. They can be physically and tactically prepared but if their attitude isn't right, they'll never experience The Zone. The biggest worry for a sports coach is having your team at a peak physically but trailing mentally. Then you start worrying because it's your job to tune them in all senses.

Not all the memorable performances by Auckland and the Blues involved them hitting The Zone. Auckland's classic Ranfurly Shield victory against Canterbury at Lancaster Park in 1995, for example, was a triumph for tactical planning. That performance wasn't pretty; in fact, our guys never got anywhere near The Zone. But they went out that afternoon to play rugby chess and succeeded in masterly fashion. We did things that day we never did again – like consistently kicking the ball dead, thus forcing Canterbury to take 22 drop-outs from which we regathered possession. We possibly influenced the lawmakers with our attitude that day. Now, of course, if you put the ball across the deadball line, it's a scrum back from where you kicked it.

Another unforgettable performance, the Blues' epic victory over Natal in 1996, was also achieved without embracing The Zone. It was never going to be a Zone-type game. We were too desperate for that. It was a game the Blues had to win, to secure a home semi-final. Given the circumstances – Durban's heat and humidity, a partisan home crowd and a South African referee – it was a game we had to win by 20 to 25 points to win by one! Again, it was a tactical victory. Because of their great lineout strength, we decided we would not jump on their throw-in but instead would commit every forward to the post-lineout maul, thus negating the drive which had become a feature of their play. I must say the execution of our tactical plan on that occasion gave me and the team enormous pleasure. Especially when the final whistle went and we knew we would be hosting the semi-final at Eden Park the following

Saturday. It is common in the game these days to not compete at lineouts to prevent the drive, and have the halfback in the "tramlines" and two loosies off the back forming a two-man defensive screen. Auckland's game against Natal was the first time these tactics were used.

As a coach, you don't manufacture The Zone. You create the environment from which it will flow.

My most challenging times as coach of Auckland were when the All Blacks returned from their international commitments and had to re-focus on the NPC. There's a substantial drop from test to representative level. And we're not talking throwaway tests here. Springbok coach Nick Mallett is on record as saying that the Tri-series is more competitive than the World Cup. I believe he's right.

To the layman, it probably seems pretty straightforward, dropping from international to representative level. After tangling with the might of South Africa and Australia, taking on lesser-skilled players from the provinces should be a piece of cake. And technically, that's true.

If only it were that easy. The international players who reported for Auckland NPC duty in 1996 and 1997 had been putting their bodies on the line, as Super 12 players and All Blacks, for six months virtually without a break. If their bodies were hanging together – and in many cases they weren't – mentally they were exhausted.

Almost without exception, they'd had a gutsful of rugby. They'd been under relentless pressure for many months and no matter what I did as the coach – even if I stood on my head – it made no difference. What needed to be done was to remove them from the competitive environment for a time. Give them a week in Fiji, say.

How do you determine who's ready to come back and play? The lights are on but nobody is at home. They want to perform but they are jaded and the more you as a coach push them, the worse they get.

There have been a lot of articles written, relevant to professional sport, about over-training and over-using players. They all come to the same conclusion – there's nothing you can do, until the player is mentally refreshed. Offer him a break and wait till he's enthusiastic about playing again.

It was hardest for Auckland because we had the greatest number of players involved in the All Blacks. That began to alter a bit in

1998 (after my departure for Wales) when Otago, probably for the first time in 50 years, finished up with more test players than Auckland.

The 1997 season was the most difficult of all. Auckland had won four NPCs in succession so naturally everyone wanted to knock us over, particularly teams like Canterbury and Otago. It was easier for them because most of their players were fresh. But not for us. I wanted to say to the test players, "Go take a break in Fiji," but I couldn't afford to because we had so many injuries. The All Blacks had been through the Super 12 and the Tri-series. And in November there was a tour of the UK coming up. It was worse than normal and the guys were buggered.

Quite frankly, it was only tradition that was keeping us up there. Other sides like Waikato, Canterbury and Otago had improved their standards immensely, which was good for New Zealand rugby. There had been a levelling of strengths and there was a hunger among the sides who hadn't won the NPC for a long time.

No team can stay at the top forever. We were shooting for a fifth straight title but things were going to change. I could see it. I could feel it. Saying all that, Auckland could still have fluked the title. There was nothing in the semi-final at Lancaster Park. It was all penalty goals and dropped goals. No tries.

A major negative for us was Zinzan Brooke announcing his retirement prior to the semi-final in Christchurch. It took his focus away from that game, a game in which he uncharacteristically engaged in a running battle with the referee. I hesitate to criticise Zinny, whose contribution to Auckland rugby over more than a decade was immense – indeed, I'd be the first name on the list if there was a petition to erect a statue at Eden Park in his honour – but on that particular occasion, he got it wrong. He shouldn't have made any statement about his future until the NPC was over. I appreciate that he was probably putting the interests of the All Blacks first in making his announcement, but it didn't do anything for the team he captained, Auckland.

The other factor which lessened Auckland's potency in 1997 was Sean Fitzpatrick's wonky knee. He was trying desperately to get it right but the writing was on the wall. Fitzy the indestructible was living on borrowed time. He'd been a key influence in Auckland and New Zealand success throughout the nineties and you can't just suddenly replace someone like that.

While there was undoubtedly disappointment in Auckland when Canterbury claimed the NPC title in 1997 – something it hadn't achieved since 1983 – it seemed to be accepted everywhere else that it was good for the game generally. Rugby supremacy had been Auckland's long enough, we were assured. I could appreciate that, although my philosophy was that excellence should always win out, regardless of the geographical and political circumstances.

Auckland's 15-year dominance of New Zealand rugby ended emphatically in 1998 when the team came home a distant eighth, with Otago, Waikato and Canterbury plainly the three strongest teams in the NPC competition.

The obvious question to ask is whether one team can ever dominate New Zealand rugby again as Auckland has done almost throughout the eighties and nineties. Personally, I doubt it, especially in light of the professional situation that now exists. Because the NZRFU has a policy of levelling out the standards throughout the country, you are seeing a lot of the second-tier players from Auckland, for example, being drafted elsewhere while the annual exodus overseas continues. To that extent, unions like Auckland are no longer masters of their own destiny.

Rugby dynasties, like Auckland's, occur when a group of young guys grow up together and create a camaraderie and spirit. That may not be possible under the new professional regime. The levelling of playing strengths is going to make it hard for one team to dominate. Look at Canterbury. It was supreme in 1997 and seemingly on the verge of a memorable era, yet a year later it was swept aside in the semi-finals by Waikato, which in turn was no match for Otago in the grand final.

The rugby Otago played over the last six weeks of the competition in 1998, when it averaged 65 points a game, points to continuing success. But, of course, straight away there are complications for the team, with Rugby World Cup commitments meaning it won't be able to utilise its All Blacks in '99. Also, the NZRFU has a policy of not allowing coaches dual appointments for Super 12 and NPC teams for more than one year, which takes Tony Gilbert out of the equation. I predated that ruling – one I'm not entirely convinced is in the greater interests of New Zealand rugby – enjoying three years as both the Blues and Auckland coach.

As far as Auckland goes, it's got to start again and rebuild, with hunger. The Auckland union has obviously identified Jed Rowlands, the man who developed Taranaki into a formidable unit, as the coach to revive Auckland's fortunes. But again, the NZRFU policy intrudes: Jed can only hold the joint appointments for one season. Presuming he retains the Blues coaching role in 2000, Auckland will soon be searching for another NPC coach.

It was interesting to read Maurice Trapp's comments after he'd stepped back into the Auckland coaching breach at short notice following my departure for Wales midway through 1998. In a hard-hitting statement, he said he was "dismayed" at the lack of fitness, focus and standards among the All Blacks in his side.

"There was a cancer in the Auckland side which seemed to have spread to the All Blacks," he said. "Their attitude was simply not hard enough."

He claimed the players were more professional before the game went pro than now. "Too many of them don't know the real meaning of the word professional," he said. "To them, professionalism has been about money first. The problem is that they are being paid comparatively huge salaries in New Zealand terms but they don't have the experience to know how to handle the money."

He claimed the All Blacks had forsaken the hard-grafting attitudes of the past. "These guys have reneged on the All Black template. If they get the attitude right, they will be formidable at the World Cup. If they don't, it will be disastrous." He said he had passed on his concerns to All Black coach John Hart.

Attitude. It's what I come back to. Plainly, Maurice's men obviously didn't waft into The Zone too many times in 1998, if at all. If his assessment of the Auckland All Blacks is accurate, it's got to be a matter of huge concern to the NZRFU. If their huge salaries are making them soft, then maybe the NZRFU will have to revise their contracts and perhaps introduce incentive-based payments.

With due respect to Maurice, when he previously coached Auckland the side incorporated a group of outstanding players all operating at the same time in the same team. They were clearly several classes above any other provincial side in the land. The current quality of the Auckland side means it is just another team. If it plays to its full potential perhaps it could do the business – the challenge is getting the team up to that potential.

A large number of high-quality players have been moving to other provinces, for the opportunity of playing regularly and to secure professional contracts. At the same time the Auckland Rugby Union needs to work closely with management to ensure that the team environment is always positive.

Because of the extended success of Auckland over many seasons, there were numerous youngsters who believed they had little or no chance of breaking into the team and therefore they decided to try their luck elsewhere. This problem has been added to by the aggressive player recruitment campaigns launched by Canterbury and Otago, efforts not matched by the Auckland union.

Players enjoy the provincial environment. They are heroes in Canterbury, Otago and Waikato but the low key attitude of Auckland and the Auckland rugby people means they don't receive the same attention. Maybe this doesn't seem important but for young men it is a factor. They want to feel important.

The announcement at the time of the Rugby World Cup in 1995 that a Super 12 competition was to be launched, embracing New Zealand, South Africa and Australia, came as a hell of a shock. There had been speculation that professionalism was inevitable but I don't believe many people were aware of the negotiations that would see an incredible $US550 million from Rupert Murdoch's News Ltd channelled into southern hemisphere rugby over 10 years. The International Rugby Board's decision to make the game wholly professional was inevitable after that.

Professionalism had vast ramifications for coaches like myself, who had been maintaining a delicate balancing act between an occupation and after-hours commitment to rugby teams. I had been an amateur rugby coach for 21 years, since my days at Auckland Grammar School. All that was going to change. I found the prospect pretty exciting.

Until Marguerite Seager, my secretary (and good mate) at Kelston Boys' High, suggested in her straightforward manner that I should contemplate becoming a full-time rugby coach, I have to say I hadn't too seriously considered it. Obviously, rugby was taking Graham Henry over... and sometimes you can't see the wood from the trees. In fact, I enjoyed my job at Kelston. I enjoyed the responsibility and the challenges of the position. The staff were good to work with and many I considered my mates. The kids, although always a challenge, were generally achieving. I had become so accustomed to functioning in my dual capacity that the prospect of abandoning the teaching profession hadn't crossed my mind. It was a very important job, far more important than coaching a rugby team and I guess it gave me security. Coaching, I always understood, was a year-by-year proposition. You started losing and those officials who sat in judgment on you would pretty swiftly start looking for a replacement.

First things first. I had to win the Auckland Blues job which involved a series of interviews, dealing mostly with the NZRFU's commissioner, Peter Thorburn, who was forthright in his desire to involve the best coaches in the land. I had imposing qualifications, having won three consecutive NPCs, and I had the support of the Auckland Rugby Union. My appointment was duly rubber stamped.

Next came the matter of selecting the players. I was a little anxious when I realised this was effectively out of my hands because of the NZRFU's desire to field five teams of uniform strength, involving a draft system. As a coach, you like to be in charge of your own destiny. You want players you believe will do the job for you and therefore you like to have a major say in the selection.

Generally, things worked out well. A couple of Auckland's promising back-up players were shipped off to the Otago Highlanders which didn't seem to matter at the time, but Kees Meeuws and Isitolo Maka would take such a shine to their southern setting they would return and play regularly for Otago. They would be seriously missed in Auckland, particularly Meeuws who should have been Olo Brown's successor.

Of course, the franchises were a matter of some controversy. Because the NZRFU believed that an amalgamation between Auckland and North Harbour (both teams being flush with All Blacks) would produce a Super 12 side of excessive strength, it paired Auckland off with Counties-Manukau while poor old North Harbour was lumped in with Waikato. While that in itself wasn't a bad thing, geographically it was ridiculous. It was a wrong decision and it took the NZRFU three years to correct it. It was only ever a makeshift arrangement. Personally, I didn't mind because the liaison with Counties-Manukau brought Jonah Lomu and Joeli

No sponsor's name on the leather ball I've just forced to score a try for University against Otahuhu at Eden Park in 1974 (the year we won the championship).

In an interview I gave in 1984 I said I was either mad or a rugby nut. I was trying to justify spending almost the entire year coaching rugby, having charge of the Auckland University club team and the New Zealand secondary schools team at the time.

Hmm, looks like my Auckland University team must have been trailing at halftime. An Eden Park scene from 1983.

The Auckland Grammar School first fifteen of 1979 which completed 15 matches without defeat. That's Foxy next to manager Allan Faull.

The 1980 Grammar first fifteen which won all 21 games it played, Foxy having advanced to the captaincy. Two along from manager Allan Faull is Martin Crowe, who would dazzle as a cricketer, while the pair cross-legged in front would make their mark at representative level – Mark Adam and Iain Wood.

Did you ever feel like the Pied Piper? That's me leading the Auckland Grammar rugby boys in the march past in Taiwan in 1980. Foxy's found something more interesting. Don't look too closely at the flag – it was loaned to us by Lion Breweries!

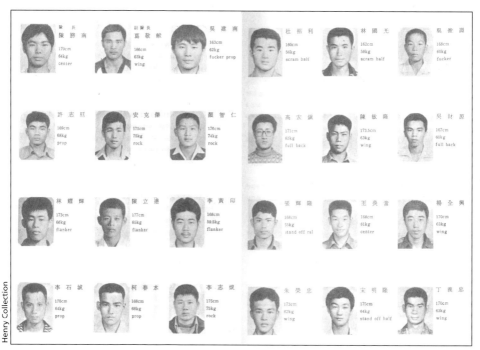

The Taiwanese, who hosted the Pan Pacific schools tournament in 1980, entered into the spirit of things and made an attempt to present part of the programme in English. They had a bit of trouble translating some of the scrum positions!

Home sweet home – the Henry property in Epsom, Auckland.

Watching a rerun of the 1997 Super 12 final against ACT Brumbies with my youngest son Andrew.

At our daughter Catherine's 21st birthday party.

Outside the new Henry residence in Wales - the appropriately-named Coach House

David 'Mr Contract' Jones.

Auckland's says farewell to Fitzy.

Vidiri, the two most dangerous wingers in New Zealand, arguably in the world, into our franchise. Between them, they would score 43 tries for the Blues in three seasons (and that was with Jonah being grounded in 1997 with kidney trouble).

I retained my post as principal of Kelston while the Super 12 was played out. However, by the start of the third term I had made the decision to commit myself 100 per cent to rugby. It was a scheduled tour by Auckland to the UK between seasons that finally forced my hand. Ironically, that trip would would fall over, although in February, as a prelude to the 1997 Super 12, Auckland would play two matches in England and one against the European champion, Brive.

It wasn't easy parting company with Kelston. I had spent 25 years in education and valued my job highly; it was a responsible position and I enjoyed being the boss. It offered security whereas a professional sports coach had his position reviewed from year to year.

There was the satisfaction of leaving Kelston in an excellent state. The school had been an achiever, both academically and outstandingly in sport. One year, we had two students in the top 10 in the country for University Bursary and examination results were usually positive, which was richly rewarding for the staff. The nature of the clientele meant life was always a challenge at Kelston. Many of the students claimed English as a second language and were from a lower socio-economic strata, and a lot of them didn't find school all that stimulating. It was vastly different from Auckland Grammar School where there were a lot of intelligent boys competing against each other. Having said that, it was challenging to the teachers to get the kids up to speed.

We achieved remarkable success in sport. Kelston won the national first XV rugby title on a number of occasions and, in 1998, took out the world schools tournament held in Zimbabwe. At soccer, the school also often claimed national supremacy while there were rich successes for the school's basketball and touch teams. We had a lot to be proud of, for the vast majority of the kids were good people. Obviously with a roll of 1250, you had to be on your toes for there was always something likely to flare up.

John Graham had had a huge influence on me when I was teaching at Auckland Grammar School and I had adopted many of his attitudes and philosophies. He'd always given teachers the opportunity to develop their talents and abilities, and that was also how I operated. As I've mentioned, several of those under me went on to become headmasters in their own right.

Suddenly, I was a full-time professional rugby coach, holding contracts with the Auckland and New Zealand unions which made it an attractive financial package. It was ludicrous, I felt, that I should be getting more to coach professional sport than I had commanded when I was in charge of 100 staff and 1250 kids. But that obviously was the way of the world.

I must say it was a marvellous sensation to realise I had only one role to fulfil. It meant I was more relaxed, that I could attend the gym and keep myself fit and do many of the fringe things that had always previously been shelved. I started communicating with my players far more, which probably came as a shock, and started spending time with the media, which obviously came as a hell of a shock to them.

In the recently-concluded amateur days, I used to identify the critical games and give major attention to them. The lesser ones I tended to skim over. But now in the Super 12 arena, every fixture was an important one for which the preparation had to be thorough.

The nicest spin-off was that I was able to settle down at nine o'clock in the morning and analyse videos as I commenced my preparation for the game ahead. Previously, the only time in my crammed schedule when I could work videos in was usually around midnight. I went through withdrawal symptoms there for a while, not quite knowing what to do with myself in the evenings at home.

Obviously one series of video analyses the Auckland coach interpreted incorrectly concerned the Queensland Reds, our eighth opponent that first season. We were coming off a useful victory over the Waikato Chiefs while they were obviously hurting after losing to the ACT Brumbies in Canberra (where every visiting team lost for two whole seasons).

We took an unbelievable pasting, by 51 points to 13, and I seem to remember we scored the last try! The thrashing was every bit as comprehensive as the scoreline suggests. We started poorly and never remotely looked like getting into the game.

To this day, I cannot account for such a wretched performance, except to say that the Queensland Reds have inexplicably been an underachiever for the three seasons the Super 12 has operated, because they can field virtually a full international fifteen. It was my considered opinion that they were the best team in the Super 12 that first year. At their best they were capable of taking any team to the cleaners, as they did us that night. I've never been through a game where my team took such a mauling.

We rebounded from that astonishing result to win the championship whereas they didn't progress beyond the semi-finals in 1996, then plummeted down the ladder the next season.

As a coach, I believe it's important to take something out of every game. While Brisbane was a painful experience, positives did come out of it. Any time we lost, it made me more determined than ever to get everything right. Losses certainly screwed up the Blues coach who in turn screwed down the players. That 50-point hammering, which was pretty humiliating at the time, provoked some serious thinking from the coach, a lot of it lateral. It must have worked because we came away to put 56 points on the New South Wales Waratahs five days later.

Although the Blues would take out the championship and produce some stunningly effective rugby in the play-offs, I was disappointed with much of that 1996 season. Super 12 had come upon us so suddenly, it hadn't allowed us to prepare properly. In a sense, it was a journey into the unknown, having to play 11 high-pressure matches in three countries in 10 weeks. The organisers didn't get it right that first season, either, expecting travelling teams to play midweek matches. For instance, we took on Transvaal at Ellis Park on a Tuesday night and had to regroup for the all-important fixture with Natal in Durban four days later.

We came of age as a team in that Durban game when there was enormous pressure on us. We'd played like idiots against Transvaal, which was at the bottom of the competition. At least against Queensland we'd tried hard, but at Ellis Park the guys just weren't there. Whether the travel and altitude were factors, I don't know, but it was the type of performance that makes coaches consider taking up some other pastime.

I found out several months later that Doc Paterson and Richard Fromont had been arm wrestling in the days prior to the Transvaal game. Doc was always trying to prove he was fitter and stronger than the players. It was a bloody obsession, the only weakness in a top person and an outstanding professional. Fromont took the field at Ellis Park with one good arm and played like a clown, which he didn't have to try hard to do. With attitudes like that, no wonder we struggled. Doc and Richard told me several months after the incident – it was humorous then but, hell, I don't know how I would have reacted if I'd been told at the time.

The Transvaal loss was annoying because a victory would have clinched a home semi-final. Instead, we now had to beat Natal, a daunting prospect at King's Park.

Zinzan Brooke, our captain, reckoned we would be okay, that Auckland teams always played well when their backs were against the wall. While he was correct in this line of thinking, as a coach I couldn't help but wonder why Aucklanders needed to encounter adversity before producing their best.

REX DAVY
Auckland Blues manager
I was associated with Graham for seven years and although he always hated losing, that Ellis Park defeat in 1996 was the only time I recall him reacting personally. Normally, he saves his comments for the next team session but in Johannesburg that night he was confronting people in the bar demanding to know why the team had performed so poorly. He was very upset.

As professionalism bedded in, Zinny and I became more professional ourselves. One of our greatest strengths was to exploit the opposition style and weaknesses. I'd do the initial homework by video, providing information that the players would assimilate and we'd play accordingly.

It's all very well having a plan on paper but what your team puts into effect doesn't always equal to the theory. So we'd practise till we had confidence in our strategies. Guys like Michael Jones and Zinny in particular were outstanding in assessing what was right and what was theoretically flawed, with Zinny developing into a great leader. Their instincts were second to none. As loosies, they knew the lines to run for maximum effect. It was stimulating to work with these people. Along with Mark Carter, Andrew Blowers, Junior Tonu'u, Carlos Spencer, Eroni Clarke and Lee

Stensness, we'd work out defensive patterns that were awesomely efficient. They were a group right at the top of the tree who created a fabulous environment in which to work.

We worked out Natal for that crunch game in 1996 but to combat them meant changing how we had been playing. I had to get the guys to buy into my strategies. Fortunately, I had a group who had confidence in me that my daring theories would work.

REX DAVY
Graham got me to run the first team meeting in Durban. He didn't want to be out front. Instead, he stood back and listened as the players had their say. Then he came forward with his radical plan for upsetting Natal.

We went to a little club south of Durban to put our blackboard concepts into effect. Two of the most potent weapons Natal possessed were flyhalf Henry Honiball as an attacker and Mark Andrews and Steve Atherton as a locking combination. Honiball ran a lot and his team consistently drove off lineout takes. We had to neutralise both of these strengths. There were a few raised eyebrows among the troops when I suggested we would not jump at the lineout on Natal's throw but commit every forward to stopping their drive. It's a common ploy now but it was quite revolutionary back then. Our second defensive ace was to have Michael Jones shadow Honiball from every set piece, ensuring he never had room to run straight or cut back. We left him with a solitary option – to run outwards, where we could cover him.

We operated, for the first time I believe, a two-pronged defensive screen at the back end of the lineout, using Michael Jones and Andrew Blowers. We concentrated on Honiball, ensuring he didn't get close to the advantage line. Andrew went directly for Honiball while Michael, utilising his freakish anticipation skills, knocked over whoever Honiball passed to. Usually, it was an inside pass. This put a serious dent in the major components of Natal's game plan – the drive from the lineout and its ability to consistently bridge the advantage line through Honiball and players around him.

We also stacked our three loosies at the front of the lineout on our own throw, with the jumpers at the back. Usually we threw short to Michael Jones. It was done to confuse the enemy, to keep them thinking. The home advantage was enough in their favour – we never wanted them thereafter to feel comfortable.

REX DAVY
We didn't spent much time practising these innovative methods because we were worried about who might be spying on us. Most of the planning was done on the blackboard. After the Wednesday training, Graham ordered a 5.30pm meeting in the bar. No one was excused. It wasn't a drinking session, just a social hour, an important bonding time. It was when the dismal performance of Ellis Park was put behind us and the challenge of King's Park became our total focus.

Notwithstanding our innovative methods, Natal proved a doughty opponent and hung in grimly but a classic late try by Eroni Clarke, created by Lee Stensness, secured the victory. I've never known a happier dressing room. The guys were chuffed because they knew they'd implemented a game plan to perfection to overcome one of the most formidable provincial sides in the world; and they were enormously relieved to be going home. I doubt I could have got them up to win the semi-final if they'd been quartered in Durban for another week.

It was an entirely different scenario at Eden Park a fortnight later when we re-engaged Ian McIntosh's men in the final. Now the 40,000 fans were all behind us, the referee was neutral and the players had been experiencing normalcy in their homes instead of living out of suitcases in a hotel in a foreign country. You can't beat a home advantage, particularly at play-off time when the odds are stacked against the travelling side which has 48 hours to organise itself after the final pool match. For those South African teams, it involves an exhausting 23-hour journey across the Indian Ocean and the Tasman Sea.

Without being able to justify my argument with scientific evidence, I can tell you jetlag is a greater problem for rugby teams returning from South Africa than going. But in 1996 the excitement was so high after qualifying for a home semi-final that it overcame all these challenges. Experiencing a full house at Eden Park –

something which only intermittently occurred even for test matches – and having all New Zealand cheering for Auckland created the perfect environment for a top-notch performance. We received countless messages of goodwill from around the country. As the only New Zealand team to qualify for the play-offs in that first season, the country was firmly behind us. It was an unusual situation but most reassuring.

I think we probably expected to be playing the Queensland Reds in the final because, as the top qualifiers, John Connolly's men had the home semi-final advantage. But Natal played outstandingly in Brisbane to come through, a win every bit as meritorious, I considered, as ours had been in Durban the weekend before.

I knew the guys were right for the final. I've never experienced three weeks where a group of players was on such a high – we would have beaten any team in the world. The players were in The Zone for three weeks effectively… confident, excited and wanting to express themselves, with the senior pros at the peak of their powers. Even though test matches are the ultimate in rugby, it would be hard to derive greater enjoyment and satisfaction than what we as a team experienced at that time. Even the coach was relaxed! Especially when the boys slipped into The Zone against Northern Transvaal in the semi and Natal in the final. They collected 14 tries in those two games to confirm their status as the best team in the Super 12 in 1996. Their confidence and class would roll over into 1997.

For the two play-offs we went through the usual analysis of the opposition. After the successful tactics employed in Durban, we had made a quantum step forward in our defensive pattern and it was a matter of perfecting this for the finals. We were on a high mentally and there was a collective desire in the team to take these two South African sides apart. We were in The Zone. The confidence among the group was enormous – we wanted to play our game and express ourselves with the ball, from all parts of the field.

After the pain of Transvaal and the win against Natal – achieved by sheer guts and determination – added to by the "new" defensive strategy, there was a huge focused attitude among the group that the blood, our blood, left on the field at King's Park in Durban was not going to be wasted by defeat at home. Attitudes were on the edge of the edge, and attitude is everything if you are going to play in The Zone.

Despite that, Henry Honiball did break us on a One Double Two (when the first-five doubles around behind the second-five) for an outstanding try. So absolute perfection in rugby may never be attained but, oh, what huge satisfaction in trying to achieve it with a team at the peak of its powers.

REX DAVY
In 1995, Auckland played before largely empty stadiums. It was the year the Warriors were launched and the floating sports population of Auckland were all obviously going off to Ericsson Stadium.

A year later, when the Auckland Blues played Northern Transvaal in the Super 12 semi-final, you couldn't fit another person into Eden Park. It was the same a week later for the final against Natal, an incredible experience. You had the feeling not only everyone in the ground was cheering for Graham's team but the whole of New Zealand was behind the Blues.

One of the great strengths of the Blues, particularly in 1996 and 1997 when Zinny and Fitzy were involved, was their ability to improvise, to change tactics on the field. It's paramount to have this flexibility because although a coach can outline several ways to play, the guys in the middle have to have the nous to know which tactical plan is going to work. We were lucky to have individuals like Zinny, Fitzy, Robin Brooke, Junior Tonu'u – who was always a good decision maker – and the props, guys who were always thinking as well as playing.

What wins most games, involving teams of comparable strength, is your ability to stop the opposition playing their game. It hurts them psychologically when you shut them down. Australians are naturally confident and cocky and approach matches so positively they appear personally affronted if you disrupt their battle plan. The Aussie attitude has won them a lot of tests when they weren't necessarily the better team and they've simply out-psyched the opposition. While that brazen attitude could be their great strength, it could also become a weakness, one as a coach I always enjoyed challenging.

A classic example was the Blues' clash with the ACT Brumbies at Pukekohe in 1997. The Brumbies had been tearing opponents apart across in Canberra. They were superbly coached by Rod Macqueen and in flyhalf David Knox they had one of the most talented attacking footballers in the world. Knox had defensive deficiencies but tactically he was a master, possessed of skilful hands and deft touch. He was a super passer of the ball, with seemingly dozens of options at his grasp. He operated flat enough to embarrass any opposition.

Some opponents were easy to work out because their game plan was so narrow but the Brumbies presented a major challenge, Knox being the catalyst for goers like Stephen Larkham and Joe Roff. Analysing the video of Knox and the Brumbies' backline from the week before, I was confident that we could read them.

If you're working on a plan to neutralise Knox, who better to implement it than Michael Jones, Zinzan Brooke and Mark Carter? I spent a lot of time analysing videos of Knox and the Brumbies backline in action that week before I was confident they could read him. We then devised a strategy, involving the three loosies and the inside backs, to curb the Brumbies attacks. Our video study of the Brumbies backline also yielded a bonus, a defensive weakness we felt we could probe at centre.

We were coming off a thoroughly unconvincing performance against the Canterbury Crusaders in which we'd sneaked home, as much by good fortune as good play, by a solitary point. As a consequence of that, combined with the Brumbies' smashing form, many of the pundits were predicting a loss for the Blues.

Well, Zinny and Michael and Mark smothered the Brumbies' backline operations so effectively you could almost hear the Aussies shouting, "What the hell's going on?" While we were shutting them down, we were prospering ourselves by penetrating their midfield with almost ridiculous ease. We finished up scoring six tries that afternoon, winning 41 to 29. Their 29 included three tries scored inside the final 10 minutes when we took our foot off the accelerator.

Our next opponents, the Gauteng Lions, had obviously studied our performance against the Brumbies and concluded that the way to close us down was to stand up flat and knock us over. If we'd persisted with Plan A, they would have strangled the life out of us. But that's where a captain like Zinny was so mighty. "Stuff this," he told his players, "they're making a meal out of us. We're switching to pick-up-and-go. See how they handle that!" Changing tactics isn't something you can do from the grandstand – although admittedly it's easier now in this electronic age – so to observe your players seizing the initiative like that was enormously satisfying. The Transvaalers had no answer to Plan B and eventually lost 63-22.

REX DAVY
Graham had an established matchday routine which seldom varied, whether his team was playing home or away. After breakfast and having overseen the players doing a few drills in the carpark or at a nearby park, he would adjourn to his room around 10.30am to prepare his team talk, always pouring himself a cup of tea. I'd hang around for no more than 20 minutes then leave him to it. He'd invariably ask if I had any "gems", any buzz-words appropriate to that day's encounter.

I wouldn't see him again until the team meeting when he always spoke from his notes, constantly referring to them. His team talks were marvellous to listen to. He never swore and hardly ever raised his voice. He delivered his talks rather with all the skill of a top headmaster addressing a college assembly, often hanging his comments around a word or a theme, constantly reminding the players of what they'd practised during the week.

He sometimes asked me if he really needed to produce a team talk and I always said yes. Some players don't need them but for many they provide reassurance and are part of the ritual of match day. Most of the players would be tense but some, most notably Mark Carter, were relaxed. Carter was the most relaxed individual I ever encountered. He and Graham usually winked at each other before the session started.

The bus trip to the ground was always undertaken in silence, a time for reflection.

Once at the ground, Graham was always quiet, almost serene. If it was the Blues, he'd leave the words to Mac McCallion and the players. If it was Auckland, he'd let John Graham, or whoever was his assistant, do the talking. He might just have a quiet word with someone like Carlos Spencer but generally he never said anything in the dressing room.

During the game he would never yell or scream or demonstrate any emotion, certainly not in the manner of England coach Clive Woodward, one who never hides his feelings. He'd follow the play closely and instantly note if a defence wasn't organised. He'd see tries coming quite a bit before they were scored.

During the Ranfurly Shield challenge against Canterbury at Lancaster Park in 1995 when the score was 22-nil, he leant across and said nervously, "Do you think we've got it won?" I assured him we did. In fact, we'd strangled them to death long before that.

After games, if he was pleased he'd let the players know. If we'd played poorly and perhaps lost, he would never berate the players. He never singled out individuals for criticism; in Graham's book, if the game was lost, it was the whole team that lost it. He always gave credit to the opposition, choosing to sort out his own team's problems later.

The only occasion he ever displayed emotion after a poor performance was following the Super 12 loss to Transvaal at Ellis Park in 1996. He was really angry that night, knowing the players' sub-standard performance – against the bottom team – could well have cost them a home semi-final.

Graham always took defeats personally. The team room would be like a morgue for the next 24 hours. Then he'd refocus on the next assignment and set about ensuring it didn't happen again. Such was his ability as a coach and motivator that in the seven years I was associated with him, he only once suffered two consecutive losses (and that was in 1996 when the All Blacks were in South Africa). Zinzan Brooke had a phrase which Graham later borrowed: Remember what it's like to lose – and make sure it doesn't happen again.

I like to think that an important ingredient in the success of both Auckland and the Blues was the qualities of assertiveness and ownership installed in the players. It's easy for a coach to over-direct and one thing I learnt along the way was to place responsibility for the team in the players' hands. At the end of the day, they're at the coal-face, having to make the critical decisions. As a coach, you can't be with them 24 hours a day. So individual ownership and responsibility is a most important part of developing a team, and it's something that is applying more and more as professional rugby beds in.

The players who come to the fore are those with balance in their lives. Some are natural leaders but others have to be developed. They have to take control of themselves and take on the responsibilities that go with being a professional sportsman. That means having interests outside rugby, be it self-employment, working for a company or studies. Those players who limit their personal involvement purely to rugby run the danger of becoming stale, or "brain-dead" as former All Black prop John Drake very appropriately described them. You can't have guys sitting around watching videos and working out at the gym as their only interests beyond rugby

When Sean Fitzpatrick and Zinzan Brooke stopped playing, we went through an important phase with the Blues to ensure that the surviving senior players in the side took over the leadership. It was important that guys like Craig Dowd, Robin Brooke, Olo Brown and Eroni Clarke, who'd been marvellous support players for Zinny and Fitzy (at representative and international level) stepped up to become leaders. For a couple of weeks, with the assistance of a sports psychologist, we worked solidly on this important aspect prior to the start of the 1998 Super 12 series. If we hadn't done it, I don't believe the Blues would have qualified again for the play-offs.

You've got to empower the individual to take responsibility for themselves and the team, rather than you, the coach, forever being the main man. The coach has to keep emphasising this. This attitude doesn't apply only to rugby (or sports) teams. I used it most effectively as a headmaster at Kelston Boys' High, empowering those under me to take greater responsibility. If people have that ownership they perform better.

Assertiveness – it became the culture of Auckland rugby, a culture that demanded that Auckland would be the best provincial team in the world. It was an attitude introduced when John Hart took control of the Auckland team in 1982 and maintained when Maurice Trapp succeeded him. It was an objective more easily fulfilled as time went on because of the remarkable sequence of successes built up through the eighties and on into the nineties. The Ranfurly Shield held a permanent place at Eden Park from 1985 to 1993 while the NPC was won in 1982, 1984-85, 1987-88-89-90 and 1993-94-95-96.

Eleven NPCs in 15 seasons, an amazing record. I doubt we'll ever see such domination by one team again, partly because of the professional scene which has led to the dispersement of talent. Auckland's situation has been unique. There has never been one team dominate to the same extent in South Africa where Natal, Western Province, Transvaal and Northern Transvaal have all had their terms as top dog.

I expected more of the South African teams when the Super 12 was introduced. Although Natal (who later became the Coastal Sharks and are now simply the Sharks) has always been competitive and has fashioned an excellent record, generally speaking the South Africans have been hugely disappointing. For two reasons – they haven't travelled well and since regionalisation was introduced, there seems to have been a lot of infighting. With Nick Mallett now heavily involved in team selection and, one imagines, in general preparation, we can expect improved showings. Considering the shortcomings of the South African teams, Mallett has done a marvellous job, in a remarkably short time, to pull things together with the Springboks. Not only has he fashioned a magnificent record which will see South Africa go into the 1999 Rugby World Cup as the favourite but his team has produced a great brand of rugby.

Mallett isn't a person I've had any dealings with, but I have a feeling our philosophies and attitudes would run along parallel lines. The South African coach with whom I developed a strong relationship was Ian McIntosh, who didn't retreat into his shell after being dismissed as Springbok coach but, because of his love of and commitment to the game, has given huge service to Natal and the Sharks. Rod Macqueen in his days with the Brumbies was another with whom I had a good, positive association. There was never a negative situation between us. Some coaches you respect more than others and whenever I encountered Ian or Rod, we would also discuss current issues and wish each other well.

The team I respected most over the years in which I was coaching at first-class level was Otago, because on the paddock the southerners never saw themselves as second best. That was because Laurie Mains and Gordon Hunter (and obviously the latest coach, Tony Gilbert) were always so positive in their approach. More often than not, Otago would play to its potential, which always reflects generously on the coach. I experienced defeat once at Carisbrook and although my teams always managed to come out on top at Eden Park, we were desperately fortunate a couple of times, especially in 1995 when Mr Hawke awarded that now-infamous penalty try.

The Auckland guys always enjoyed playing at Carisbrook, because of the stimulating atmosphere that existed there. The fans were always patriotic, but fair. That support undoubtedly meant a huge amount to the Otago players. It was something I often missed at Eden Park; indeed, I would have loved to have taken the Otago public to Eden Park.

Unfortunately, I can't offer the same degree of enthusiasm for the city in which I was born and bred, Christchurch, where the spectators were consistently boorish and over the top, to the point of being embarrassing. If you won at Dunedin, they treated you with respect, but that wasn't always the case in Christchurch, where crude banners and personal insults reflected the very opposite. Some of the adult behaviour at Lancaster Park (now Jade Stadium) was the very worst role model for kids. As a person involved in the education system, I recognised that and as a one-time Christchurch citizen always found it most disappointing. It was probably only a minority involved, but they certainly made their presence felt.

Chapter 4

So long Zinny, farewell Fitzy

If you're not part of the steamroller, you're part of the road.
Rich Frank, studio president, Walt Disney

FROM THE MOMENT THE SUPER 12 was introduced in 1996 it was obvious that teams like Auckland were going to get less and less value from their international players. For the very obvious reason that by August when the NPC bursts into life, the leading individuals, coming off six months of intense rugby action – for their Super 12 franchises and the All Blacks – are stuffed. They need rest, they need to re-activate themselves before tackling another succession of extremely competitive provincial contests. Unfortunately, the structure of the season now doesn't allow them that rest time.

It hadn't been too bad in 1996 because the old firm of Zinzan Brooke and Sean Fitzpatrick were still at the height of their powers and there was no end-of-season tour (apart from a cameo visit by the Barbarians club to England) to act as a distraction to anyone.

But it was a completely different scenario once the Tri-nations series was wrapped up in 1997. The old maestro Fitzy was carrying a knee injury that would be terminal as far as his career was concerned, captain Zinny was deep into negotiations with the Harlequins club of London, Michael Jones was recovering from another monumental knee reconstruction and all the international players (except for Zinny, who was wondering whether to announce his retirement) were thinking about the All Black tour of the UK coming up in November.

It was bloody hard work for the coach, too, I can tell you. Perhaps I'd had enough, anyway. Who knows? But it's not easy trying to revive a cluster of All Blacks who are mentally flat and physically battered to operate at a level several notches below that at which they have been competing.

The situation was compounded in '97 because, while we were plainly weakened, a number of other unions were patently much stronger. Obviously into this category fell Canterbury, Waikato, Counties-Manukau and Otago, although it would be another year before Otago would blossom fully. The number of injuries associated with the Auckland squad meant it wasn't possible to give the All Blacks the rest time they needed. On top of which Fitzy was a virtual passenger and Zinny was having trouble getting focused.

For all that, we still qualified for the semi-finals but through finishing only third, behind Waikato and Canterbury – having lost to both those teams – it meant that for the first time since 1994 (when a different system operated, with the play-off venues being the opposite to where the round-robin game was staged) we would have to try and qualify for the final away from home. And at Jade Stadium, before a partisan (capacity) crowd, that was a daunting assignment.

We lost 15-21, with neither side managing a try. We probably had more opportunities than Canterbury and could have fluked a victory but in the the context of the season, the result was probably fair enough. Unfortunately, Zinny, our captain, became frustrated with referee Paddy O'Brien and allowed his normally steel discipline to loosen. Not that Paddy was blameless, for it seemed to me he over-reacted also.

I had the impression, from my position in the grandstand, that most of the 50-50 decisions went against us. We were certainly up against it. Auckland had won four successive NPCs and the first two Super 12s which, from a New Zealand rugby marketing viewpoint, was not considered a good thing. While Auckland followers were obviously on good terms with themselves, the feeling elsewhere was that the game would prosper more if success in the major competitions was shared around.

I had attended a meeting at the NZRFU where it was suggested I should give serious consideration to taking over the coaching of the Otago Highlanders, who had finished last in 1997. It was made abundantly clear that the game's administrators, and certainly the marketing people, felt that Auckland's continued domination was not a good thing.

I heard their comments and would give serious consideration to the move. The prospect of a fresh challenge had appeal. But I came away from the meeting with a feeling of unease. If the administrators were feeling this way, and wanted the spoils shared around, were the referees of like mind? I remember thinking that perhaps there should be neutral referees for NPC finals and even for Super 12 play-offs if two New Zealand teams were involved. Perhaps I was being paranoid but I couldn't help feeling that things were building against us.

Paddy O'Brien is a most accomplished referee, who merits the tag of New Zealand's No 1. But he was a South Islander handling a semi-final contest between teams from the North and South Islands. Is it not possible he was hearing the NZRFU's desire to wrench the major titles away from Auckland? I'm not suggesting for one moment that Paddy went out with a preconceived concept of how he would referee the game. But subconsciously might not that pressure have affected his decision making? I think anyone who watched the video of that contest at Lancaster Park would have to acknowledge that Paddy, who is normally so unflappable, was wound up like a clock that evening.

Canterbury's victory – its second at our expense that season, the red and blacks keeping us try-less on both occasions – produced a grand final at Lancaster Park with Counties-Manukau which made all the rugby people of Canterbury ecstatic and undoubtedly heartened the good people at the NZRFU who were marketing the game nationally.

The offer to move to Dunedin and coach from the commencement of the 1998 season had appeal. As I've mentioned, I'm a great admirer of the rugby scene down south and envious of the passion and enthusiasm they generate. It would be bloody marvellous for a coach to have that sort of support. Financially, it was attractive because there was talk of a double contract which would have meant coaching Otago as well. While I was reasonably keen, logistically it didn't work out. Raewyn had commitments as a teacher and as coach of the Auckland netball team while Andrew had important exams coming up at school. I was only prepared to move on the condition the whole family came with me because I wasn't interested in spending 12 months without them.

Around the time I was concluding that a transfer south was improbable, the Auckland Rugby Union tabled an offer making it worthwhile for me to stay put. Their perceived loyalty merited loyalty in return. And the fact the family couldn't go south clinched it.

The person responsible for keeping me in Auckland was the ARU chief executive officer, Peter Scutts. Peter did a lot for Auckland rugby in his short time as CEO. He was an excellent entrepreneur and built a strong working relationship with the Auckland A team and the Blues. He was able to underpin the team with positive contracts. There was a confident buzz when Peter was CEO and the Auckland team and management missed him when he was headhunted for a top position in advertising.

It's interesting to ponder how things might have developed if I had taken up the Otago offer. For a start, I almost certainly would not now be in Wales. Another slant on it is that Tony Gilbert wouldn't have been given the opportunity if I'd moved south. And look what a sensational success he has been, with both the Highlanders and Otago.

When the new season rolled around, I was once again in charge of the Blues and Auckland, in addition to which the NZRFU had appointed me coach of the New Zealand A team, with Frank Oliver as my assistant. That was fine, with the defeat in the previous year's NPC fuelling my desire to prove myself once again as a coach. My contract with the Auckland union was signed and sealed but my contract with the NZRFU was not. There were several items which, on the advice of my lawyer, David Jones, my adviser on contractual matters, had been referred back to the national body. Many months later, when I entered into negotiations with the Welsh Rugby Union, the contract had still not been returned to me.

Winning a third Super 12 crown became a massive challenge when it was apparent we would have to operate without Zinzan Brooke, who'd taken himself off to the UK, and Sean Fitzpatrick, who wouldn't announce his retirement until May but who was severely handicapped with a worn-out knee. These two guys had made almost 300 appearances between them for Auckland and another 228 for the All Blacks, as well as providing essential leadership, punch and inspiration to the Auckland Blues throughout the first two seasons of the competition. We are talking two of the great rugby players of all time. You cannot extract that sort of experience and talent from a team and expect that things will carry on as before.

The first challenge was to select a captain. For this purpose I brought together the senior members of the pack, Robin Brooke, Craig Dowd, Olo Brown and Michael Jones, to discuss the matter. I initially promoted the unique concept of having different captains for particular games. The players considered it wouldn't work, although I felt it would. But, obviously, if I couldn't sell the idea to them, it wasn't worth pursuing.

Michael Jones became the captain, an appointment about which the other three were adamant. I was delighted to have someone of his standing leading the team. It was a case of whether the captaincy was going to be a difficulty for him. Could he play enough rugby? That was probably the major concern because he'd been plagued with injuries, major and minor, for several seasons, not because of any brittleness but because, having such a huge heart and being so totally dedicated, he put his body on the line so fearlessly.

While Michael was the captain, in the absence of Zinny and Fitzy who had been such dominating personalities, we spread the leadership among the senior players, involving Robin, Craig, Olo and Eroni Clarke. It was a case of making more people responsible. Programmes were set in place to achieve this and I believe it was a success. Though we didn't achieve the phenomenally high standards of 1997, when we were undefeated, we still performed outstandingly, qualifying top and making it through to the grand final for the third successive season. Against the best provincial teams of New Zealand, Australia and South Africa, that was an achievement of which we could be mightily proud. We actually performed better in the round-robin than in 1996 when we lost three matches and took that buffeting from the Queensland Reds in Brisbane.

Robin Brooke made great advancement as a leader. Perhaps it was the departure of brother Zinzan that gave him the freedom to express himself. He was totally supportive of Michael and masterminded the lineouts for us. His efforts were rewarded with the appointment as vice-captain of the All Blacks.

With Zinzan gone, Charles Riechelmann was obviously going to play an important role in the competition but he survived only 90 seconds of the first practice game at Coolum before breaking his ankle. Not only was it a devastating blow for our team, it was enormously sad for Charles, because he is a marvellous guy to have in a group. I have huge admiration for him. He's had a wretched run with injuries but never puts his baggage on to anyone else, which is quite remarkable.

Charles was an invaluable utility forward, equally adept at lock as blindside flanker. Choosing a replacement presented obvious problems, with the best dozen or so locks and utilities already allocated to the various franchises. The options included Richard Fromont, who, although he'd worn the All Black jersey, wasn't right physically, I believed, and Blair Larsen. The guys wanted Fromont, not least because he's a humorous character who does good things for team spirit.

On instinct, I phoned Kiwi Searancke, Waikato's forward coach, and Alistair Scown, the former All Black also based in the Waikato, and asked what they could tell me about Royce Willis, who was on the draft list. They both recommended him, for his strength, scrummaging ability and attitude. They were impressive qualities so I went for him, which turned out to be an inspired decision.

It's extremely rare for a player not ranked in the top 15 in his position at the start of a season – particularly in a specialist position like lock – to make such phenomenal progress that by season's end he is commanding a regular test spot. But that was Royce Willis, who at 22 was one of the younger (if not the youngest) players in his position in the entire Super 12. He made an instant impact and immediately gave me valuable options in the lineout. Against power-scrummaging sides, we used Royce as Robin Brooke's locking partner. But if the greater need was quick lineout ball, we included Leo Lafaiali'i who had a similar spring to Ian Jones. At least, that's how we launched ourselves into the competition. Pretty soon, however, it became apparent that Willis was so effective in all aspects of his play that we couldn't leave him out. Weighing 120kg and supremely fit, he was a footballer going places.

In preparation for the 1997 season, we'd zoomed off to the UK for three matches, against Bristol, Harlequins and the European club champion, Brive. That was an interesting experiment. It's essential you meet quality opponents in the build-up to a competition like Super 12, which we certainly did, and indeed we had the satisfaction of putting 47 points on Brive. But coming away from searing summer heat in New Zealand, it was a shock to be plunged into near-zero temperatures in England. We'd scarcely acclimatised after a stay of two weeks when we were winging our way south for our Super 12 opener at Pretoria where the temperature was back up in the thirties!

We anticipated heat, altitude and a fired-up Northern Transvaal side would be the major challenges at Loftus Versfeld but our greatest concern was a virus which struck the team soon after we arrived in South Africa. Shades of the All Blacks before the 1995 World Cup final! For the Wednesday training session, there were only 10 players standing, but we managed to battle back to reasonable health and played out a cracker on the Saturday, the final score being a remarkable 40-all.

From there, we moved on to Bloemfontein where we defeated Free State. It wasn't a memorable performance; in fact, it was a bore. We never threatened The Zone, just did what we had to do. Then beat it back to New Zealand. Without being too unkind about South Africa, where the sporting facilities are magnificent and the rugby people wonderful hosts, the level of crime throughout the country is horrifying. You get into a syndrome there – play, hopefully win and get out of the place as fast as possible.

The build-up to the 1998 Super 12 was more appropriate. We joined the Crusaders, the Waratahs and the Reds at the delightful holiday resort of Coolum, on the Sunshine Coast north of Brisbane, in what was billed as the Southern Cross tournament. Because the All Blacks had endured a major tour of the UK, running through till December, I delayed the Blues' assembly until February and took a deliberately low-key approach at Coolum. So low-key, I think many of the guys thought they were there for the the golf, the beach and the sunshine! Which is how they played first up against the Crusaders, when we suffered an embarrassing 33-0 hiding. Cycling to the ground from our hotel indicated that we weren't exactly treating the occasion as a test match. That result sharpened us up and we actually finished first equal in the tournament, which meant nothing really.

There's no point in Super 12 teams peaking in February and March when the crunch games come in late May, but our gentle approach proved costly when we crashed to the Coastal Sharks in the tournament opener in Durban. With Zinny and Fitzy gone, the doomsday merchants had a ball after that result. They would have had more fuel but for what ranks as the most unbelievable comeback of my coaching career, at Ellis Park a week later. Well, I guess Auckland's effort in scoring 21 points in the final 10 minutes to rescue a Ranfurly Shield match against Bay of Plenty at Eden Park would rival it. But considering the venue (mighty Ellis Park), the opposition (a Golden Cats team dripping with Springboks) and the circumstances (the Blues had taken out two championships without ever losing two matches in a row), this performance comes right out of the believe-it-or-not category.

We were effectively dead and buried. But I guess as long as you've got people like Michael Jones, Joeli Vidiri, Eroni Clarke and Robin Brooke in your team, anything is possible. We began playing high-risk rugby and got away with it while they lost their focus completely. When your team is 37-11 down, you're squirming and wondering how much worse it can get. When half an hour later the scoreline reads 38-37 to your team, it all seems totally unreal. I guess we were fortunate to have a neutral referee in Wayne Erickson whose brave decision, in a hostile environment, to award a penalty try at the death sealed the Cats' fate.

"If" is the most useless word in the English language, I know, but it's interesting to contemplate how the Golden Cats' season might have developed if they'd finished us off, as they should have. They never recovered from that demoralising setback and lost their next eight matches, finishing last in the competition!

One of the tryscorers and leading contributors to the victory at Ellis Park was Eroni Clarke, a player for whom I have the greatest admiration. He's been a mighty servant of Auckland rugby for a long time and was hard done by the All Black selectors. He was a commanding individual at centre as Auckland won four NPCs and the Blues took out two Super 12s, and I was personally disappointed he received no recognition until well into the 1998 season when the national selectors had exhausted all other options.

When Eroni and Frank Bunce opposed each other, they were classic contests. There was never a clear-cut winner, yet Frank played 55 tests virtually in succession while Eroni was abandoned after 1993. Despite his rejection by the All Black selectors, he never lost his poise or enthusiasm and I never once heard him utter an unkind word about them. He was a great role model who always played particularly well for us. What a cruel twist that after finally regaining his test jersey in 1997 he should suffer such a crippling injury in the opening Super 12 contest at the commencement of the new season.

Another player who suffered a shattering injury when he seemed poised to break into the big time was Paul Mitchell, the hooker who linked with the Auckland Blues when Fitzpatrick's future was in jeopardy at the start of 1998. Mitchell by then was 30, with 129 games for King Country behind him. Not the qualifications you'd think would point to a rosy future. But Paul, brother of John who is making his mark as the forward coach of England, had proven himself in a leadership role with King Country. And with Fitzy and Zinny gone, we desperately needed players who could lead. In the Blues environment he got himself fitter than he'd ever been. As a player, he went from strength to strength and, I believe, could have become an All Black in 1998. It was a very sad morning when he came to grief. We were doing cross-training at Red Beach when Paul, concentrating on pulling his life-jacket on, collided with a riderless jet ski. His leg was shattered and he was in a plaster cast for some months. If he can reproduce his 1998 form, there's no reason why he couldn't follow his brother into the All Blacks.

Hooker was an enormously troublesome position for the Blues in '98. With Fitzy retired, Paul Mitchell in plaster and Andrew Roose injured, we eventually finished up with 19-year-old James Christian doing the job. A promising kid, he'd graduated from the Auckland Colts and not only held his own in the Town Hall company but had the satisfaction of scoring our only try in the final.

Notwithstanding all those difficulties, we still managed to progress satisfactorily to the play-offs, losing only one game after Durban, predictably the clash with the Queensland Reds in Brisbane, where, for some reason, Auckland always seems to have problems. This time we conceded only 33 points, an 18-point improvement on 1996! Once again, we would go on to play in the semi-finals and Queensland would miss out.

We had another ding-dong go with the Wellington Hurricanes. In the three seasons of the Super 12, our matches with them finished 36-28, 45-42 and 45-34, always, fortunately, with the Blues in front. The best of those contests was the 1997 game at Eden Park when we just held on 45-42. There was more hype for that game than any other I was involved in at Super 12 or NPC level, with the two teams effectively top of the competition. We were unbeaten and the Hurricanes had won six of their previous seven games. The marketing people and the media had a ball building the game up. Often in those circumstances matches can disappoint. But this was a cracker.

The Hurricanes possessed some mighty gamebreakers – Christian Cullen, Tana Umaga and Jason O'Halloran, O'Halloran being a player I've always had a lot of time for. We had the game pretty well under control, then went to sleep. Which is not a thing you should ever do when there are Cullens and Umagas lurking in the opposition, players who could split a game wide open. Before we knew it, they'd almost overhauled us. I know the crowd thought it was a fantastic game and from the viewpoint of spectacle I'd have to agree with them. But as a coach who set high standards, I was personally disappointed that our guys had let their concentration slip.

In the modern game, if you relax and a team gets on a roll, there can be 14 or 21 points scored before you know it. I admired the spirit of adventure which Frank Oliver and Graeme Taylor built into the Hurricanes. If they were behind, they would run the ball from anywhere. It was high-risk rugby but extremely hard to handle and could embarrass any opponent. I recall them coming from 17 points down to bury Queensland at Ballymore (I was terribly envious of their ability to smash the Reds on that ground) and they almost did the same against us.

That Wellington has never qualified for the NPC play-offs is plainly a source of frustration in the capital. It was a disappointment therefore that Oliver's men couldn't sustain their excellent form in 1997 and make it through to the final for a rematch on Eden Park. But they couldn't get past Rod Macqueen's well-drilled ACT Brumbies side, losing to them first at Athletic Park and then, in the semi-final, at Canberra.

So our opponents in the '97 final became the Brumbies, the team we'd outwitted at Pukekohe. It was a great misfortune that torrential rain fell in the build-up to the game, condemning both sides to wet-weather rugby. The two teams presented contrasting attacking styles which were obviously limited in the conditions. The old traditionalists loved it, I'm sure, because it was a close, low-scoring game, unlike most of our other Super 12 outings that season. Personally, while delighted to have won again, I was somewhat disappointed that the game never rose to the high standard of the 1996 final when the weather was perfect.

The Brumbies were a fine side, clever and extremely well prepared, as good a team as I ever encountered as a coach. They'd given us a hiding in Canberra in 1996 when the Blues, like everyone else, believed all the pre-championship publicity which insisted they were the weakest of the three Australian sides. We quickly came to appreciate that that was a load of baloney. We misjudged their ability that first year, but never again.

The 1998 Super 12 final pitted two New Zealand teams together for the first time, after the Canterbury Crusaders nosed out the Coastal Sharks in a high-scoring thriller in Christchurch and we narrowly survived a storming finish by the Otago Highlanders on Eden Park.

The 1998 final was a frustrating experience. I remember all the players, coaches and fans, including the Canterbury guys, couldn't actually believe that the Crusaders had come out as the victors. We dominated the majority of the match and should have put the game out of the Crusaders' reach with that series of scrums near their line in the third quarter.

Most people thought there should have been a penalty try awarded but Paddy O'Brien didn't agree with the multitude. Or was it the subconscious recall of the flak that Colin Hawke took for awarding Auckland a penalty try in the NPC final against Otago a few years earlier? Or did it boil down to a North-South thing and the fact Auckland and the Blues had been dominating for too long?

Personally, I consider there is too much pressure on referees in situations like this. No matter how efficient a referee is, off-the-field baggage can affect his on-the-field decisions. I was so concerned that I asked for a neutral referee for the '98 final – an Australian or a South African – which I believe was allowed for in the rules of the tournament. The ARU approached the national body about this but the NZRFU insisted a New Zealand referee officiate in the final. This was a wrong decision, I believe. The appointment should have been based on what was best for the final, not what was best for New Zealand referees. Unfortunately, egos got involved.

Notwithstanding all that, full praise to the Canterbury Crusaders who had a poor start but showed character and strength to recover and play some outstanding rugby to win the tournament. I always had a lot of time for the Crusaders management and team as a group of people. The Auckland guys respected them enormously. Just a pity about their supporters!

We were below strength for the final, because Jonah Lomu, Paul Mitchell, Andrew Roose and Andrew Blowers were all sidelined. It was a great misfortune that Jonah had to miss the Super 12 final for the second year in a row. The previous year, of course, he'd been laid low with that debilitating liver disease. This time, he was carrying a foot injury. So we had three teenagers in the starting fifteen – Caleb Ralph, Xavier Rush and James Christian.

Even though we were beaten, I was proud of the team. It was our third final in three years and we'd demonstrated character throughout the competition. I thought the guys gave everything and as a coach you cannot ask more than that. Without Zinny and Fitzy, they achieved well beyond most people's expectations which was a credit to all involved.

In the wash-up there was some criticism of me for not making more extensive use of the reserves bench. Frankly, I didn't consider replacements necessary because we were controlling the match. The Crusaders made changes because they were always playing catch-up rugby. Also, I think an analysis of the two squads would reveal the Crusaders had by far the stronger group of reserves.

In three seasons, there had been six Super 12 play-offs at Eden

Park – three semis and three finals. What a windfall for the Auckland Rugby Union. Although when it came to the bottom line, did they appreciate it?

Having Jonah Lomu in your side was an experience in itself. I felt sorry for him in 1996, when Lomu-mania was rife. He was a natural hero and everyone, but everyone, wanted a piece of him. I remember we went to the West Coast for a pre-season outing. If there were 3000 in attendance at the game in Greymouth, 2000 of them wanted to be close to Jonah! I wondered how he would ever handle all the hysteria.

He was a different boy in 1998, more mature, more confident… at peace with himself. How he got through 1996 as a rugby player with his liver deteriorating, I'll never know. Graham Paterson, the Blues' doctor, said he must have played as if a bag of coal was on his back.

Jonah was always capable of winning any game for you. I've worked with hundreds, perhaps thousands, of rugby players in my time but never encountered anyone with his size and pace combined. He could do things no one else could. Initially – as we saw at the World Cup in 1995 – no one could handle him. Then his illness struck and he's had to battle back.

As for Joeli, well, what a finisher. He could conjure up magic. He cost Waikato a place in the NPC final in 1997 with three tries and he knocked Canterbury out of contention a year later with an even better effort, scoring four times on Jade Stadium. Actually, he made only three NPC appearances in 1998 – and scored eight tries. But that's the sort of player he is. Sometimes his handling lets him down but if you create half a chance for Joeli, pity the enemy. He's a great guy with a lovely personality who could contribute a lot to New Zealand rugby. If he got a few tests under his belt, he'd be a huge force.

There's no greater sight in rugby than Joeli in full cry. I still have a vivid memory of the try he scored after exploding clear from his own 22 against Natal at Eden Park in 1997. Joeli and Jonah were two of the unifying forces in a very positive relationship between Auckland and Counties-Manukau.

Another was my assistant coach Mac McCallion. We weren't exactly two peas in a pod. I tended to be calm, methodical and undemonstrative whereas Mac, who'd built Counties-Manukau into one of the most respected teams in the country, was the original straight shooter with no hidden agendas. He used a lot more expletives than me, but the guys always knew exactly where they stood with Mac. The guys enjoyed him and worked for him.

I admired him because besides being an extremely able coach, he was totally supportive. He may not have agreed with every team selection – I know he dearly wanted George Leaupepe to be involved but it was hard to go past Eroni Clarke and Lee Stensness – but he backed me 100 per cent. Whenever we met with John Hart he always supported me. We had an excellent relationship and forged a strong friendship.

He deserved to get the Auckland Blues coaching job for 1999. I don't know anything about Jed Rowlands, although I would assume he has excellent credentials. But Mac merited the appointment after what he'd been through. I felt for him, and I sent him a fax when he missed out. At least he's retained as the assistant coach, although he deserved better.

As a professional rugby coach, my year obviously revolved around the Super 12 and the NPC but late in 1997 came an interesting diversion – a couple of months in England involving myself with the Blackheath club. I went across there along with one of the Auckland union's coaching co-ordinators, Steve McHardy, and executive member John Baird, who acted as CEO of Blackheath for that period. The purpose of our mission was to ascertain whether Blackheath represented a good investment for the Auckland Rugby Union, which was prepared to put up about $1 million.

It was the brainchild of the chief executive officer of the time, Peter Scutts, and had the conditional support of the executive. In principle the purchase of Blackheath, one of England's longest-established clubs, had merit. In light of the dozens of players defecting to English clubs, it would certainly have been desirable to have a twin club across there to divert them to.

Steve and I were required to present a report on the club's coaching and playing standards. I certainly enjoyed the experience because there were a lot of good people associated with the club at the time, including a strong New Zealand association. Hika Reid was the coach and John Gallagher was involved as a player still and an administrator.

It was apparent the club's playing strength was modest. It held second division status with no immediate prospects of gaining promotion. Hika was essentially a forward coach and he had the pack going great guns. The problem was the backs didn't quite seem to know what to do with the ball when they got it. I lent a hand for a while, and sought to introduce more adventure, more ball in hand, more structure.

The Blackheath set-up was pleasant enough, with two little grounds and a grandstand that held no more than 200. In its favour was the location, to the south-east of London, with no other high-profile rugby clubs in the vicinity. But Blackheath needed a serious injection of capital... more, I fancied, than the Auckland Rugby Union was prepared to invest.

Clubs in New Zealand have their roots firmly embedded in rugby, with almost no exceptions. While that might have been the situation in England when the game was amateur, with the advent of professionalism several clubs have been taken over by wealthy entrepreneurs, among them Newcastle, "bought" by Sir John Hall. He spent millions developing the facilities and buying glamour players from around the globe, including Samoans Inga Tuigamala and Pat Lam, both former All Blacks. The injection of Hall's money certainly paid off in 1998 when Newcastle won the English club championship. But less than 12 months later, he'd become disenchanted with rugby and was intending to pull his money out, leaving big question marks over the future of the club.

To compete with the Newcastles, the Harlequins, the Saracens and the other elite clubs of England, Blackheath would require a serious injection of capital. The way the game is presently structured there, it's the only way to be competitive in thhat environment. It's not the best in a rugby sense, but that's the reality. Auckland might have been prepared to invest $1 million, but Blackheath didn't have the backers to match it. And I concluded, once I'd checked out what was happening, that a million from Auckland wasn't going to be enough.

I enjoyed my time in England, even though it meant missing out on a large portion of the New Zealand summer. By the time I returned home, I was thinking the UK would be an interesting place for a professional rugby coach to operate. It just needed the right club or union with the right offer!

Photosport

Chapter 5

Weighing up the offers

Man cannot discover new oceans unless he has courage to lose sight of the shore.

André Gide

THE FIRST OVERSEAS UNION to approach me about coaching overseas was England. At the conclusion of the 1997 Super 12, I fielded a call from Don Rutherford, then the union's director of rugby. He simply asked if I would be interested in coaching in England. I simply replied I could be.

After that, there were a few faxes floating between London and Auckland. I was keeping the lines of communication open until I knew precisely what was offering. Rutherford, a thoroughly likable fellow and one of the most experienced rugby directors in the world, was showing a keen interest. I wasn't sure how much authority he had but I presumed he had the backing of the movers and shakers within the England union.

Anyway, he came to New Zealand and took me out to dinner. There wasn't anything cloak-and-dagger about it. I'm a rugby buff who loves to talk the game with others. And obviously I was going to get a fresh slant on the UK side of things from one of England's leading rugby people, someone with whom I got on well. As far as coaching offers went, well, if he hit me with an offer that was too good to refuse, obviously I would give serious consideration to it.

Unfortunately, the media got hold of the story, as they do. The timing was shocking because England was preparing to play Australia in Sydney and obviously Jack Rowell wasn't hugely impressed to hear that his coaching director was apparently heading Down Under to interview a likely successor for his position. Apparently Don had told Jack, so he knew about the approach.

In fact, what Rutherford was offering was not the England coaching job. He was interested in having me work with the under-21 and England A squads as well as having an input into the national team, eventually taking over as coach.

Rutherford's visit and the fact England was targeting me became common knowledge, which was not favourably received by New Zealand's top administrators. The chairman, Rob Fisher, and the chief executive officer, David Moffett, spent time in the UK and, in discussions with England's leading administrators, quashed any suggestion of me coaching there. Moffett told me personally what they'd done, so I had to assume that was right.

While I was flattered to think England wanted me, negotiations never proceeded far enough for me to have to give any serious consideration to a deal. No finance package was ever discussed.

When I was across in London checking out the Blackheath club later the same year, Raewyn and I had an enjoyable evening out with Don Rutherford, Clive Woodward and their wives. Clive would pretty soon take over England from Jack Rowell and make his mark. Don, unfortunately, would be made redundant in 1998 when the England union, concerned at its diminishing bank balance, trimmed its staff by almost 30 per cent.

The England experience proved valuable when Wales approached me in 1998. By now I'd learnt the smartest way to handle proceedings was to say nothing. To deny everything. Although, ironically, the first point of contact was from a Welsh journalist, at the time the 1998 Super 12 was winding up. He asked me if I'd been approached about coaching the Welsh national team. I said no. He assured me I soon would be.

When Terry Cobner duly phoned, I therefore wasn't caught by surprise. I said yes, I was interested, if there was a full business package offered me. I told him I wanted negotiations kept under wraps, on which matter he gave an assurance. I must say, at that point I understood the offer was to coach Wales through to the 1999 Rugby World Cup or perhaps on to the Five (or Six, as it would become) Nations championship early in 2000.

I advised Terry that I had a signed contract with Auckland but that I was optimistic they would be supportive of any move. I had not concluded a contract with New Zealand Rugby and I was naive enough to believe they would not be obstructive as long as I gave an undertaking that I would be returning to New Zealand in the year 2000. That was how I viewed the situation, seeing it as part of my professional development. It was a stimulating challenge. I was a professional rugby coach wanting to operate at the highest possible level. While the All Blacks were the team I most wanted to coach, obviously with John Hart contracted through to the end of the 1999 World Cup (and on record as saying he didn't see why he couldn't extend that), there was no short-term opportunity for me to coach internationally. But here was a passionate rugby nation, a traditional rival of New Zealand's, struggling. The NZRFU had been on about developing the game globally, and I saw this as a marvellous chance for some PR that would benefit both nations. In effect, I saw it as an extension of my role with the NZRFU.

Well... silly old Graham Henry. It soon became apparent that I was the only member of the platoon in step. I first broached the subject with Bill Wallace, New Zealand's director of rugby services. He was lukewarm on the idea, which was about as enthusiastic as anyone got. I should have realised I was backing a loser at that stage and quit. Next I talked to David Moffett, the chief executive officer. He was absolutely opposed to the concept – 100 per cent negative. His chief concern seemed to be that I would be taking New Zealand rugby ideas to another country, which I felt was in conflict with the New Zealand objective of developing the global game. I found it hard to rationalise this. Frankly, I was amazed at David's attitude because he became extremely agitated. I wasn't sure whether he was acting or being genuine, but quite frankly I found his outburst laughable. But I got the message – no way was he going to support me.

My initial enthusiasm was crumbling and I was now pretty demoralised about the whole thing. I'd wanted to coach Wales for all the right reasons. I'd done my bit for New Zealand rugby, I considered, operating for 23 years as an amateur coach, having seven seasons in charge of an NPC team and three with the Super 12 franchise. No coach can continue at the same level, with the same teams, for ever. Players need fresh ideas, coaches need fresh challenges.

There obviously wasn't an opportunity to coach the All Blacks for 18 months – although I wasn't to know John Hart would come unstuck so spectacularly in 1998 and almost get himself sacked – and I was looking for a fresh challenge in the meantime. I had expected a level of support for my concept but received none, the game's top administrators being totally negative. Maybe I should have approached the executive with a formal proposal.

Moffett told me he had spoken to Kevin Roberts and Tim Gresson, two highly-regarded members of the executive, and that they were opposed to my suggestion. Moffett then told me if I even went to Wales to discuss the proposal, I would never coach the All Blacks.

I made a personal approach to Rob Fisher, the chairman but, being a very political animal as usual, he sat on the fence. He said he would discuss the matter with fellow administrators and get back to me. I had considered there was a ray of hope because Rob had popped into my office at Eden Park one morning and intimated there was a possibility of me gaining approval for my proposal. But I never heard from him again. I also telephoned Kevin Roberts, busy, globetrotting person that he is, and left a message on his answerphone. But I never heard from him either.

My best endeavours had got me nowhere. Very obviously the NZRFU officials saw no merit whatsoever in me coaching in Wales. I either abandoned the project and reactivated myself for an eighth NPC season or proceeded with my negotiations covertly. There were a few sleepless nights as I weighed the options. My greatest ambition was to coach the All Blacks but obviously that wasn't possible inside 18 months. And there was no guarantee I would be John Hart's successor anyway. Was the NZRFU prepared to replace an Aucklander with an Aucklander? That was questionable. Also, what's the shelf life of a coach? I was 52 which meant I would be approaching 54 before I could take on the All Blacks.

There's a classic old saying about a bird in the hand... John Hart had waited eight years to win the All Black appointment. No one could give any assurance that I would do better. If I waited till after the 1999 World Cup and didn't win the appointment, what then? The Welsh coaching position would be filled and I'd be left with nothing. Notwithstanding the NZRFU's desire to retain my services, I couldn't rely on them. After all, we couldn't settle on the terms of a contract despite almost a year of to-ing and fro-ing. For that matter, I don't think any of the Super 12 coaches' contracts had been ratified at that point.

Meanwhile, Wales was genuine about contracting me to become its national coach. And I was genuine in my interest. Which I conveyed, after much soul-searching and discussion with my family, to Terry Cobner. I made him aware of Moffett's threat, that I would be persona non grata with the NZRFU if I went anywhere near Cardiff. So we arranged to meet in Sydney immediately after the game in Wanganui on 28 June between the New Zealand A team, which I was coaching, and Tonga.

A most convivial occasion it was, too, at the Sydney Hilton Hotel, with Wales represented by its chairman, Glanmore Griffiths, its secretary, Denis Gethin, and the man I'd been doing all the talking to, Terry Cobner, the union's director of rugby. I was largely there to listen to their offers but there was one condition upon which I was insistent: If I was to take over the national team, I had to have an input into the whole structure of Welsh rugby and the various competitions that were being run. They were a mess, with the nation's best players involved in competitions that were never going to adequately prepare them for international rugby. This was terribly important. You can't coach a national side without having a say in the competitions that the contracted players get involved in.

I was completely up-front with the Welsh. They appreciated I would be making huge sacrifices in moving to the other side of the world, not least the opportunity to coach the All Blacks. I spelt out the package that would secure me. I said this is what I want – you guarantee it, and I'll come. There'll be no stuffing around, no further conditions.

I had been under the impression that Wales wanted me for about 18 months, through till the conclusion of the Five (or Six) Nations tournament in 2000. So it was a shock in Sydney to realise they were offering me a five-year contract, which would span two World

Cups, involving me until the year 2003. Originally, I understood I would be freed up after 18 months, at which point I would be available to coach the All Blacks, if I was deemed good enough. Of course, my discussions with the decision-makers of New Zealand rugby had by now made me realise that that was a pipe dream. If going to Wales meant severing my links with the NZRFU, then I might as well go the whole hog and sign up for five years.

The Welsh offer was enormously appealing. Financially, it promised to be attractive, but more importantly it gave me the opportunity of doing what I wanted to do – to test my ability at international level.

Obviously, there was plenty to think about when I returned from Sydney. Raewyn and I sat down and contemplated our futures. The first major consideration was that we would be uprooting ourselves from Auckland where our family and friends lived and re-establishing ourselves in a completely different environment, about which we really knew very little. Raewyn could resign her teaching post at Baradene College easily enough but she was coaching the Auckland netball team, something she was enjoying hugely. Our youngest son, Andrew, had Bursary exams coming up. And I was on a pretty sound financial footing with Auckland and New Zealand. In fact, my financial package was a lot more lucrative than the Welsh Rugby Union initially appreciated. When I first put my demands to them, they received a bit of a shock.

For several weeks after the Sydney meeting faxes were flowing backwards and forwards between Auckland and Cardiff.

DAVID JONES

I first met Graham when rugby went professional in 1995 and he spent a considerable number of hours in my office, and at home, persuading a number of the Auckland players to stay with the NZRFU. After that introduction he began recommending me to players who needed help with their contracts. Then he asked me to help him personally – initially with his Auckland contract and subsequently with his contract negotiations with the NZRFU. He confided in me when he was approached by England and quite early on when approached by the Welsh. I met with him at his home shortly before he went off to talk to the Welsh in Sydney. The very first question he put to me was whether I thought he should stay in New Zealand or go to Wales. Unhesitatingly, I told him to go.

Why? Because his prospects of becoming the All Black coach were in my view remote. All his friends were telling him that, too. He'd done it all in New Zealand and needed a fresh challenge. He wasn't a particularly popular figure with the Wellington hierarchy and NZRFU officials weren't prepared to make a commitment to him. They were, in my view, playing him along. They were saying, "We'll give you New Zealand A but we're not prepared to make any commitment about coaching the All Blacks."

The NZRFU wanted a coach with international experience but was only prepared to give a commitment to Graham with the New Zealand A team. The NZRFU had rejected his approach to coach Wales to the end of the World Cup in 1999 – surely that was the international experience the NZRFU should have jumped at.

Graham asked me to take over the negotiations with Wales on his behalf because he said everything was getting too complicated for him. Wales in turn tossed everything over to Phil Williams of De Loitte & Touche (a firm of chartered accountants the union retained) and between us we worked through Graham's contract. Graham was right – it was complicated. We weren't just talking a simple pay-the-coach deal. Because Graham was going to live in Wales for five years, there was tax, national health and fringe benefits to consider. There were endless night conferences between myself and Phil Williams, sometimes with Graham involved, before the deal was resolved.

Actually, the first telephone hook-up was a laugh when Graham said, "I'm here with my lawyer David Jones... boyo!" With my name, I could have been representing Wales.

The heat was starting to go on because the Welsh press were saying I was the leading contender to win the coaching appointment. Suddenly, I started to field calls from rugby media throughout the world who were wanting to know what was going on. I simply said I didn't know.

I attended an NZRFU meeting in Wellington on a Sunday involving referees and NPC coaches where people were looking at me sideways. That very morning the radio stations had been booming out the news, emanating from Wales, that I had signed with Wales. Jackie Maitland, the NZRFU communications manager, asked me what was going on, then Bill Wallace took me aside and asked if the news bulletins were right. Smarter for my experience with the English offer of a year before, I simply said I had not signed a contract with the Welsh union. Which was true. I tried to carry on as normal as though nothing was happening, which was the only way I could handle it. To have said, "Yes, they've made this great offer which I'm thinking of accepting" would have created an uproar. So I played dumb.

When journalists approached the NZRFU on the issue, they were told I was contracted till the end of 1999. I'm not sure whether that was to throw them off the scent or just plain bullshit. But I knew that I did not have a contract with New Zealand; in fact, a contract had not even been prepared, let alone presented to me. Nor for that matter, from my understanding, did any of the other Super 12 coaches. When rumours that I was not contracted began to leak out, which was obviously a source of embarrassment to the NZRFU, it was claimed by the NZRFU that as I had been banking the union's monthly cheques for the coaching duties I had carried out each month, that that was tantamount to my having signed the contract.

New Zealand had first made an offer to me in August 1997. I couldn't live with it. My major beef was that they were contracting coaches on a lesser scale than the players, which I objected to. Some of my potential liabilities were also of concern. For example, I was not indemnified if any player I dropped decided to sue for loss of earnings. Virtually for 11 months, there had been no correspondence relevant to my contract. Now – with the NZRFU obviously alarmed at news reports I was considering an offer from Wales – I received a letter from the NZRFU, signed by the contracts manager, Tony Ward. He had been recuperating from a serious rugby injury, I appreciated the problems, but obviously nobody had taken over the reins in his absence.

His covering letter read: "Contract. Please find attached in duplicate copies of your contract for promotional services for you to sign and return to this office. The contract encompasses the letters sent to you by Bill Wallace on 18 August and 6 October [1997] respectively. Should you have any queries regarding the content of your contract, do not hesitate to contact me. Yours sincerely, Tony Ward, Contracts Manager."

After reading the letter, I ripped it up and threw it into the rubbish bin, retrieving the pieces the next morning and taping them together. I decided, upon reflection, that it was a letter to preserve, for posterity!

DAVID JONES

The incredible thing about the contract which had been sent to Graham at this time was that a disclaimer was stamped on the front, stating: "All Black Promotions and the NZRFU will not be bound by this contract until it is signed."

In his reply, Graham, who'd asked me to help him draft the letter, said that he would not be bound by any contract either – until he signed! It was blatant bullying by the union which was saying, "You're bound, but we're not". There was an ironic history to the NZRFU's disclaimers.

The NZRFU had been burned previously when the game went professional and it approved boot contracts for Ian Jones, Jeff Wilson and Josh Kronfeld. On that occasion, the players had signed the contract offers made to them by the NZRFU, containing the exception for their individual boot contracts. Subsequently, the NZRFU found that this presented a problem with its boot sponsor – but it was too late, the offer made to the players had been accepted, the contract done.

In Graham's circumstance, the NZRFU had gone public, saying he was contractually bound. Later, it amended this to say the contractual position was not clear. But it was perfectly clear to me and I advised Graham accordingly. He was not bound to the NZRFU until he signed that contract, and he hadn't done that and he hadn't accepted the terms offered.

I personally didn't want to get into a legal scrap. All I wanted to do was further my coaching career. My loyalties were to New

Zealand rugby where I had coached for 25 years, giving my time and energy selflessly. Only in the previous 15 months had I become a professional and been rewarded financially for my efforts. It's probably irrelevant to say that had rugby remained amateur, I would have continued coaching at representative level. And no doubt I would still have been operating a double shift as the headmaster of Kelston. I had given a huge amount of my energies to New Zealand and Auckland rugby and I was looking for a little support in return. After the reaction to the England offer the year before, when the old boy network took over, I was hoping the same administrators would this time be sensible. Some hope!

London's *Sunday Times* of 19 July carried a story which went out on the internet and in short time came to the attention of the NZRFU. It announced that Wales was about to make me the highest paid coach in world rugby and that I would be named successor to Kevin Bowring within the week. It said Wales was determined to get its man and was prepared to shell out a reputed £250,000 a year for a five-year contract.

Vernon Pugh, the Welsh rugby boss, was supposedly flying to New Zealand to sort out the details that very weekend.

The story sparked another rash of calls from the media. I tried to field as few of them as possible and to sound genuinely surprised at what was being written.

DAVID JONES
21 July
I phoned Phil Williams and asked him what the hell was going on, reminding him that our negotiations were supposed to be confidential. He said that he was sorry if Graham was compromised but he had no control over the leaks from within the union and it was not true that Vernon Pugh was coming to New Zealand – that had never been discussed.

My advice to Graham was to continue to keep his head down and let everyone guess. It was the strongest defensive weapon he had. He was under enormous pressure because he was about to undergo a major lifestyle change and he was worried about the legal threats, wondering whether he would be sued.

We were getting towards the end of the negotiations. A lawyer representing the Welsh union was preparing a draft heads of agreement. The lawyer raised the issue of Graham's involvement with Auckland and New Zealand unions. He was concerned Wales would be liable for damages for inducing a breach of contract. He wanted us to ensure there was no risk.

It was a worrying time. I was preparing to abandon Auckland, with its semi-tropical climate, for Cardiff, where it seemed to rain a lot, and I was not entirely convinced there would be any worthwhile rugby talent there when I arrived. Now there were all these legal ramifications. It wasn't what a simple rugby coach needed.

NEW ZEALAND HERALD
21 July
Auckland rugby officials admit they have made back-up plans in case Graham Henry takes a massive offer to guide the Welsh rugby side, and expect to talk to their coach about his future tomorrow.

Reports at the weekend claimed Henry has signed a five-year deal. The Auckland and New Zealand unions insist Graham Henry has told them he has not signed.

Henry could not be contacted last night.

He has contracts with the Auckland and New Zealand unions although there are suggestions his New Zealand contract has not been re-signed this year and that Henry is operating under old terms.

Auckland chief executive officer, Geoff Hipkins, said Auckland knew of the Welsh and other offers and was prepared to consider granting him a release.

"We believe he has a contract with New Zealand and Graham has a signed and binding contract with us until the end of 1999. But we have had discussions about his career opportunities. We have a superb relationship with Graham which is very upfront and honest."

Not surprisingly, with my name featuring in news bulletins almost daily, the NZRFU was obviously becoming anxious, having by now realised that it did not in fact have me contracted to them. Thus, it was not surprising when the following letter was faxed to me. The salient points of that letter were:

ALL BLACK PROMOTIONS LTD
22 July 1998

Dear Graham

I acknowledge your letter of 16 July with surprise and disappointment, in particular as it relates to compensation. We accept that submitting a final contract document has been delayed for a variety of reasons. We are naturally happy to talk through the detail of the document, but in the meantime we regard you as contractually bound to the NZRFU.

We are concerned about the recent publicity regarding Wales and have informed the Wales RFU that you are contractually bound, to ensure it is aware of your contractual commitments to us.

The points you make in your letter about remuneration have been discussed at length and were responded to as long ago as my letter of 6 October 1997. You entered into the engagement of coaching the Auckland Blues for 1998 on that basis and have accepted payment accordingly.

Bill Wallace,
Director, Rugby Services

You can imagine I saw red when I received that letter. New Zealand had pulled the Big Brother tactics a year earlier to spike my negotiations with England. Now it was trying to do the same with Wales. I replied the same day.

GRAHAM HENRY
22 July 1998

Bill Wallace,
All Black Promotions,
Wellington

There is little point in dwelling on the question of income. Obviously it is an issue which goes to the heart of any contract. Given my letters and conversations with you over the last year, you are well aware that I do not accept the income you offered. It has to be said that simply by paying me less than I was prepared to accept for carrying out the coaching duties, you cannot bully me into accepting what you have offered or, for that matter, conclude that I am contractually bound to a deal, the material conditions of which I had not seen until last week, let alone agreed to.

In the face of the fact that, first, you have presented me with a contract on which you have printed a disclaimer that you are not bound by the contract until you have signed it and, secondly, that essential terms have not been agreed, it is simply specious to suggest that I am contractually bound. You cannot on the one hand say that I am bound but on the other say that you are not bound...NZRFU has in the past attempted to spike approaches made to me from overseas...If you do not advise the Welsh RFU immediately that I am not contracted, I will have no choice but to seek legal advice on my rights against All Black Promotions Ltd and NZRFU. I look forward to your confirmation that you have advised the Welsh RFU accordingly.

Having regard to your conduct...I have no further interest in continuing discussions with you at the present time regarding the contract. However, as a matter of courtesy, and for the sake of completeness, I have briefly responded to the points covered in your letter...

Yours faithfully,
Graham Henry

I had been dealing with the NZRFU on one front and negotiating with Auckland on another. And with the NPC coming up in August, it was imperative matters were resolved. Now Auckland was a completely different scenario from New Zealand because I *did* have a signed contract. However, I'd kept the chief executive officer, Geoff Hipkins, advised of events from the moment Wales first approached me. He said he would not stand in my way and would be totally supportive of whatever move I made. I had also talked to Reuben O'Neill, Auckland's chairman, who assured me that because of what I had done for Auckland rugby, he would also back me. Both indicated their readiness to release me from my contract.

I was more than a little perplexed, therefore, when Geoff Hipkins telephoned to say the board members wanted to talk to me.

DAVID JONES
The Auckland Rugby Union attacked Graham when he was at his weakest. I've got not the slightest doubt its actions were prompted by the NZRFU. I told Graham that I suspected that the board might now say that he would not be released despite the fact that the chief executive officer had told him (as he had power to do, in my view) that he would be released.

Because Graham considered he had such a harmonious relationship with Auckland, he decided against taking me, as his lawyer, to the meeting. That, as it turned out, was a serious mistake.

I fronted up to the Auckland board and explained what was happening and that I required a release from my contract. They heard me out, after which I left. Later that day, Geoff Hipkins telephoned me, spelling out the three conditions on which they would free me of my contract.

The first was that I must coach Wales and nobody else. I couldn't, for example, suddenly divert my attentions to Canterbury. The second was that with the severance of my contract I would relinquish the two grandstand seats and car park space at Eden Park which had been granted to me for life. The third, which came as a massive bombshell, was that I had to pay the Auckland Rugby Union a $250,000 release fee.

Can you believe that? They wanted a quarter of a million dollars from the individual who had coached their representative team for five seasons for nothing (and won goodness knows how many trophies in that time). I'd done it for the love of rugby. For one and a half years, following rugby's transition to professionalism, I'd been paid a generous but not massive salary. In return, the union wanted me to give it $250,000. As for taking away my lifetime seats at Eden Park and the car park, which really hurt, I saw that as sheer petulance.

I'd gone through two months of negotiations during which the chief executive officer (who'd been kept fully briefed) had been totally supportive. Now suddenly there was a massive impediment to my resigning. By now, the contract with Wales was finalised – I wasn't going back to them to ask for more. I'd negotiated openly and honestly with Wales and they'd given me what I'd asked for.

Legally, I believe, if the CEO agreed to release me, that meant I had the support of his union. If I'd got shitty and fought it, I don't believe they could have demanded the payment. Needless to say, I was pretty grumpy about this unexpected development and I understand not all the executive members were behind the decision. It's comforting to know at least a few administrators were aware of the effort I'd put in on their behalf over more than six seasons, appreciating that I might have been responsible for a few extra spectators passing through the turnstiles. Unfortunately, the greater majority of the committee saw a way to make some easy money. Perhaps they thought the money would come from the Welsh Rugby Union. But this was my affair, nothing to do with Wales. That deal had been completed. Graham Henry was being asked to hand over a quarter of a million dollars for severing a contract.

The newspapers continued to speculate on what was happening.

NEW ZEALAND HERALD
23 July
Graham Henry appears set for a fiery showdown with the NZRFU in a bid to take up a multi-million dollar contract to coach Wales. As the scrap looks likely to escalate, the union has written a please explain letter to its Welsh counterpart while Auckland is

canvassing for caretaker coaching staff if they are needed for the start of the NPC.

The NZRFU message may come too late in Wales where there is speculation the coach will be named tomorrow.

Yesterday, CEO David Moffett agreed Henry had sought but been denied leave of absence to work with the Welsh team.

The Henry/NZRFU battle first surfaced in early June when Henry twice tried to negotiate an early release from his contract which carries him through till the end of 1999.

It is understood Henry has not signed his current contract. Sources believe the Welsh Rugby Union could buy out the rest of his New Zealand and Auckland contracts.

DAVID JONES

Although we were now only a day or two away from signing, Wales' legal advisers were still concerned with Graham's contractual obligations to Auckland and the NZRFU. They asked me what I thought. Without troubling them with the details, I assured them the Auckland matter was being resolved personally by Graham and that there was no problem at all with New Zealand because the contract was unsigned. However, to put their mind at rest, I suggested they seek an independent opinion and referred them to David Howman, a prominent barrister in Wellington.

David Howman faxed a letter to the Welsh Rugby Union on 24 July which cleared the way for us to complete our negotiations. He said that in his view the matter was "a very simple one to analyse" and that he was sure Wales' lawyers would reach the same conclusion. He assured them that I had no written contract with New Zealand rugby although an implied contract was possible. There would be short notice required to relieve me of any responsibilities under that implied contract.

As far as possible damages were concerned, he said he would be extremely surprised if any judge would contemplate a mandatory injunction forcing a person to perform a contract for services and that in his view the union would be most unlikely to achieve an injunction.

On a personal note he wrote that it was obvious to him that the

NZRFU should have adopted a sensible and sensitive approach "bearing in mind its position in the world game of rugby and continuing need to ensure that the assets which the world game has, namely its players and coaches, are properly and appropriately handled." He said that this example showed to him that rugby had not yet moved into the age of professionalism that it asserts it has and that internationally this must be of some concern

I believe this was an example of the NZRFU's lack of experience in dealing with such issues. If someone else approaches New Zealand with a similar request in the future, I'm sure they will handle it differently and approach it in a more positive manner, mindful of the individual as well as themselves.

Before I could finalise negotiations with Wales, I had to resolve this irksome matter with Auckland. I deemed the amount of compensation to be entirely unreasonable. Writing with no little passion, I prepared the following letter to present to Geoff Hipkins.

23 July

Geoff Hipkins,
CEO,
Auckland Rugby Union

Dear Geoff,

Two months ago you agreed to release me from my ARU contract so that I could take up an approach made by the Welsh RFU. Apart from our understanding that I would keep you briefed on the progress of my negotiations, which I have done punctiliously, and that I would give what assistance I could to my replacement, that release was unqualified. Specifically, the release was not qualified by the requirement for board approval.

I was astonished then that at the board meeting yesterday the board purported to impose terms on my release, in particular to demand compensation of $250,000. If as you now suggest you did not have the authority to give me the release that is a matter between you and the board. My position is clear – you had the authority to give me the release as the CEO of Auckland.

In the circumstances, not only is the introduction at this time of

the idea that the board's consent misconceived, the demand for compensation is opportunistic and wrong. The board's demand for compensation appears to be predicated on your assumption that the Welsh RFU will pay what you have demanded. This assumption is completely wrong. Consistent with what I have said above about my release, I negotiated with Wales on the basis that I was "clean".

Since my negotiations with Wales have finished, and a deal has been agreed in principle, there is no way I can go back and impose another condition. In the circumstances, you are effectively asking me to personally pay the compensation which you have demanded. This is inappropriate.

You have suggested to me the compensation is to cover potential business disruption following my departure. This claim has little merit. Similar claims are often made in relation to a great player who leaves the game or shifts unions. There is no empirical evidence to support such claims. The game is a little bigger than one player or one coach.

That said, and without prejudice to my position, I am prepared to consider paying compensation up to the sum of $100,000 on terms of payment to be agreed if after a period of one year you can show me that the ARU has suffered losses which can be attributed to my departure.

Yours sincerely,
Graham Henry

DAVID JONES

Graham and I spent some time composing the letter with a view to giving it to Geoff Hipkins at a meeting that day. In the end, he spoke to the letter but didn't present it. Fortunately, he had some mates on the board who were able to convince the others that a quarter of a millions dollars was excessive. They agreed to a lesser figure on reasonably favourable terms.

It still represented what Graham and I considered to be unprofessional behaviour by the board. Obviously, the huge sums being aired in the media regarding Graham's salary in Wales engendered jealousy on the part of some individuals.

The interval is an important time for a coach, when you either reinforce the game plan or introduce variations to overcome a difficult opponent.

Zinzan Brooke, Grant Fox and Shane Howarth head the lap of honour following Auckland's defeat of Otago in the 1993 NPC final at Eden Park.

Eroni Clarke... year in, year out voted Auckland's most valuable player.

There's nothing more rewarding for the management after all the hard work that has gone in than having your team claim the championship, as Auckland did in 1993, 1994, 1995 and 1996.

Lomu-mania was rife after Jonah's astonishing exploits at the 1995 World Cup.

It was great having Jonah Lomu and Joeli Vidiri in your team. Between them, they scored 43 tries for the Auckland Blues in three seasons.

"We've got the World Cup, but you can have this one for winning the Super 12." Louis Luyt probably said something like that to Zinzan Brooke after the Blues defeat of Natal in the 1996 final. Zinny then led his troops on a lap of honour around Eden Park.

Zinzan Brooke… there's never been anyone who led more by example.

Sean Fitzpatrick… the ultimate professional.

The Auckland squad all smiles after putting away Otago in the 1995 NPC final at Eden Park.

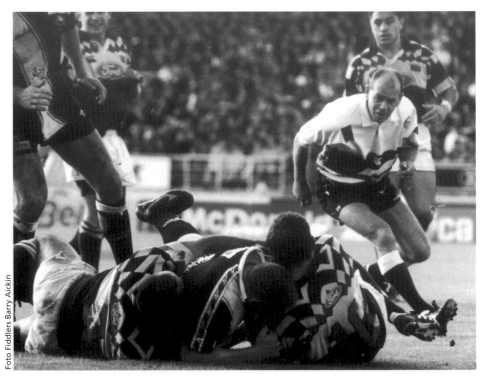

Referee Paddy O'Brien… reluctant to award a penalty try in the 1998 Super 12 final.

The national emblem of Welsh rugby, if you didn't know, is a dragon... a red one. We're trying to rekindle his fire-eating qualities.

The poster that caused a commotion in Wales. Religious groups maintained that it was blasphemous.

GREAT REDEEMER

WALES, BREAD OF HEAVEN

The question must have been whether I thought Wales could win the 1999 World Cup. Having been in Wales 24 hours when the question was asked, it merited a good laugh.

There's nothing much more a coach can do once the team talk is completed but ponder what might be in store.

There was no greater challenge in rugby than taking on the job of national coach of Wales.

Winger Gareth Thomas across for Wales' first try against the Springboks at Wembley.

Scott Quinnell (8) shares brother Craig's golden moment after his try against France in Paris.

An emotional occasion after Neil Jenkins had landed the vital conversion that defeated England at Wembley.

Shane Howarth… the advent of professionalism has been the making of him as a rugby player.

Welsh manager David Pickering and I in sombre mood before a Five Nations encounter.

Lyn Howells and I nervously awaiting the England international at Wembley.

I was bold enough to declare after the England victory that Neil Jenkins was a better goalkicker than Grant Fox.

Inviting my daughter Catherine to join me in Cardiff when I first arrived was a great idea. She got more publicity than me.

The board agreed to reduce the amount of compensation to $150,000, payable over three years. That was something, I guess. It still means that $50,000 comes out of my Welsh Rugby Union salary each year until the year 2001 to help the Auckland Union's coffers. Oh well, they've got that new North Stand to pay for. I hope I've helped furnish a few of the corporate boxes.

If the Auckland union had finished with the matter, the NZRFU certainly hadn't, because it released a most remarkable press statement following its board meeting in Wellington.

NEW ZEALAND HERALD
25 July
Should Graham Henry be appointed national coach of Wales, he will never be given the All Black job.

In a move which looks to be the direct result of the current Henry furore, the NZRFU yesterday announced a new policy which precludes any New Zealand coach who has been in charge of another national team from getting on to the All Black staff.

The decision is immediate but not retrospective, so therefore it will not affect John Mitchell (assistant coach of England), Warren Gatland (national coach of Ireland) or Brad Johnstone (national coach of Fiji).

"We are simply protecting our investment in coaches," said chief executive officer, David Moffett, "in the same way we protect our investment in players."

That decision lacks logic, thought, sensitivity and maturity and I'm sure they'll change it when they have time to consider it. It doesn't correlate with the global objectives of the union. Most professional companies in New Zealand prefer to employ individuals with overseas experience. But if you seek that experience as a rugby coach, you are penalised to the point of being banned for life from association with the All Blacks. Isn't that simply an unenforceable restraint of trade? There's one law for the corporate world, another for rugby. I had thought New Zealand rugby was progressing and was becoming more enlightened but this decision is right out of the sixties.

Thanks to the brilliant negotiating skills of David Jones, the heads of agreement deal between myself and the Welsh Rugby

Union was finally concluded in the small hours of Thursday 29 July. The final decision to commit myself to five years with Wales had not been taken lightly. I had talked the move through with several of my mates, people whose opinions I respected, and they all said go.

One hilarious sidebar to the whole issue was that right up till the time Raewyn departed for Wales – almost four months after me – she was still driving around in an NZRFU Ford car. I had successfully negotiated the car as a perk the previous year and naturally expected the union to reclaim it once I announced my intention of heading to Wales. I'd been using an Auckland union car, leaving the NZRFU vehicle available for Raewyn. Because no one reclaimed the car, Raewyn drove around in luxury until she flew out to the UK in December. The Ford people actually rang in late November but didn't pick up the car until after she left on 11 December. The car was left on the road with the key on the front tyre!

I also found out, following my departure, that the NZRFU had demanded a release fee of the Welsh Rugby Union. Of course, it had nothing to do with me and didn't stop me taking up the coaching position, but I did think it was rather cute that at the same time I was asking the NZRFU for what was owing to me for my Super 12 coaching.

Fortunately, I was able to leave all this behind me. I just wanted to get away to Wales without too much blood-letting. It was a pity, I felt, that the NZRFU didn't handle the whole affair professionally.

Chapter 6

'I'm off to Wales!'

Coaches who can outline plays on a blackboard are a dime a dozen. The ones who win get inside their players and motivate.

Vince Lombardi, coach, Green Bay Packers

MURRAY DEAKER, Newstalk ZB's celebrated sports talkback host, was a friend I'd known for a long time. We went to university in Dunedin together, played cricket together and I'd taught with him at Auckland Grammar School. Because he's a bit like a dog with a bone once he sniffs out a contentious issue on that weekend radio programme of his, I'd phoned him a few weeks earlier and asked him to "get off my case". Which he very kindly did, understanding where I was coming from. Now that D-Day was looming, I felt he was the best person to approach about how I should handle the announcement. Deaks was great. He could have been selfish and organised the news break for his own benefit, but he insisted on setting up a press conference, selecting the Centra Hotel in central Auckland as the venue. He appreciated the significance of the occasion more than me. At one stage, I asked him, "What if no one turns up?"

Deaks negotiated with the hotel and we issued invitations to the print and electronic media, happy to involve representatives from all the newspapers and radio and television stations. I expected to see the usual dozen or so faces I'd regularly confronted at press conferences following Auckland and Blues matches at Eden Park, so when Raewyn and I arrived, I was surprised to find more than 50 packed into the room. We had given some consideration to having John Graham chair the meeting but because John was now president of the Auckland Rugby Union, we considered that might be a tad insensitive.

Deaks offered a little private tutoring on what to say and how to say it. "These are professional journalists whose attention you must capture from the start," he told me. "Don't waffle. Hit 'em straight between the eyes."

We agreed to start by telling them I was off to Wales and I was going tonight. Which is precisely how I launched into my announcement. There probably was a bit of waffle after that, but there were a lot of things I wanted to say and I was determined to put them on record.

I told the gathering that it was a dream opportunity to coach a national team through until 2003, spanning not one but two World Cups, and that I was a simple soul who wanted to coach and not get involved in politics.

I explained that my heart told me to stay but that my head said to go, that if I hadn't accepted the offer I could have finished up a grumpy old man in 18 months because I might miss out coaching the national team in both countries. Explaining why I'd accepted the offer, I said there were only two nations in the world where rugby was the national game – Wales and New Zealand. Both were totally passionate about the game.

The Welsh team I was about to take responsibility for was coming off a 96-13 hiding from the Springboks, which obviously was ominous, but I assured the gathering I was confident that once the team had all its best players available, dramatic improvement was possible. Well, you could only improve on a 90-point licking, couldn't you?

I reminded them that the Auckland team had created a culture back in the early eighties where it expected to be a winner. I had been associated with a lot of winners and I was naturally expecting that to continue in Wales.

The NZRFU had stated that if I took up the Welsh coaching appointment, I faced a lifetime ban from ever coaching the All Blacks. I said I thought that decision lacked sensitivity, logic and maturity.

There was a good feeling evident among the gathering and only one question tarnished it. Someone questioned my loyalty to New Zealand rugby. Not anticipating such a question, I gave a hopelessly inadequate answer. What I wished I had said was that I had given 25 years to coaching within the amateur game, from schoolboys and colts through to NPC and Super 12. If that's not loyalty to New Zealand rugby, what is? It was a shitty question and I was annoyed that I didn't answer it better.

There was little reference to the incumbent All Black coach, John Hart, although in the seemingly endless one-on-one interviews that followed the formal press conference, I was asked a couple of times whether I thought I could have operated in tandem with him.

The simple answer is yes. I didn't consider I would have a problem working with John. But he seemed to have a problem working with me. He went on record as saying he didn't feel I was assistant coach material. He's entitled to that view, but I was arrogant enough to believe I could have made a difference to the All Blacks if I had become involved. I probably operate differently to the majority of coaches, in the manner in which I prepare for games. I'm technical, John's motivational. Together, I genuinely believe we could have formed a strong partnership.

John and I spoke to each other, one on one, on numerous occasions, dealings that were always positive. From those discussions, however, it was apparent that he approaches life differently to me. I had the feeling he was always looking into the future to see if the path was clear whereas I was only really concerned with the next assignment.

I didn't appreciate John's attempted interference with the Auckland Blues at times. Carlos Spencer's status as a goalkicker was a prime example. I was prepared to do as much as I could to help the All Blacks without it being detrimental to our team. I was happy to give Carlos goalkicking opportunities if he could maintain a reasonable success rate. But he couldn't. So Adrian Cashmore was used. I wasn't prepared to risk losing Super 12 games through not using Cashmore. I wasn't against Carlos kicking, but my first responsibility was to my team, not John's, and anything I didn't consider was in the best interest of the Auckland Blues, I didn't entertain.

It also annoyed me that the All Black management operated behind our backs in using their medical staff to instruct individuals not to play at times, instead of coming directly to us. They were questioning our professionalism. It irritated our doctor, Graham Paterson, and it irritated me. If John believed Michael Jones, say, shouldn't play the next game because he wanted him for an upcoming international, surely the proper procedure was to come and discuss it with me or the Blues or Auckland management.

Endless people assured me I would be John's successor but none of them could guarantee that. If John had continued on his winning way and triumphed at the next World Cup, who knows, he could have been there for life.

I certainly believe I had the qualifications to coach the All Blacks. I was perhaps the only guy in New Zealand rugby with extensive experience in coaching at the top before professionalism kicked in who was still going strong three years later.

There were two things I was trying to achieve as a coach. First, obviously, was to coach to the best of my ability, using technology as an important tool. Over the years I had come to appreciate the need to make training sessions as exciting as possible, to bring flow and urgency to sessions. You want the guys to find training so stimulating they want to be there for the next one. It's vital that practice sessions are varied and meaningful and relate to what you are doing in the game. It's important to mix fun and humour with all the seriousness, not to become too deadly serious as a coach. I'm always learning, to the extent I consider myself a better coach now than I was last year. The second aspect of coaching is to be aware of the bigger picture and to create the right environment for the team to function. While you demand professional standards are set in terms of dress, behaviour and punctuality, you must also allow your players the opportunity to relax and have a few beers occasionally, particularly after a big game. That's what we did with the Blues, where manager Rex Davy played an important role, and it's how we are now operating with Wales, where managers David

Pickering and Trevor James are doing the job. Camaraderie and team spirit are ingredients every bit as important as tactical nous in the development of a successful rugby team. Developing a rugby environment which allows no release of tension breeds negativity which in turn doesn't allow teams to function to their full potential. A coach has to know when to lighten up.

When Laurie Mains, who did wonders for New Zealand rugby and who was highly respected by his players, stumbled at the final hurdle at the 1995 World Cup in South Africa and chose not to seek re-election, I decided to stand for the All Black coaching job, as did John Hart. I campaigned diligently, which is my way, travelling around the country talking to people I regarded as decision makers in New Zealand rugby, guys like Colin Meads, John Sturgeon and the past president Rodney Dawe.

At the end of the day, I realised it was a waste of time, because the decision was made by a coaching sub-committee whose recommendation I originally thought had to be ratified. I was wrong. If I'd realised they were the ones to lobby, I'd have turned my attentions to them. Obviously I didn't have them in my pocket and was out-thought. One of those I attempted to lobby finished up as John Hart's manager, which demonstrated my political shortcomings! It's why I'll stick to sport. Anyway, there seemed to be a feeling throughout the land that with rugby now professional, John Hart was the right man for the job. His background with Fletchers obviously counted highly. I was only ever referred to as a schoolteacher. The fact I was responsible for 100 teachers and 1200 pupils didn't seem to qualify me for business status. John Hart was in the corporate world. That elevated him well above humble schoolteachers.

Perhaps there was an over-emphasis on business qualifications to go with rugby's new age. At the end of the day, a coach's job is to coach a team to produce the goods on the field. Back in 1996, rugby sometimes appeared to be relegated behind the corporate image.

To be fair, the All Blacks performed superbly for two years, claiming an historic series victory on South African soil and taking out the first two Tri-nations championships. A change is always good and initially an attitude of positiveness pervaded the national team. John had the perception of involving famous former All

Blacks as mentors, which I'm sure assisted the current players. More significantly, he possessed individuals in Fitzpatrick, Zinny Brooke and Bunce who had few peers in the world in terms of international experience, expertise and qualities of leadership. He utilised their extraordinary talents to help make the All Blacks supreme through 1996 and 1997.

John gave the players responsibility and ownership of the team. They were enjoying this consensus approach. However, the more a team wins, the more pressure is exerted, and here I can speak from experience. It's the ultimate challenge to a coach to remain at the top, because, as everyone knows, it's one-way traffic when you're on the summit.

The Springboks and the Wallabies, humbled in 1997, appointed new and successful coaches who were determined to restore their countries' pride. Nick Mallett and Rod Macqueen were correct appointments, coaches with the right credentials. There was little pressure on them in '98. It was all on Hart and the All Blacks. It's not easy when you're top of the pile. There are classic examples – the Liverpool soccer team and the Boston Celtics basketball side among them – of champions which have dominated for three or four years failing to sustain their dominance. Human nature enters the equation. Each year you are the champion, the pressure intensifies to reproduce your level of performance. Other sides are hungry for success and naturally target the champion. Every outing therefore becomes a test match. The marketing people don't want one team to dominate so will go to lengths to disadvantage the champion. And sometimes even the referees can get caught up in the hype.

The reality was the All Blacks lost three key players (Fitzpatrick, Brooke and Bunce) who were impossible to replace. New leaders had to be found and developed and a considerable number of injuries didn't help the cause. Added to this, the pressure of trying to reinvent the wheel for the third year in a row proved extremely difficult. That's the biggest challenge for any coach. We tried to win a third Super 12 without Fitzy and Zinny, and failed. Never underestimate the impact of leaders such as them.

I programmed the Auckland press conference so I could walk out of the hotel, and virtually head straight to the airport and fly out to Wales. The theory was impeccable until the city council intervened – they'd towed my car away from outside the Centra. Maybe the NZRFU had tipped them off! Leaving my trusty lawyer David Jones to retrieve the car, I departed in a taxi, calling at home to collect my suitcase, in the process removing the telephone, which was going mad, from the hook. As I was checking in at Auckland Airport, there were TV cameras up my nose. I maintained a dignified attitude as I disappeared through the check-in zone, reasoning that the last thing I needed to do was to embarrass the NZRFU at this point.

As I entered Air New Zealand's first-class lounge, desperately wanting to flop down and unwind, I found the place packed and there, large as life on the TV screen being interviewed by Paul Holmes, was Graham Henry. Oh, hell! All I could do was laugh. Grant Dalton, who'd achieved fame as a round-the-world yachtsman, was in the lounge and offered me a seat. He and I sat together, as it turned out, all the way to Europe and shared a few sporting experiences.

He was totally supportive of what I was doing. In fact, it occurred to me as the jet powered away from New Zealand, that the only negatives had come from the NZRFU and the Auckland Rugby Union, which had wanted to make some money on the side.

Photosport

Chapter 7

Come in, the Redeemer

The goal of planning is to remove from a tough situation the panic element of "What the hell are we going to do now?" The less thinking people have to do under adverse circumstances, the better. When you're under pressure, the mind plays tricks on you. It's a terrible mistake to let outside forces influence you more than the pragmatic realities of the situation already are.

Bill Walsh, coach, San Francisco 49ers

MY ARRIVAL IN WALES had been planned with military precision. Rather than have me land at Heathrow following an exhausting 24-hour journey from Auckland, then three hours up the road in Cardiff confront the media in a jetlagged state, it was arranged that I would overnight in Amsterdam where I linked up with Welsh rugby officials. They presented further documents for me to sign which confirmed my status as rugby coach of Wales.

Refreshed and signed up, I flew into Cardiff the next morning to confront the media. They'd packed the room at the Centra in Auckland and this looked like another sell-out conference! Fortunately, having had seven seasons with Auckland and three with the Blues, I was accustomed to talking into a proliferation of microphones, peering down the end of television cameras and answering questions that varied from the cute to the acute. I'd learnt to say the right things over the years, not to make boastful claims I couldn't fulfil.The formal press conference lasted an hour but the individual interviews and photo shoots went on for another four hours. I'd arranged for my daughter Catherine, who was living in London, to come through and join me, which was an inspired move. She softened the occasion and finished up getting more media attention than me!

I fielded some pretty straightforward questions. What did I hope to achieve? Well, obviously I wanted the Welsh team to play to its potential and with passion. At that stage, of course, I had no concept of what I was getting myself into. There was no question that the results in South Africa, where the test was lost 96-13, had plunged the nation into depression. That tour was patently not a fair reflection of the strength of Welsh rugby but at the end of the day, the results were there for all to see. Some of the Five Nations defeats the previous season had been pretty calamitous too. But I'd resolved not to concern myself with the past. Coming from New Zealand with no rugby baggage whatsoever, I was determined to start afresh, to take players as I found them. No coach utilises videos more than me, but I refused to watch anything of Wales' performances in South Africa or during the previous Five Nations championship. To focus on those games would, I considered, be a negative.

The reception and publicity that attended my weekend in Wales – I would return to New Zealand for a couple of weeks before setting up house in Cardiff – was quite overwhelming. Considering the national team's record in recent times, it was surprising to encounter such an air of expectation. It was hard to tell whether it was excessive confidence or sheer hope. Still, I felt if the Welsh had gone to all this trouble to get me, they were taking a positive approach.

TERRY COBNER
Welsh Rugby Union
We looked at rugby coaches all over the world before deciding to approach Graham Henry. We knew with his qualifications he was the right man for the job. Our initial inquiries led us to believe he was not available but

fortunately that information was wrong. He's made a dramatic impact in an extremely short time in Wales. Not only is he an exceptional rugby coach but he has the ability to cut through the periphery and get straight to the core of a matter. His presence has created a tremendous impetus. People are talking rugby far more animatedly – even my wife, who is a school principal.

As a coach, you have a vision of how rugby is best played and you try and find the appropriate individuals to achieve that. Sometimes it's hard to find the right player for a particular slot, but generally, if you're operating from a wide catchment area, you are usually able to fill in most of the gaps. And for all the problems that had beset Welsh rugby in modern times, there didn't seem to be a shortage of capable players.

In Auckland, I always built on the year before. Considering what had been achieved every season from the early eighties, with the Ranfurly Shield a permanent fixture from 1985 to 1993 and the NPC taken out 11 times in 15 years, that was common sense. I never had to burn the place down and start again. But in Wales, dealing with a team coming off a 96-point hammering against the Springboks – who just happened to be my first opponents – meant that obviously I was going to have to start building from the ground up. It would, for me, be a novel and stimulating experience finding players to make the vision a reality.

The original scheduling gave me a month back in Auckland to put all my affairs in order but that was condensed to a fortnight when, after discussions with the Welsh Rugby Union, it was apparent that the only time trials could be staged were in mid-August. Trials were important to give me the opportunity to observe as many players as possible and to let the Welsh players know we were starting from scratch and so every one of them had the chance to stake a claim.

My brief stint back in New Zealand coincided with the Springbok test at Athletic Park in Wellington, which I attended as a guest speaker for Corporate Host, along with former All Black captain Graham Mourie. I have to confess I was a shade apprehensive about the weekend. What if people started giving me a hard time about abandoning New Zealand, an anxiousness that had been planted in me through my dealings with the NZRFU? Far from that, everyone was totally positive. Graham Mourie wished me luck and considered it a natural stepping stone in my coaching career. And there were only positive vibes from the fans at the game. "Good luck, boyo," was a popular comment. You never know how people are going to react but every person I talked to was of common mind, that it was an individual choice, which was important in the scheme of things. They were all extremely friendly and supportive, a reminder of what great people Kiwis are.

Obviously, the first requirement in building a new Welsh team was to put the management in place. Because I was a New Zealander, I insisted from the start that the balance of the management team had to be Welsh, or Brits the Welsh related to. Although I was going to be providing the playing strategy, it was important the new structure wasn't perceived as a New Zealand takeover.

During my stint at Blackheath, I'd undertaken a journey north to Scotland, calling in en route at the Newcastle Rugby Club where I caught up with Pat Lam, Inga Tuigamala and Ross Nesdale, three players I'd had a bit to do with back in Auckland. They asked what I was doing in town. "You're the reason," I said. "Newcastle's top of the heap. I thought I'd call in and find out what makes you better than the rest."

The answer, which wasn't the one I was expecting, was a Geordie called Steve Black, the club's conditioning coach, the person responsible for their mental and physical preparation. I filed that piece of information away for future reference. Then about six months later, when my Welsh coaching appointment was imminent and I was in Apia preparing the New Zealand A team, I renewed my discussion with Pat Lam, now wearing his Samoan captain's cap. Black was, he assured me, a remarkable person with the capacity to fire players.

When I finally set up shop in Cardiff, one of the first phone calls I made was to Steve Black. Yes, he was interested in becoming involved with Wales, so I arranged for him to meet Terry Cobner, Jim Blair and myself, which became an occasion of high entertainment. Steve – Blackie to everyone – is 40, looks like Friar Tuck and is into positive reinforcement in massive slices. He's thoroughly exuberant; in fact, at that first get-together, Terry and I couldn't shut him up. I had to tell him to be quiet at times so I could get a question in.

There are two sides to Blackie – one, the conditioning coach, the other a feel-good motivator. He asserts that players must have a full tank, physically and mentally, going into a game. I have to say I've changed as a coach since becoming involved with him, particularly in the manner in which I now prepare the squad for a test match. Blackie hovers like a mother hen, ensuring we don't overtrain, being continually at me and forward coach Lyn Howells to look after the players physically. Less is better than more, in Blackie's book. Not that I've ever been one to flog players, but he made me trim twice-a-day practices to a solitary session.

Blackie conditions players as opposed to physically training them and in this he's great because he makes the players feel good about themselves. He's at his best one on one; in fact, he doesn't like dealing with more than four players at a time because he's working on their minds as well as their bodies. He's a great believer in love. "You've got to love your players, Graham," he keeps reminding me. It's that feel-good factor coming through all the time, which has impacted emphatically. Because of Blackie, I'm probably closer to the Welsh squad members than I ever was to the Auckland players, amazingly.

Blackie had a major influence on Pat Lam's career at Newcastle. Pat's career was continually interrupted with leg trouble until Blackie got hold of him. Now he's one of the outstanding No 8s on the world rugby stage.

Blackie's now fully employed by the Welsh Rugby Union and has been a marvellous acquisition. He and I complement each other perfectly. I'm low key, he's upbeat. I devise strategies, he unearths quotations and happenings that provide inspiration and motivation. I was fortunate to find someone of his exceptional talent.

With a New Zealander and a Geordie involved, it was important to have a Welshman who'd been there, done that as the manager. David Pickering, 37, a sometimes-captain in his 27 tests for the Scarlets, was the ideal appointment. A successful businessman with a major shareholding in three safety and engineering companies, he is both authoritative and personable, someone the players have no difficulty relating to or, when necessary, confiding in. He and I have become close mates. I regard him as a younger version of Auckland and Blues manager Rex Davy.

We brought on board Alun Lewis, the current coach of Newport, who was, everyone assured me, the best back coach in Wales (he, David Pickering and myself comprise the national selection panel), Lyn Howells, the Pontypridd coach, an expert on forward play who'd survived the traumatic trip to South Africa, and Trevor James, a full-time employee of the WRU, as the administrative manager of the team. Trevor, enormously loyal to the players, is a tireless worker who puts in endless man-hours to ensure everything runs smoothly. Unfortunately, he doesn't have the control he should have because of the committee structure which continues to burden Welsh rugby. All paid employees of the union are accountable to the committee which limits their ability to get on and do the job. They don't operate according to laid-down policy but on what the committee wants, which is a weakness of the system. In most other major rugby nations now, 90 per cent of what paid employees do is based on policies laid down by the committee.

David Pickering and Lyn Howells came to New Zealand on a fact-finding mission in the wake of Wales' disappointing tour of South Africa in 1997, working closely with the Auckland Rugby Union. I got to know them, little thinking I would be helping form a management team with them within the year. For any sports team to succeed it's essential to have a strong management group in place. We've been able to achieve that in Wales, bringing together a selection of individuals, none of them with hidden agendas – I'm big on this – who would create the ideal environment for the players, which has been possible because they're all team people. Creating that positive environment is critical and allows the players to enjoy what they are doing. It struck me back home in 1998 that the environment was one of the problems with the All Blacks. David and his delightful wife Justine have helped to make both Raewyn's and my transition from New Zealand to Wales enjoyable.

I was guilty in my early days in Wales of listening to too many people and allowing myself to be influenced against some of the players who would eventually become key components of the Welsh squad. Fortunately, as I journeyed around watching club teams in action – not all of them on the Welsh side of the Severn

River – I came to recognise that a good deal of what had been uttered was based on bias, village-ism or feeble judgment. I was annoyed with myself for taking on board other people's assessments of players because I'd come determined to start afresh, to take every player as I found him. I pretty soon put out of my head everything that had been spoken to me about contenders for the Welsh team. It was a huge advantage for me to have no preconceived opinions about players. I had no roots in Wales, no club allegiances. At the end of the day, I made up my own mind based on what I saw in front of me. I would select players I considered could help me fulfil my vision for the team. In some instances, I would rely on gut feeling. After 25 years rugby coaching, I felt I knew the sort of player I was looking for.

One person I did listen to who talked a lot of sense was Derek Quinnell, someone who has achieved an almost legendary status in Wales similar to that held by the great Colin "Pinetree" Meads in New Zealand. Derek's the father of Scott and Craig, two hulking forwards who would become vital members of my pack. But it wasn't the future prospects of his sons we were discussing. The more urgent issue was the state of Welsh rugby.

He was concerned that divisions had formed within the Welsh team because half the players were on contracts and half weren't. He gave the example of the match against England at Twickenham the previous season: about seven of the players on the pitch were commanding salaries of £30,000 or £40,000 while the other eight or so were on nothing. There was a win bonus system operating, which was of limited merit since the team was losing more matches than it was winning. Not unnaturally, friction was bubbling under the surface.

The first thing I did, in association with the rest of the management team, was to restructure the whole system, putting every squad member on the same basic contract with increases directly proportionate to the number of caps. Now they were all operating on the same formula. The more tests they played, the more rewarding it became for them.

It was a much more player-friendly arrangement. No longer was Wales treating some players as stars and others simply as numbers in the programme… hardly the way to produce a dynamic team effort.

There were other factors requiring attention. For instance, it had been the practice to assemble the Welsh squad in Cardiff every Wednesday throughout the rugby season. Now theoretically this might have been advantageous in terms of developing camaraderie but what was happening was that the players were hammering hell out of each other and then going home.

I didn't see any benefit in this whatsoever. When you bring a squad together, you must have specific objectives and ensure the sessions are meaningful and exciting. Otherwise, as a coach you're simply trying to justify your existence. Since the advent of professional rugby, there are too many people, I consider, trying to justify their existence in the eye of their employers. They're paid large salaries, so they consider it important they be seen to be doing a lot.

I quickly deduced, because of the heavy commitments that were being heaped upon the Welsh players, that less was better. Leading into the Springbok game on 15 November, we organised only two squad sessions, at the beginning of October and again in the first week of November. That was it until we assembled the week of the test. Players are better off, in my opinion, champing for knowledge rather than being saturated with it. It was something we worked hard at with the Auckland Blues. I know there's a body of opinion that says rugby players should always be caressing a ball so that it becomes an extension of them, but when you're dealing with a squad, balance is essential. The mental thing of working with the ball all the time can become counter-productive. It's important to stimulate your players by occasionally doing something different, something completely unexpected, like swapping a training session for a workout in the gym, or eliminating rugby balls from the session altogether. In this, I was often guided... perhaps nudged is the term... by the team's senior pros.

For the Springbok game, we came together at midday on the Monday and went through a gym session in the afternoon. On the Tuesday we staged a long training session in the morning and a lighter workout in the afternoon. Then I sent them home.

The players had Tuesday and Wednesday evenings in their homes, which I'm sure was more beneficial than stifling them in a team situation. It allowed them to relax while maintaining their intensity. After reassembling on the Thursday, we went through the team plan before travelling across to London (for the game at Wembley). Friday was about fine-tuning, ahead of the game on the Saturday. The final result, as everyone knows, was 28-20 to the Springboks, the eight-point winning margin being achieved in injury time.

That particular preparation worked for us. Some coaches believe more is better, which I don't necessarily condemn because all any coach is surely trying to do is create an advantage for his team. Personally, I'm convinced I can best achieve this in short, high-powered sessions, keeping the players on edge and creating excitement.

The first training session I oversaw with Wales was an eye-opener for me, because the players were walking from phase to phase. I had to tell them to run. They were in what I quickly identified as the "Plod Syndrome", which has a lot to do with over-involvement in trainings and matches to the extent that no one is ever giving more than 80 per cent effort.

While Wales may not possess game breakers of the calibre of, say, Jeff Wilson, Christian Cullen, Ben Tune and Joost van der Westhuizen… not at the moment, anyway… the nation is blessed with some good quality players. The problem was that they had been knocked around by the press and the public and placed under pressure by coaches who had obviously gone for the over-physical approach.

People expected me to be familiar with all the leading Welsh players when I arrived in Cardiff. I think I startled them by saying I hardly knew the names of *any* current internationals. And I certainly didn't consider watching a replay of the team's horror performance against the Springboks at Pretoria was the place to start.

Because every Welsh rugby person is so passionate about his team – which I quite understand – they all have definite views on every player in, or in contention for, the national side. Naturally, they all wished to convey their opinions to me the minute I arrived in their country. As I say, my initial mistake was to listen to some of them.

I can nominate seven players who weren't named in the original squad because I was stupid enough to listen to other people's opinions – Jonathan Humphries, Chris Wyatt, Craig Quinnell,

David Llewellyn, Shane Howarth, Neil Boobyer and Mike Rayer. Their introduction was based on my own observations. Blatant parochialism lay behind the advice conveyed to me. It's not exclusive to Wales but I do consider it's more ingrained here than anywhere else. Everyone is outrageously biased towards their own club, as a consequence of which the poor selectors are placed under enormous pressure. I don't know how my predecessors, with club allegiances, ever managed. It's a huge advantage not to have any preconceived opinions, I can tell you.

SUE MOTT
Daily Telegraph
He is, above all, not Welsh. He has no baggage to declare but his chattels from New Zealand. He is above internecine Welsh rugby politics. The mere sound of his New Zealand accent commanded instant player respect.

The biggest problem confronting rugby in Wales lies in the infrastructure, with players committed to schools, clubs, districts, counties and their country. I spoke with one 17-year-old who had played 93 games the previous year. The poor blighter had to train for them all, too. Compare that with my son Andrew who, when he was in the first fifteen at Auckland Grammar School, played no more than 25 games in the year.

Fortunately, I'd insisted on being directly involved in rugby at all levels before I signed my contract with the Welsh union. It was terribly important to do that because you cannot coach a national side without having a say in the development of competitions through the levels. And it's a wee bit of a mess in Wales, you'd have to say. The top players are not involved in competitions conducive to churning out individuals of international standard. Meanwhile, the younger fry are overwhelmed by the number of fixtures they find themselves committed to.

The rugby development issue is a can of worms which I hopefully can work through because there's got to be a pathway to the top for the best young players. When they emerge, they need to be stimulated, not exhausted by the horrendous schedules presently confronting them.

The other major concern in Wales is the implementation of

professionalism. In New Zealand, while there have been a few hitches, generally the game has completed the transition efficiently and effectively. But in Wales – in fact, in the UK generally – they've taken the professionalising of rugby too literally. I visited the tiny club of Cefn Coed, which plays in the sixth division of the national league, and was astonished to learn that the players are on a win bonus of £50 per player, so every victory costs the club £1100 for the 22 squad members. No wonder clubs are going into receivership all over the place. Sixth division in the UK is about equal to senior reserve B in Auckland, where the guys are 100 per cent amateur.

If a lower grade club has a player of rare talent, it's often difficult for him to advance because of the transfer fees involved. The fifth or sixth division club, identifying a player as the next Barry John or Gareth Edwards, puts a price of maybe £5000 on his head, which other clubs simply can't afford to pay. So he's stuck down the grades.

It's stimulating to be involved in all of this. We're basically dealing with good people who want Welsh rugby to progress. It's just they've got themselves into one hell of a mess. The Welsh are a lot like New Zealanders where the success of the national rugby team means everything. Nothing causes despondency back in New Zealand more than a loss by the All Blacks, and it's the same in Wales. Except the Welsh have been losing a lot more consistently than the All Blacks over the past couple of decades.

Greater parochialism exists in Wales. While there is fanatical support for Canterbury, particularly, back in New Zealand and a North-South debate always gets a few hackles raised, the Welsh scene is amazing. Here you find them defending street against street, club against club, east against west. They all want Wales to win, especially when the Five Nations championship is happening, but a lot of people have difficulty sacrificing their own agendas for the sake of the national team. I recall the All Blacks of 1989 expressing astonishment at the rabid fervour of the locals when they played Neath. Well, while things might be a shade more intense in Neath than elsewhere, what the All Blacks experienced is symptomatic of what is happening throughout Wales. Now while you never want to undermine a nation's passion for a sport, it's important that these energies be directly positively, for the ultimate benefit of the national team.

Welsh rugby supporters have been living off the glory days of the 1960s and 1970s, when fabulous footballers like Gareth Edwards, Barry John, Gerald Davies, John Dawes, JPR Williams, JJ Williams, Phil Bennett and Mervyn Davies abounded. They dearly want to recreate those times when Welsh teams set rugby fields alight. Yet by their blind parochialism, they have been doing everything to ensure that never happens.

Every club in Wales wants to be a super club, whether it's Cardiff or Swansea or Pontypridd or a remote little village in the seventh division. While their pride and loyalty are to be admired, their objectives are often completely unrealistic.

It's my job to identify the best 22 Welsh players and prepare them for test matches and, hopefully, without offending too many people – because I'm pretty new in these parts – I can help streamline the processes along the way. It doesn't worry me that it might involve a lot of work, because I've got an appetite for work. I enjoy it. What is important is that we structure rugby in Wales correctly so everyone is happy and the game flourishes. It's hard enough competing against the major rugby nations of the world as it is, without handicapping yourself internally.

The huge advantage I've had is being free of club and regional affiliations. Cardiff, Swansea, Pontypridd and Neath are just four clubs to me who play in different coloured jerseys. I'm only interested in how the individuals perform, not the final scorelines whenever they engage each other. Perhaps that's where my predecessors in Wales have had problems because they would naturally bend towards the people they know whereas I breezed in from New Zealand with no fixed ideas or prejudices.

I quickly appreciated that there were significant numbers of players eligible for the national team who were operating outside Wales, predominantly in England. In the first few months in my new role, I watched Richmond play four times. Club officials expressed surprise, saying they'd hardly ever sighted a Welsh coach previously.

I called in on London Welsh, a club I consider should become a centre of excellence for Welsh rugby in England. Prior to Christmas, I spent a weekend with the club at its headquarters at Old Deer Park. I was most impressed with what I encountered. I see the club playing a major part as we bid to maximise our strength at national level. The great Welsh teams of the seventies were built on players from the club, individuals like JPR Williams, John Dawes, Mervyn Davies, Gerald Davies and John Taylor, but the club fell into the doldrums and has only just begun to pick up.

There are a great many Welsh-qualified players in the Greater London area and there's a club there for them. We have to work on that. At the Welsh union, we've been working hard to establish a worldwide database of players in a bid to ensure that all Welsh qualified players are monitored. I see London Welsh as having a crucial role to play in that area.

One of my earliest meetings in Cardiff was with Kevin Bowring, the previous coach, who went out of his way to be helpful. I appreciated that, because it can't have been easy for him. He's obviously a good student of the game who knows his players. He pointed out some of the plusses and minuses of the game in Wales.

It was around this time I was making the mistake of believing what other people were telling me about some of the potential candidates for the national side. Almost half the team would differ from what we as selectors initially sketched in. Sorting out a starting fifteen was a matter of some urgency because although I hadn't finished unpacking my suitcases, there was an international coming up against South Africa in 10 weeks time. The same South African team that had triumphed in the Tri-nations (which included a double success against the All Blacks), would go 17 tests without defeat until the hiccup against England at Twickenham, was now the bookies' favourite for the World Cup and had put 96 points on the men in scarlet at Pretoria.

People kept asking me if I was daunted by it all and seemed surprised when I answered no. It was hugely stimulating because I had taken on the greatest challenge in rugby – restoring Wales to its rightful place on the international stage. Far from being awed, I was excited about it all. This wasn't some rugby backwater I was coming to. This was Wales, which ranked right alongside New Zealand in its passion for the game. Just as pulling on the black jersey is the ultimate for every young player in New Zealand, so running on to Cardiff Arms Park (which I suppose we now have to call the Millennium Stadium) is what every aspiring rugby player in Wales dreams of.

STEPHEN JONES
London Sunday Times
The Welsh can see that he is doing more for their rugby than any previous coach. He's taken coaching sessions at some of the tiniest clubs in Wales. They're so tiny that not even many Welsh people have heard of them. And he's certainly infected the players with his own excellent form early on. He's been incredibly thorough, re-motivated them and made them want to play again. Henry's uncomplicated methods had restored organisation and confidence to Welsh rugby. There's not been a single word of criticism of him.

There was a time when Welsh rugby was being perpetually ravaged by the league clubs of northern England. But since the professionalising of rugby, that trend has been reversed and gifted footballers like Scott Gibbs, David Young, Alan Bateman and Scott Quinnell have come back to the game. I hope there are many more.

I was spoilt with riches back in Auckland, certainly in the early nineties, although perhaps not so much in recent years. There were people who claimed a donkey could have coached Auckland to NPC success. I guess I had to come to Wales to prove I wasn't a donkey!

Because of the wealth of talent in Auckland, maybe I sometimes lost my sharpness and zeal. It took challenges like Auckland's Ranfurly Shield bid at Christchurch in 1995 and the Blues' must-win Super 12 contest at Durban in 1996 to get me totally focused at times. But that was a natural human frailty. When you prepare the same team for seven years, obviously there are going to be occasions when you operate a little on remote control.

From the moment I touched down at Cardiff Airport on 31 July, I was as energised as I could possibly be. No matter who takes on the coaching of the All Blacks, they are expected to achieve instant success and to win every international. Qualifying for the final of the World Cup won't be enough. Hark back to 1995 when Laurie Mains' team succumbed to the Springboks at Ellis Park after extra time. They were gallant losers, but the nation was thrust into depression. Although the public recognised the spectacular quality of play produced throughout the tournament and gave Mains' men a heroes' welcome when they returned, the '95 campaign has been consistently referred to as a failure since then.

Becoming coach of Wales presents a completely different challenge. Here is a nation that has not achieved any sustained success for more than 20 years. Apart from the huge totals conceded to France, England and South Africa in recent times, the team failed to qualify for the World Cup quarter-finals in 1991 and '95, and in one widely-circulating publication was ranked only eighth in the world (behind New Zealand, Australia, South Africa, France, England, Samoa and Argentina) at the beginning of 1998… an unflattering commentary on a country that regards rugby as its national game.

To have the opportunity to prepare this team through to the 2003 World Cup, an event to be jointly hosted by Australia and New Zealand, was, for me, the ultimate challenge, the chance to start again and reformulate ideas. Although inevitably the locals wanted instant results – which seemed to have a bit to do with my reported salary – my main objective, besides shaping a powerful test fifteen, was to strengthen the whole infrastructure of Welsh rugby so that when I finally step aside after five years, the nation has hopefully not only re-established itself among the game's elite but that the future is assured.

I was pleasantly surprised with some of the quality of talent on display once I dropped into the Welsh (and English) club scene, which was a relief. This only emphasised that Wales' problems lay in the developmental and competitive aspects. Instead of having a professional structure in place that underpinned the national team, the set-up was counter-productive at international level. The top side was copping all the backlash. As far as I could see, the Welsh had been papering over the cracks for a long time instead of getting the foundation stones in place.

So where to start? First I met with the premier coaches and fitness advisers, the movers and shakes among the administration, the top-ranked players and the officials who had taken the team to South Africa. I asked a lot more questions than I issued instructions at that point.

My first priority as national coach was to establish a rapport and a relationship with the coaches throughout the country. To facilitate this, I attended as many club trainings as I could work in, sometimes having a bit of an input. It was important for me to involve myself in the rugby environment of Wales as soon as possible. I wanted the coaches to know where I was coming from, that I wasn't in the UK simply to sing the praises of the All Blacks or rugby back in New Zealand. It was essential to build a positive relationship with them. From some of the mail I had received, it was apparent not everyone throughout the land considered my coming a blessing. A few disgruntled Welshmen regarded me as "a bloody foreigner". I wrote back to them all, assuring them I was totally committed to the cause and that I was determined to build a national team of which they could all be proud.

Besides calling on clubs throughout Wales, some of them surely among the tiniest and most remote in the entire UK, I also visited Bath, Leicester, Sale and Richmond and flew to Ireland to check out a few players as well. The only way I could determine whether players were worthy of selection was to watch them in action. It was no good me delegating this responsibility because I was the one with the vision for the Welsh team and only I could determine whether a particular player fitted the pattern or not.

I was enthusiastic when I sighted some of the talent available. Chris Wyatt had played the vast majority of his rugby at No 8 but I saw him as a middle-of-the-lineout jumper with his soft hands. And Craig Quinnell, Scott's brother, I saw as the Royce Willis of the pack, the No 2 lineout jumper with power. He could obviously run with the ball. They were a couple of greenhorn locks who I considered would develop into a top international combination.

For fullback, I suddenly had available Shane Howarth, who had worn the No 15 jersey for the All Blacks back in 1994 and since tried his luck at league. I became aware of his qualifications – his grandfather comes from Cardiff – at my press conference in Auckland. Roger Mortimore, a sports agent, approached me and asked if I was aware of Shane's Welsh heritage, which I wasn't. Shane had played more than 50 games for me with Auckland and we had developed a strong personal relationship. John Mitchell also assured me Shane had aspirations to play at international level again. He was now playing rugby for Sale and I phoned him once I arrived in the UK. Things took off from there.

Wales had had a squad system operating, with up to 50 players assembling in Cardiff once a week throughout the rugby season. I immediately scrubbed that because it was counter-productive for the players who had so many demands on their time already. It was also obviously costly for the union. After the South African and Argentinian games in August, the squad didn't come together again until January, for the build-up to the Five Nations championship.

One of the players I needed for the Springbok challenge was No 8 Scott Quinnell, who'd been ordered off for a late charge on Lawrence Dallaglio in club play. I went along to the hearing because I consider it's important for a coach to support his players and was disappointed when he received a two-week suspension. I felt the penalty unwarranted and Scott's club Richmond appealed.

In an hilarious sequence of events, the appeal was postponed until after the Springbok test – which freed him to play – because his wife was expecting a baby on the very day the hearing had been scheduled. We all complimented the couple on their impeccable timing! As it turned out, the hearing quashed the penalty, ruling that the ordering-off was sufficient penalty.

With props David Young and Peter Rogers – a former Transvaal representative who'd been born and bred in Wales – both injured, the tight five we would field against the mighty Springboks couldn't rustle up 10 test caps among them!

To launch my career as the new coach, the Welsh Rugby Union chose to indulge in some innovative marketing and produced a poster which would receive worldwide publicity. The brainchild of the young ladies employed in the marketing division of the union, the striking poster had me standing in front of the full Welsh squad, all nattily kitted out in scarlet jerseys and white shorts, and a message that proclaimed, "Guide Me, O Thou Great Redeemer" and a secondary line reading: "Wales: Bread of Heaven."

It was their idea, not mine, although I supported it enthusiastically. After the setbacks the national team had sustained, the objective was to conjure up some passion among the game's followers and hopefully bring back the singing to Welsh rugby. The poster appeared in various guises throughout Wales and produced an amazing variety of reactions. While most people seemed to think it was appropriate, a number of church people didn't. Some branded it blasphemous.

Instead of answering questions about rugby, for a few days I did nothing but defend the poster. I told the media I thought some people were reading far too much into it, that the purpose of the poster was purely to promote the game against South Africa and to help bring some fervour and excitement back into Welsh rugby. There was never any intention to be blasphemous.

The Advertising Standards Authority investigated the poster after receiving a complaint that it was "blasphemous and offensive". However, the authority found there was not a case to answer under the British Codes of Advertising and Sales Promotion. "We believe the advertisement is unlikely to cause serious or widespread offence," it replied.

PISGAH, EBENEZER AND MARTLETOY
BAPTIST CHURCHES

I feel obliged to write in connection with the new national coach. Like yourselves, we wish to see Welsh rugby successful again, but ultimately our God will not be mocked by such language. There is only one redeemer and that is JC our Lord, not GH. I suggest that Welsh rugby and the powers that be will do well to honour His name and the titles that are rightly His and His alone.
Signed: Rev Phylip Henry Rees

PRESBYTERIAN CHURCH OF WALES
HOPE CHURCH MERTHYR TYDFIL

I write to protest in the strongest possible terms at the poster. At least, the poster is in bad taste; at the most, it is blasphemous and will inevitably cause hurt and offence to practising Christians and, I imagine, agnostics. Anyone with the slightest acquaintance with Christianity will understand that redemption by the sacrifice of Christ is central to the faith of millions. Does the WRU see Graham Henry as a Christ figure or more? We are bordering on the unthinkable.
Signed: R Morris, secretary

PRESBYTERIAN CHURCH OF WALES
GWENT

I write to object to the ad in the Western Mail. I would point out that there is only one redeemer and when William Williams and Peter Williams wrote the hymn 'Guide Me, O Thou Great Redeemer' in the 18th century, they were praising their redeemer,

Our Lord Jesus Christ. You have imported a New Zealander and you may consider that you will be redeemed by him, and that's all well and good, but I'm sure God, through our Lord Jesus Christ, would do a better job for Wales. We would be pleased if you would publish with the same enthusiasm an apology for blaspheming our Lord.

Signed: A.E. White, clerk

NEBO BAPTIST CHURCH
ABERDAR

We the members of the above church wish to express our objection to the Welsh RFU's promotion of the game against South Africa through the use of the word Redeemer in connection with the new Welsh coach. We understand that the original wording of the hymn used is 'Guide Me, O Thou Great Jehovah' and not 'Redeemer' as seen on the poster. We feel that the use of the word redeemer is at least in bad taste and touches upon the whole ethos of our Christian faith which proclaims that JC is the only redeemer.

Signed: Rev Roger Thomas

Whether the Welsh crowd burst into song at Wembley, which is possible considering that we were leading the Springboks until the dying moments of the game, I honestly could not say, because once a game is under way, be it at Eden Park, Ellis Park or Wembley, I am totally focused on the rugby action. I have no awareness of anything else and I certainly wouldn't know what the crowd was doing to entertain itself.

Unfortunately, there was one distraction towards the finish of my first assignment that I became all too aware of because it held up the game – the appearance on the field of a streaker, a bearded bloke who, stark naked, ran 50 or 60 metres down the field before he was apprehended by about eight security people. I hope he wasn't a Welshman because the distraction played right into the hands of the Springboks, who were 17-20 behind at the time with about a dozen minutes left on the clock. The streaker did us no favours whatsoever, breaking our concentration and giving the Boks time to regroup. South Africa had rarely been in the game until then. Whoever he was, he obviously knew nothing about rugby.

Foto Fiddlers Barry Aickin

Chapter 8

A woman's perspective
by Raewyn Henry

Put your own ego aside. Don't be concerned with people writing about what a great coach you are. Make the team the focus. If the team wins, you have done your job. I did not need any more satisfaction than that.

Bud Grant, football coach, Game Plans for Success

IF SOMEONE HAD SUGGESTED EARLY in 1998 that by the end of the year I would be setting up house in Wales, coaching the Cardiff netball team and indulging in walking tours in Tuscany, I would have thought they were bonkers.

But that's the new existence for the wife of the coach of the Welsh national rugby team. I've had to shake my head a couple of times to convince myself that while our sons Matthew and Andrew, our cat Tiga and dog Zak are still living in Auckland, we're now UK-based, a part of the world I had never even visited until less than two years ago.

It's been a bit of a culture shock, I have to admit, but I'm regarding it as part of the great adventure. We're here for five years, so I'd be crazy to sit around hankering for my old Auckland lifestyle. I've adopted the "When in Rome" attitude…

A sweet old woman who was our new neighbour in Cardiff

invited me across for morning tea shortly after we'd settled in, which was charming of her. However, it being 10.30 in the morning, I was a bit taken aback to be offered a whisky or a Bailey's Irish Cream for starters. I figured the Bailey's was the lesser of two evils! She then served up immaculately prepared sandwiches made from her home-made bread. Concerned that I would be lonely when Graham was away with the rugby, she offered me a couple of videos to help while away the hours. Gosh, thanks, I said. She selected *South Pacific* and *Gigi* for me. And there's a lot more where they come from, she assured me!

I've quickly appreciated that I've landed in a man's world. Wives are into looking after their men and sons in a big way, doing everything for them, putting them on pedestals. Women's sport has no profile – it isn't seen as important. For example, soon after I arrived Wales played England at netball, a sport which is huge back in New Zealand with every international telecast live. Not only wasn't this game telecast, the score wasn't even in one of the papers I read the next day.

When it comes to rugby, however, they're amazingly passionate and into adulation in a way which would astound New Zealanders. You wouldn't believe how they treat Graham. I say to him, 'You're only a bloody rugby coach!" but the Welsh regard him like a pop star.

When we attended a game at Pontypridd, there was lovely Welsh lady who approached Graham as we crossed the road. She had this bag of home-made Welsh mints which she had been taking to every game in the hope of meeting him.

If I go to the supermarket, it's not worth taking Graham – it's too disruptive. Everybody wants to talk to him, from little kids to grandmothers. It's incredible. Back in New Zealand, notwithstanding the fact he'd won more Super 12s and NPCs than anyone else, he maintained a comparatively low profile. He'd get a few "Hello Grahams" and the odd rugby enthusiast would engage him in conversation but basically people left him alone.

In Wales, though, he's a national celebrity. He attended a sportsman's luncheon in March shortly after Wales had defeated France in Paris for the first time in 25 years, entering the function alongside boxer Lennox Lewis' manager Frank Maloney, who was the keynote speaker. Graham received a standing ovation. Frank

Maloney couldn't believe it.

It was probably inevitable that I would end up married to a rugby person having grown up in a rugby-mad household. There *were* other topics of conversation but when winter rolled around nothing competed with rugby. To say my father, Alan Cochrane, was a staunch rugby person would be the understatement of the century. If I tell you he christened his first son Calvin Fraser Cochrane, so that the initials CFC matched those of the Christchurch Football Club, of which Dad became a life member, you get the picture. I got away with Raewyn Gail.

Dad played a few games for Canterbury during the war years and both my brothers played representative rugby as well. Calvin was good enough to win an All Black trial while Bruce, the youngest, was selected for New Zealand Juniors. Although my parents were supportive of all their children, if it was a toss-up between attending a first fifteen game or the netball, rugby always won out.

With all this rugby madness going on around me, my mother, Jeannie, maintained a good, balanced approach to life. She went back to work to ensure there was enough money for her children to complete their educations. Tragically, when he was only 50, Dad died from complications stemming from bowel cancer.

For three years from 1967, I flatted in Dunedin while working my way through a physical education degree at Otago University. The only other Christchurch person involved in the same course for the same years was a guy called Graham Henry. We were a couple of sports nuts. He was into rugby and cricket in a big way while my interests were netball, basketball and athletics, particularly sprinting. Initially, I wasn't impressed with this Henry fellow, but because our studies brought us into contact so regularly we eventually became good friends. Very good friends. Such good friends that we married in 1970, the year after graduating. Graham was 23, I was 21.

Three years later we found ourselves in Auckland, which was pretty traumatic. I'd been teaching at Aranui High School when Graham won an appointment at Auckland Grammar School. It was a career opportunity too good to resist, so we uprooted ourselves from Christchurch and headed north.

The early months were a challenge. We existed in a terrible flat,

I swear it rained every day for six months and I wrote our car off in attempting a U-turn in a narrow street without noticing that another driver was bearing down on me. The car was a mess but I managed to clamber out uninjured, if shaken. My mother had remarried and moved to Auckland, which was a blessing because Graham was unbelievably busy. If he wasn't playing sport, he was coaching it. One summer he was away for six weeks managing the New Zealand schools cricket team, another he finished up on crutches after snapping his Achilles tendon playing senior club cricket.

For four years our home was the Auckland Grammar School hostel, of which Graham was the house-master, before we eventually bought a house in Mt Eden. While Graham concentrated on his teaching and coaching, I dedicated myself to our three children, Matthew, Catherine and Andrew, eventually returning to teaching at Baradene College, a Catholic school in Remuera. I sort of drifted into the job as a reliever. Before I knew it, I was full-time and coaching the netball team, something which came fairly naturally. When you're a phys-edder in New Zealand, coaching sports teams goes with the territory and I'd helped prepare teams from a young age.

Unlike Graham, who was always ambitious as a coach, I tended to fall into coaching appointments. I'd been helping out at the Carlton club when the senior team's job became available. They couldn't get anyone, so I agreed to take over. From there, I became the Auckland under-19 coach and in 1998, I somehow finished up as the Auckland representative coach. As I say, Graham always set goals whereas I finished up doing things because I was in the right place at the wrong time or the wrong place at the right time!

It was good material for the media, husband and wife coaching the rugby and netball teams in New Zealand's biggest city, but any resemblance between the two roles was purely accidental. While Graham had ample talent from which to select his Auckland rugby team, my arrival on the representative netball scene coincided with an entire club defecting to a rival association, which took away three or four key individuals.

Just as I was immersing myself in the coaching role, and thoroughly enjoying the challenge, Graham began serious negotiations with the Welsh Rugby Union. I have to confess, I didn't take the developments seriously. The previous year, he'd been talking with England and that all fell over and I sort of expected Wales would be the same. The difference this time was that some of our close friends who were aware of what Graham was working towards were really excited. I thought if they're feeling this way, perhaps I should be too! But because I was embroiled in my own sporting world, I didn't give Wales much attention until Graham returned from his secret rendezvous in Sydney and explained what was going on. The revelation that we could be spending the next five years in Wales certainly grabbed my attention, especially as Graham was talking of making the move at the end of July. It was then the end of June!

If I'd had to move with him, it would have been chaotic. Logistically, it wasn't possible to transplant ourselves to the other side of the world in such a short time. There was the house, the pets, the children, my commitments as the Auckland netball coach and several other issues to consider. Graham was the only one who needed to move instantly. Once we worked through a schedule which would give me another three and a half months in Auckland, I relaxed a little - not that I was ecstatic about having my husband 10,000 miles away for the rest of the year.

As it turned out, I had a brief sample of Wales in August, completely out of the blue. To meet certain legal (and tax) requirements in the UK, it was necessary for the Henrys to arrive as a husband and wife team. Fair enough, except that I had only about 72 hours warning. Suddenly, I was winging off to the UK with Graham, unsure when I would return. It was all very complicated, a complete whirl. Graham had already been across to Cardiff once, for the grand announcement, and expected to have a month back in Auckland before taking up his duties as coach. But the month became a fortnight when he realised the only time he could organise trials was in mid-August. So here we were, UK bound. Fortunately, I was back home in less than a fortnight, linking up with Graham permanently a couple of weeks before Christmas, by which time I'd set up a family trust, organised the animals' welfare and made suitable arrangements for Matthew to stay in our house with a couple of flatmates. After a stint playing rugby in Italy, Andrew would return to complete his schooling at Auckland Grammar and join them.

During that first little sojourn in Cardiff, we were accommodated in a hotel, while for the next four months Graham survived in a rather cramped apartment until December, when he moved into a delightful property seven miles out of Cardiff on the old Newport road. Called quaintly "The Coach House", the building is 500 years old… three times as old as New Zealand! Completely modernised, it's ideal for our needs – spacious, warm, cozy, private and with generous gardens that allow me to put my green fingers to use. After initially renting, we decided to buy. I'm starting to feel like Rachel Hunter – one home in Auckland, another in Cardiff!

After Graham's contribution to Auckland rugby, I was terribly disappointed with the Auckland Rugby Union's attitude once they knew he was going to Wales. Taking back the seats and the car park at Eden Park which had been allocated to him for life was petty and the article which appeared in the Auckland-Canterbury programme was insulting.

GEOFF HIPKINS
Auckland RFU chief executive officer
Quoted in an Auckland programme:
"Maurice [Trapp] adds a new element which may well be what is needed for Auckland to perform creditably. He has a tremendous rugby background and knowledge, and is a great leader, and we're absolutely ecstatic to have someone of his calibre.

"Maurice is not a person to skim over problems and he's better in an organisational sense than Graham [Henry]. If you have a meeting with Maurice, he'll be there at 2.30 whereas Graham would come at 2.34.

"Maurice is probably a stricter disciplinarian on himself and the team and probably demands higher standards from the team than Graham would, which I think is a good thing."

Graham actually paid for his own farewell, staging it at our home in Epsom while I was away at the netball nationals. A male-only show, he invited all his mates along. The chief executive officer of the ARU was not among them! There was talk among ARU officials of holding an appropriate farewell for him, but Graham said "thanks but no thanks" in the circumstances.

I'm sure Graham would have challenged the union in court over the indecent amount of money they demanded for breaking his contract (after the CEO had originally assured him he was free to go) but the time constraints with Wales didn't allow it. The union had him over a barrel, and knew it. It made me really angry and if I ever meet the officials concerned, I'll tell them what I think.

I wonder if the committee members appreciate the painstaking preparation Graham put into every match he coached on behalf of Auckland, from colts to A representative level and on to the Auckland Blues. He says he often worked through till 2am analysing rugby videos. Well, he was quite often up again at 4am on rugby business before heading off to work, in his days at Kelston Boys' High. I'm sure because of the rich success of all his teams, he was responsible for putting a lot of bums on seats at Eden Park.

Being privy to Graham preparing for an important encounter is quite an experience. He can read a game so well, which is an important start, and he loves the game. In fact, he's as passionate about rugby as the Welsh, and that's saying something! He spends hours and hours analysing his opponents' strengths and weaknesses and his own team's mistakes, from which he prepares precise schedules before confronting his players for the next challenge. He also reads a lot, not just about rugby but motivational books and about achieving success in other fields.

Graham's not great company for 24 hours after his team loses. He always blames himself, never the players. If it's a bad loss, he won't sleep; in fact, after major fixtures – NPC and Super 12 finals, Ranfurly Shield challenges and now test matches – it takes him about three days to wind down before he can sleep normally again. He really takes defeat on the chin. Fortunately, in all the time he coached at representative level, there were precious few defeats. And only once, in 1996 when the All Blacks were in South Africa, did Auckland or the Blues ever lose two matches in a row.

Did I say he's not great company after a defeat? Well, before a big match, Graham is focused and quiet and best left alone. The family has learnt not to trouble him with trivialities in the countdown to kick-off; in fact, it's best when there's just Graham and me at home on such occasions.

The rest of the time he's very easy to live with. Well... I think he is. Over the past couple of years we have enjoyed being able to spend more time together. I wouldn't say he was grumpy before a match nor actually grumpy after a loss… just very disappointed and wondering what he could have done differently.

I hate going to matches when Graham is the coach. People say to me, "Why does Graham pick so-and-so?" as though I sit in on his selection meetings. It would be worse being the referee's wife, though – spectators can be so cruel with their comments. I used to sit with Grant Fox's wife, Adele, and we'd often cringe at what we heard. As far as the papers went, if I identified a negative article, I wouldn't read it. I'm afraid I take criticism too personally. Graham maintains a more philosophical attitude, which is important if you're going to coach at the highest level.

You'd think with both of us having been born in Christchurch that we'd have a soft spot for Canterbury, but far from it. Because of the animosity of the spectators there, I wouldn't go back. I attended one game at Lancaster Park in 1997 in the company of Zinzan Brooke's partner, Alison Imm, who was wearing an Auckland jacket. Canterbury prevailed – for the first time against Auckland, I might add, in about 15 years – whereupon poor Alison was subjected to intense abuse. I felt really embarrassed for her. I don't know what it is about Canterbury crowds but they are, without question, the most unsporting in New Zealand, which is a shame because the officials and leaders of the Canterbury team are great people. You expect supporters to champion their own team but not to display hatred towards the opposition. Auckland fans by contrast are always fair and acknowledge quality play by the opposition.

Our son Matthew attended university in Christchurch, and there were times when locals tried to beat him up because he was from Auckland. I don't know what it is about that part of the world, but I'm embarrassed on occasions to call it my home town.

Wales by comparison is something completely different. The passion for rugby has to be experienced to be believed and Graham, as the coach, acquired a higher profile here in six weeks here than in six years back home. Of course, through bringing respectability and pride back to the national team, he's come to be regarded as a saint. People have accorded him an almost cult status, which is why he decided we should base ourselves outside Cardiff, away from the public glare which is not something he seeks. Graham is actually a self-effacing individual who prefers to let his teams do the talking for him.

Life in the Henry household back in Auckland was never what you would call structured. With both parents teaching at one stage and involved in coaching sports teams, meals were often taken on the run or at unorthodox hours. I'm sure we were bad role models for our children although they seemed to adapt to the chaos that was home life. There were always people coming and going, if Graham wasn't on the phone organising something, I was and our sports teams invariably seemed to be taking precedence over our children. Thus far, our children seem to have turned out reasonably normal citizens and not inherited too many of our worst traits!

Family life in Wales is much more formal with dinner times well established. Our endeavours to introduce a degree of casual Kiwiness haven't had a huge impact, I'd have to say. We've explained that it's a perfectly natural custom in New Zealand to just drop in on friends for a chat or a drink or both. The Welsh are deeply suspicious of this. The wife of one of Graham's colleagues listened enthusiastically, I thought, to my putting the case for "dropping in". "Well, feel free to drop in any time," she said. "But you will phone first, won't you!"

No sooner had I taken up residence in Wales, reunited with my husband, than I was approached to coach the Cardiff representative netball team. My involvement as a coach back in Auckland had been referred to in one of Graham's interviews and, Cardiff being desperate for someone to prepare their team, I was identified as the ideal person.

Protesting that my achievements were extremely modest and that they shouldn't presume because I was Graham Henry's wife, I could weave similar magic among my teams fell on deaf ears. I was available? Good, you're appointed then!

When I turned up for the first practice session, it was to find that I was personally responsible for the premier representative team, the Cardiff A team and the Cardiff under-21 team, collectively involving some 30-odd players. No coach, not even Graham Henry, can do justice to that many individuals in a session but with the assistance of an under-21 coach we managed to obtain some organisation.

As I mentioned earlier in this chapter, women's sport has an extremely low priority in Wales. New Zealanders are well familiar with how well netball is organised at home, on a par, I would suggest, with rugby's NPC. Well, there's no draw for the Welsh netball championship – our Cardiff management has to liaise with the other rep teams to arrange the fixtures at our mutual convenience!

Being the "Messiah's" wife has at least brought netball some much-needed publicity here in Cardiff, but I fear there's a long way to go.

Chapter 9

Come on, Cymru!

The game must always be special. We must be elevated from professional on the training ground to passionately exceptional when we play.

Steve Black

TAKING ON THE SPRINGBOKS as a first assignment as Welsh coach – less than three months after arriving in the Principality – probably appeared, on the surface, extremely daunting. The Springboks, after all, were the world champions, they were coming off a glorious Tri-nations series in which they had scored four telling victories over the All Blacks and the Wallabies and they had scored an embarrassing 15 tries at Wales' expense in their previous meeting earlier in the year.

However, I saw a lot of positives about playing the Springboks first up. In many respects, they were the ideal opponents for me to launch my international career against. There would be little expectation on Wales because of what had happened at Pretoria, although I personally didn't attach a lot of significance to that result because the Welsh had been seriously depleted. There would inevitably be a level of complacency about the South Africans, so we had the chance to catch them with their pants down.

Individually, they were opponents with whom I was familiar because of the Auckland Blues' involvement in the Super 12. When you're preparing for a match, it's always helpful if you know the opposition's style, and in this instance I did. On top of all that, it was probable that after the intensity of the Tri-nations, followed by their Currie Cup competition, Nick Mallett's men would be wearied.

There seemed to be a body of opinion that if Wales could hold South Africa to 20 or 30 points, it would be a major achievement, given what had gone before (the bookies were offering Wales 36-point start). Well, that might be how some people approach a game, but such negativity isn't how Graham Henry operates, I can assure you. I genuinely believed we could win the match. When it was all over, I was annoyed that we didn't win it. A loss by 28 points to 20 was heralded in most quarters as a triumph for the men in scarlet, but my immediate reaction was one of frustration. A dodgy penalty try awarded against us in the first half and indiscipline by some of our players in the second prevented Wales completing what would have been an historic first victory over the South Africans.

SIR TASKER WATKINS
President, Welsh Rugby Union
Writing in the match programme:
Former headmaster, clear of mind, plain speaking, Graham Henry will make an immediate difference. The South Africans will know about that this afternoon. His coming to Wales marks the beginning, in my view, of a new passage in the history of Welsh rugby.

The scrum from which Australian referee Stuart Dickinson awarded the penalty try should never have been. The Springboks were lurking within 10 metres when our guys took a quick tap penalty in the shadows of their own posts. Instead of penalising them, however, Dickinson ordered a scrum when their scroungers torpedoed our move. We were 14-nil in front at the time.

Equally as costly was the rush of blood from winger Gareth Thomas inside the final five minutes, when the score was 20-all. Wales had been awarded a penalty within range of the posts and Neil Jenkins was coming forward to take the kick. A scuffle erupted, Thomas rushed in angrily and as a consequence of his actions, the penalty was reversed. The Springboks didn't waste the opportunity. They kicked downfield, working themselves into the position from where they scored the winning try.

When my research revealed that they were playing a specialist flyhalf (Franco Smith) at inside centre, we decided to target him. It's a difficult adjustment from No 10 to No 12 and we were able to probe his inexperience in the position.

On the subject of experience, we were desperately light on it among the tight forwards, experiencing all sorts of selection difficulties coming into the game. Prop David Young, whose career stretches back to the 1987 World Cup, was going to be the cornerstone of the pack until he injured his knee in a club game the week prior to the test. Hooker David Humphreys had packed down in almost 30 internationals but his fellow tight five colleagues scarcely made up 10 test caps among them. Yet what they lacked in test exposure, they more than compensated for in commitment and passion, which went for the whole fifteen.

We could have done with more pace on the wings. Three times in the second half we created tryscoring opportunities but didn't have the toe to finish. At the end of the day, however, we lost because the guys didn't know how to win and because at critical moments they lacked discipline. We would work on those shortcomings as the season unfolded, but it was unfortunate that it cost the players the chance of a lifetime at Wembley to defeat the world champion Springboks. Against that, they did regain the respect of the Welsh nation... and, I suspect, of the South African players and public.

PAUL ACKFORD
Sunday Telegraph
So how did he do it? How did Graham William Henry, Wales' New Zealand born coach, transform a side who were on the wrong end of a 15-try, 96-13 thrashing into a team four months later who were leading the Boks with three minutes of the match remaining?

Any fool can work with quality but only a genius can transform mediocrity. Henry invested drive and energy across the board. The greatest tribute you could pay to Henry was that he gave Wales back their rugby nous.

JAMES LAWTON
Daily Express
The ultimate tribute to [Graham] Henry was the gut-wrenching pain in the Welsh dressing room after victory trailed away in extra time created by the moronic intrusion of a streaker at precisely that point when the idea of defeat for this great South African team ceased to be a fantasy.

"There is a lot of pain down there," said Henry. "They know they could have won, that they should have won. But I'm still proud of them."

The team lost discipline and momentum only in the final strides and Henry suggested a little maturity would overcome such problems.

The scenario favoured by all shrewd judges – and the bookmakers who gave the new Wales a 36-point start – was that South African mayhem would come in the last 15 minutes. In fact, it was the Welsh who produced the mayhem for most of the match.

For years the talk has been of the huge gap between the hemispheres of rugby. For 80 minutes that was suspended, utterly, at Wembley. Why? Because finally the Welsh had the wit to hire a man of the southern game.

GRANT FOX
Former All Black
When I watched Wales taking on the Springboks – and almost beating them – I immediately identified several Graham Henry traits... Neil Jenkins' positional play, the forwards remaining on their feet, the team's willingness to chance its arm from inside its own 22 and the organised defensive patterns.

It doesn't surprise me he achieved instant success because of his meticulous planning. He's still got a lot to do though. Graham will want his team to be consistent and that's only going to happen when Wales builds its infrastructure.

When you've been around for a few years you come to appreciate that on some occasions the rub of the green goes with your team and at other times it can go diabolically against you. You accept this as part of the deal. As if to prove the mathematical inevitability of this, I experienced the two extremes in my first two outings with Wales. Good fortune most certainly did not shine upon the men in scarlet when we played the Springboks, but a week later against Pumas at Llanelli, it was the Argentinian management who would have been gnashing their teeth when the 50-50 decisions went against them.

We didn't play as well against Argentina and were outmuscled up front, particularly in the scrums. Mind you, the Pumas have arguably the strongest scrum in world rugby, scrummaging being something of an obsession with them. They appear to focus on it to the exclusion of other, important, aspects of their game. They were unlucky to be denied a try against us at a vital stage, being recalled for a forward pass, which was debatable. Still, after the frustrations of the Springbok game, it was good to get the win, no matter how fortuitously!

Notwithstanding the pressures exerted by the Argentinian forwards, we managed to free the ball consistently enough to score four spectacular tries, with Scott Gibbs contributing mightily. While I would have traded the loss against South Africa for the win over Argentina, the result (43 points to 30) was an important stepping-stone in our team's development.

ROBERT KITSON
The Guardian

Toss Graham Henry a hard hat and, the way things are going, the Millennium Stadium will be finished by Christmas. On the field, despite Argentina's best efforts to demolish the scaffolding, the New Zealander's brief to rebuild Welsh rugby's Staircase to Heaven is so far ahead of schedule even world rugby's cosy skyline may be transformed by this time next year.

Henry is clearly from the quick-drying cement school of master builders and, give or take shoring up his front row, has achieved more in 10 days than his predecessors managed in a decade. If a formidable Pumas pack asked some pointed questions in the tight, only a pessimist could ignore the revivalist spirit poking its head out of the rubble. Henry has breathed new life into the concept of sporting gurus.

We went into Christmas – two months out from the Five Nations championship – with a reasonable level of confidence. Of concern were the injuries to midfielder Allan Bateman – who was seen as a major contributor – and prop David Young and the fact that props Andrew Lewis and Chris Anthony had been under pressure. In fact, the scrum was identified as a major concern.

When you've been through the Super 12 and NPC mill several times, you think you're pretty worldly in a rugby context, but Edinburgh in February, where Wales opened its Five Nations campaign, was a huge learning curve for me, a time of discovery. I had almost no concept, and I suspect most New Zealanders would be the same, of the passions generated by a Five Nations rugby match. This wasn't just 15 against 15 on the field, this was nation against nation. Half of the population of Wales seemed to be on Edinburgh's main thoroughfare, Princes Street, on the morning of the game. I was assured that if 20,000 Welsh people were inside Murrayfield when the game kicked off, close to another 20,000, lacking tickets, had ventured north simply to be part of the occasion.

I'd sampled rivalry between neighbours back home, I thought, with the supporters of Auckland and North Harbour in the north and Canterbury and Otago further south fiercely parochial, but that was nothing compared to this. In a New Zealand context, it would be like 5000 loyal Otago fans making the journey through to Christchurch for a Ranfurly Shield challenge or NPC final just to soak up the atmosphere, knowing they had no prospect of securing a ticket for the game.

After the encouraging performances against South Africa and Argentina, expectations were high for a strong showing by Wales. Too high. There was huge hype in Wales leading into the game, which was part of our undoing, I'm sure. I was probably to blame. It was my job to ensure the boys bought into the ideas I was trying to sell them but against Scotland we were in a halfway house.

We were also probably lulled into a false sense of security by events leading into the game. The Scots, 100 to 1 outsiders with the bookies, had been written off by everyone. They'd been well beaten by New Zealand Maori and, although the arrival of the brothers Leslie, John and Martin, had obviously strengthened the team, I don't think anyone saw them as serious championship contenders. We certainly didn't take them lightly, although deep down in the subconscious, some of our players, I suspect, regarded this as a game for the taking.

It's terribly important, in the approach to a big game, to maintain composure, to use the top three inches, to think about what you're going to do. It was a difference I immediately identified between Welsh and New Zealand players. Sometimes New Zealand players are not on edge but they're always thinking. Welsh players are *always* on edge but the thinking process is not always good enough. Perhaps it's something to do with the competitions they play in.

The Scotland game was eminently winnable, but the victory eluded us, which was a huge disappointment. I was angry with myself for not emphasising the game plan strongly enough to my players. The Welsh boys were accustomed to playing in a particular manner and when the pressure went on, they resorted to what they knew, effectively abandoning the pattern I was seeking to introduce. We wouldn't see that until Paris.

Of course, the start was catastrophic with John Leslie scoring from the kick-off. I was numb at that stage. I had spoken to Shane Howarth in the changing room before the game and told him I thought Scotland might switch the kick-off and try and hit Matt Robinson because he was playing his first test. I didn't tell Matt because I did not want to increase his nerves. But as it turned out, that's exactly what the Scots did. I had prejudged it but not the result – seven points in the first 10 seconds of my first Five Nations game. Shattering. But who would know? The face wouldn't have changed!

We had no stability at the lineout, something we have now remedied. At Murrayfield, Ed Morrison, one of the most experienced referees about, upset our fluency by challenging our methods. Against the Springboks and the Pumas, we'd sought to increase the tempo of the game by throwing quickly to the lineouts as the forwards were arriving – a concept the Auckland and Blues teams had used effectively. On this occasion, however, Ed and his touch judges questioned our methods and insisted the lineout be properly formed before allowing the throw-in. All very pedantic and unsettling to our players who proceeded to make a giant mess of the lineout. It was a shame all round because Ed is a good referee. I'm not saying his decision cost us the game but it certainly diminished our confidence and fluency.

At a crucial stage of the second half, we were awarded a penalty within Neil Jenkins' range. The guys decided to tap and go instead but the ball was intercepted by Gregor Townsend who scored between the posts at the other end. It was a 10-point turnaround, plainly the turning point in the game. Till then, I was reasonably confident we would win, even though we had never achieved any clear-cut ascendancy.

If the Scottish international was an exercise in frustration, the Irish game a fortnight later – ostensibly a home game, although it was being played at Wembley, a two-hour drive from the Welsh border – became a nightmare. I anticipated they would try to intimidate us through aggression and instructed our players to get into them physically. That command was completely misinterpreted. The guys certainly got into them all right – but with an absolute absence of discipline. We lost our cool completely, which rebounded on us in the number of penalties awarded to the men in green and our attitude understandably annoyed the referee, who turned against us. The occasion became a disaster. At one stage we were 6-26 down before clawing our way back to 23-26, almost salvaging a victory, although in all honesty on our performance that afternoon we didn't deserve a win.

So after two Five Nations outings, things were looking bleak for the coach from Down Under – played two, lost two. With the giants of the competition, France and England, looming ominously ahead of us, we were dead on target for the wooden spoon! The critics had been overwhelmingly generous after Wales' two heartening displays back in November. I hated to think what they would be writing now, so I didn't read any papers for weeks. I didn't need any negative vibes, especially at this stage of our development.

I can say now that I believe we had to go through the agony of the Scottish and Irish defeats to find ourselves as a team. They certainly represented a giant learning curve for me and the setbacks made us dissect what we were doing. Only subsequent to the Irish game did the Welsh players collectively buy into the game plan I was wanting to promote, the high-intensity, wide- ranging game I'd wanted them to execute from the start. What we were practising, we had to start implementing on the field.

A problem area that needed shoring up before Paris was the scrum, our front row having been exposed. We would take on the

French with an entirely new front row, Peter Rogers and Ben Evans, who had demonstrated their readiness with the A team, coming in as props with veteran Garin Jenkins taking over as hooker. I seriously under-estimated Jenkins who, at 31, was Wales' most capped player in the position, believing he lacked the skills to play the wide-ranging game I was promoting. It was a major selection error. Not only did he prove himself mobile, his natural leadership qualities were inspirational to the rest of the team. Rogers, who had represented the Gauteng Lions while living in Johannesburg, was short of match-play having damaged his cruciate knee ligaments the previous October. Although we knew he was struggling with fitness, we really had no choice but to introduce him. It would turn out to be an inspired selection.

So with a restructured front row and a new openside flanker – New Zealander Brett Sinkinson, claiming NPC experience with Bay of Plenty and Southland – coming in for Martyn Williams, we headed for Paris, where Wales had last experienced victory in 1975. The French, Grand Slammers the previous two seasons, hadn't lost a Five Nations match since 1996. We were, predictably, given no hope by any of the pundits. We were back to where we'd been approaching the Springbok game in November. As on that occasion, we didn't concern ourselves with other people's pessimistic forecasts. The guys knew what they had to do.

Analysis of the Scottish and Irish internationals revealed the opposition were running off our flyhalf Neil Jenkins, satisfied he posed no threat as an attacker. So part of our policy in Paris was to use him as a runner, a role he adopted enthusiastically and with such devastating effect he completely spooked the opposition. French back coach Pierre Villepreux would say later he had never thought it possible that Jenkins could run so incisively. The French were completely unprepared for his daring raids.

Our evaluation of France's play in previous outings highlighted defensive weaknesses along the backline, so we concentrated on moves to exploit these, which worked tellingly, particularly in the first half. The French appeared stunned by our relentless attacks and we built a 28-18 advantage by halftime. In the previous games, we'd thrown too many 50-50 passes but in Paris the ball retention was superb. Throughout the first half, the guys were brilliant. They'd produced the best attacking rugby by any of the Five

Nations teams up to that stage of the season. But there were still 40 minutes to go and unfortunately they tended to lose their way in the second half. Instead of continuing the relentless attack, they tried to bat out time, partly, I'm sure, because the fitness levels weren't yet right. France nearly knocked us off and Thomas Castaignede could have marred the occasion if he'd landed a wide-angle penalty goal in injury time. After initial reluctance to take the kick, he hooked it outside the upright, leaving us ahead 34-33.

Huge emotion unfolded after the final whistle, even from the coach who usually tries to maintain a reserved stance. It was a marvellous experience, Wales' first win in Paris in 24 years, probably the most satisfying moment of my career. The only other time I'd been involved with something like that was at Durban in the first year of the Super 12 and even that pales into insignificance. I told the guys to be bold and keep being bold. Being bold wins rugby matches, being shy doesn't. The Quinnell boys would, tearfully, remind me later that their famous father Derek, who played a huge number of games for Wales, never once sampled the delight of a victory in Paris. There were a lot of tears from grown men in the wake of the victory. It was a hell of an important success for Wales, giving us the confidence we needed to go forward. I think we were all a little stunned at what we'd achieved, for we'd effectively played French rugby against the French. It was a hell of an improvement on the Scottish and Irish displays, owing much to the new stability up front. You could feel the self-belief coming into the camp. We were ready to take another step forward.

The entire French experience was something I will never forget. The Stade de France, a magnificent new stadium – light years ahead of anything in New Zealand – housed 70,000 spectators and they say they could have sold it five times over. The interest in the game was amazing. I'm thrilled Wales was able to turn on a performance worthy of such an occasion. When you play that high-speed, high-risk game, you're vulnerable, but we showed tenacity to hang in, even though we couldn't maintain the tempo for the full 80 minutes. The result enthralled the nation, ushering in another new dawn. Twenty-four years is too long between successes in Paris.

TIM GLOVER
Independent

Anyone who witnessed one of the biggest upsets in France since the revolution would have been privileged to say: "I was there." It had to be seen to be believed and even then seemed unreal.

When Thomas Castaignede's injury time penalty attempt sailed wide Wales had not only won in France for the first time since 1975, they had done so with panache, elan and chic, not to mention cheek, and any other word they can borrow that symbolises the best of French fashion and style. It was tour de force, exhilarating and breathtaking in its approach and, in terms of entertainment, utterly compelling. William Webb Ellis would have loved this.

Wales were looking at a whitewash in one of the most fraught seasons to bedevil the old game. Henry, though, devoid of emotional baggage, is a good traveller and his strategy for the Paris match was a sensational if nerve-racking success.

Henry's opposite number, Jean-Claude Skrela, said that, "We saw the All Blacks playing in red jerseys. The Welsh played rugby as it should be played."

STUART BARNES
Daily Telegraph

Wales' epic victory (on a Homeric scale of 0-10, it reads 11) against a fatally over-confident France deserves a few video replays for no reason other than gratuitous pleasure. This was a classic game of rugby.

France and Thomas Castaignede were desperate to fan their peacock's plume after the attrition of Dublin. Make no mistake, this team can play, but like a boxer who dismisses his opponent too lightly, a lack of defence resulted in them being dumped on their collective butts. The men in red rained painful blows from all angles.

Graham Henry has re-established his Redeemer credentials on the streets of every town in Wales. Against South Africa, it was the hallmark professionalism of the All Black defensive pattern which pervaded throughout but in Paris we saw the unstinting self-belief of the 1995 All Blacks, one of the greatest of all teams but one that lost the World Cup final.

The rugby romantics were relieved when one of the game's arch romantics, Castaignede himself, missed with the last kick of the game, leaving it Wales and Neil Jenkins' day.

Earlier in the week, Henry considered victory in Paris as his coaching Everest, the biggest challenge of his career. On Saturday night he was re-setting his sights. "There are many more mountains to climb. This is hopefully the start." The whole Welsh nation is behind him every step of the way.

RUPERT MOON
News of the World
After the narrow defeat by South Africa, I said Hail King Henry. Unfortunately, the bubble burst after that and we had to endure defeats by Scotland and Ireland, leaving us down in the mouth.

But this was the master at his very best. Despite criticism from all areas, Henry has stuck with what he knows best and on this occasion it brought its reward. I don't think I have ever felt as excited about a game of rugby and I am not sure I ever will. For goodness sake, let's get behind Graham Henry, Rob Howley and those Welsh heroes and start to support instead of criticising.

ROBERT HOWLEY
Welsh captain
The best day of my rugby life without a doubt. The team, and my captaincy, have been under criticism for the past month but today we supplied the answers on the field. We scored three tries but it could have been seven more. It's nice to pay back the fans and coach Graham Henry for the work he has done.

PIERRE VILLEPREUX
French assistant coach
Wales has the best collective team in the Five Nations. It is playing very ambitious rugby, which can be risky, but with that approach it can challenge the world's best teams.

SIMON THOMAS
South Wales Echo
It may have taken 24 years but in the end it was worth the wait. This was a victory to rank alongside the great Welsh wins – 13-8 against the All Blacks in 1953, 10-9 against England in 1993 and 25-10 against France in Paris in 1975.

But more than being just a great Welsh win, this was also a great game. When the Welsh management arrived at the post-match press conference they were greeted with a brief outbreak of spontaneous applause from normally cynical Welsh and French journalists. The first half saw northern hemisphere rugby taken to new heights with skill levels and thrill levels matching anything the Super 12 and Tri-nations has to offer.

Just as before the autumn test against South Africa, Henry's team was given next to no chance against a French side looking for a record-equalling 10th successive Five Nations victory. Just as on that occasion, Henry's men had an unquenchable faith in themselves and in their game plan.

It would have been understandable if Wales had looked to employ a negative damage limitation exercise in Paris but that is not Henry's style. The Kiwi coach has an unshakeable belief in the way the game should be played. He told his men to be bold and bold they were.

ROBIN DAVEY
South Wales Argus
Graham Henry didn't imagine a nation could be so affected and so uplifted by such a result. But he soon caught the post-match Paris mood when he said, "It means we can have a party tonight, not a meeting." And by all accounts a party is what he had as the WRU committee took hold of him on Saturday night and he joined in the singing. It's not clear exactly what he mouthed to the Welsh songs because he doesn't know a word of the language! An even more incredulous Henry had to cope with the delay at Cardiff Airport the next day as fans, young and old, queued for autographs. He admitted he had asked for divine intervention as Castaignede lined up the final kick. "I asked the above for a bit of assistance – I don't often do that," he said.

SUE MOTT
Daily Telegraph
Somebody up there likes Graham Henry. I do not mean the Messiah, with whom he is now frequently confused in the jubilant, thronging, transformed streets of Cardiff, but somebody up in the northern hemisphere. Quite a lot of somebodies, in fact.

There are 2,921,000 people in Wales, for a start, who are thinking of changing the words Land of My Fathers *to* Land of Choice New Zealand Imports *and they would not be meaning mutton. Graham William Henry – no discernible Celtic antecedents whatsoever but "I'm Welsh enough for me" – was plucked from the land of the All Blacks and appointed Welsh coach at the end of July. In eight months, he has transformed a team and a nation.*

With that blazing 34-33 victory over France, the Welsh dragon is firing again after at least a decade of being a depressive newt. "It was breathtaking, one of the greatest games I have ever seen," said Gareth Edwards, one of the greatest names of Welsh rugby, so he would know. And everyone gives credit to Henry, the coach who has imposed southern hemisphere professionalism on a British basket case.

One doesn't like to keep making comparisons between New Zealand and the UK, but a huge advantage coaches and teams have in the southern hemisphere is once a competition like the Super 12 or the NPC (or the Currie Cup in South Africa) kicks off, you're locked in, you're in the groove. You're together as a team for the duration.

But with the Five Nations, which has traditionally scheduled matches a fortnight apart – actually there was a three-week gap to the final series of games in 1999 – it's hard for the players and management to achieve continuity. After the losses to Scotland and Ireland, for example, there were important matters I wanted to discuss and adjustments that needed to be made but I had to wait a week. That's frustration enough, but as a coach you're anxious during the weekends in between, praying none of your key players injure themselves in club action. I find myself waiting with baited breath, dreading that the phone will go on a Saturday night. I could imagine trying to sell the British system in New Zealand. The coaches would go berserk!

I've suggested to the people who administer the game in Wales that once the Five Nations squad assembles, we should keep them together. Presuming the games remain spaced a fortnight apart when the championship expands to six teams in the year 2000, the players would remain together for about eight weeks, during which time they would play five internationals. We'll see what happens.

Between the French and English games, we were drawn to play Italy at Treviso, part of the shakedown to the Italians joining the championship. The Italians have made solid progress in recent years under Georges Coste and had enjoyed a particularly good run against the UK nations, beating Ireland and Scotland, stretching Wales in 1998 to 20-23 and taking England to the wire in a World Cup qualifier at Huddersfield prior to Christmas. They're a team with some extremely talented individuals who can easily disrupt your game plan if you give them half a chance. We had to ensure that that didn't happen this time.

The setting at the Stadio Comunale di Monigo in Treviso, where about 6000 Italian fans turned up on a pleasant, sunny afternoon, was a far cry from the white-hot atmosphere in Paris a fortnight earlier. For a New Zealander, it was like a Te Kuiti experience following a Super 12 final at Eden Park! Although the scene was vastly different, the objective was identical – to produce quality attacking rugby on our terms.

Operating into the wind in the first half, we managed to establish a lead without playing particularly well. Frequent turnovers hampered progress. However, in the second half everything came together in spectacular fashion. We piled on 42 points, winger Gareth Thomas finishing with four tries to equal the Welsh test record and Neil Jenkins grabbing another bucketload of points.

In clocking up 60 points, we got our game plan operating and for the first time I saw the guys really enjoying what they were doing. Enjoyment is a crucial part of it all and confirmation that the guys had bought into the game plan.

We now faced a three-week wait to the climax of our campaign, the clash with front-runners England at Wembley. After beating the French comprehensively at Twickenham – finding tries elusive but being rewarded for immense pressure with seven penalty goals from the boot of up-and-comer Jonny Wilkinson – they were on target for a Grand Slam. They'd whipped the Welsh 60-23 a year earlier and plainly didn't see us as too serious a threat on their march to Five Nations glory.

This attitude appeared to be confirmed by an amazing letter I received in the week prior to the match. Addressed to me, it was e-mailed to the Welsh Rugby Union from London.

To Graham Henry, the Welsh Rugby Coach
Sir,
A few days ago I overheard a conversation that you may find of interest. I was on a train to London... travelling in first class... where I overheard five men talking loudly and annoyingly. They were straddling the aisle and seemed to be celebrating something. Certainly, they were full of themselves. Almost all the conversation was about rugby, which I must admit I'm not an avid follower of but know a little about.

The reason I've been told to write to you personally relates to what I heard them say about the strategy that England will take against Wales next week. For a while I tried to avoid the conversation and it was only after they started telling racist jokes that I started to listen in. I started to take notes and apologise that I didn't start earlier in the discussion.

The main ploy that they have in mind is intimidation. They have singled out Quinnell and Evans for treatment, but Gibbs, Jenkins and others were also mentioned as vulnerable. Quinnell – I've been told that there are two of them, sorry – they expect to get sent off. They referred to Dublin as an example of his temperament. They think this will be the easiest thing in the world to do. If not Quinnell, then one of them will be "sorted". They also mentioned Charvis and Sinkinson for attention. They will use Cockerill, Johnson, "Blackie" and the captain Dallaglio to effect this.

They said the backline is the best Wales has had for a long time but if they have no ball then the game will be a rout. If their scrum is able to hold Wales, then they will break off and attack Howley and Jenkins.

They talked about flatness being a threat (at least, that's what I think they said). They thought Howley was only 75 per cent fit and think there is a good chance he will go off injured, especially if hit hard. They also made a lot of fun about the way Jenkins looks.

They will use Catt to kick behind the Welsh backs every time Howarth comes into the line. They regard Howarth as dangerous but they think he is suspect under high balls from Catt and Dawson. Wilkinson will also kick behind. This Wilkinson they think will win the game on penalties.

Tactically, Catt will kick for the wingers to chase and catch, possibly on the full, especially if there's room. They think they can score tries this way. One of them said Catt has had a lot of success doing this for his club.

The body of the conversation was that if the Welsh can be intimidated and this Quinnell or someone else is sent off then the game would be won. "It should have happened in one of the other matches." They are certain that Wales will be lost because they will give England too many penalties and because someone will throw a punch and be sent off. "It's a certainty," one of them said. "We'll Beckham them," said another – and even I know what that means. I'm sure that this shouldn't be part of the game and it makes me ashamed.

That's all I noted. I hope the names are correct as I did get some help on this. I don't know how I can impress that I am certain these men were connected with the England team – they were definitely part of the planning team. They may change their plans, of course, which might invalidate some of what I've recounted. But I doubt that the tactic of intimidation will be changed.

They were so cocky about the Welsh, but it was because they were so blatantly racist that has incensed me so much. They deserve to lose. Please take this seriously and don't let them get away with this. My conscience is clear now.

One last thing. One of them has £1500 riding on this match.
Yours sincerely,
A.K.

An interesting letter, don't you think? Very obviously the writer was privy to what should have been the private musings of the English management. I referred it to our management but not to the players. It didn't tell me a lot I couldn't have worked out for myself. They obviously didn't have much regard for our collective intelligence if they believed we hadn't acted on the indiscipline that ruined our prospects against Ireland. The offenders were given a final warning – any repeat and they would never represent Wales again.

For Welsh players and supporters, England is the game of the year. I'm sure that's not the case with England. However, the attitude throughout Wales seems to be that it doesn't matter what else happens, as long as England is defeated. It's not just rugby tradition that has shaped this mentality. Over the centuries, the

English were the landowners and factory owners while the Welsh were the labourers, so it's not hard to see where the motivation comes from when the two nations oppose each other on the sporting field. If Wales beats England, it's automatically a great season.

I personally didn't see it that way. We couldn't win the Five Nations but this match represented an important stepping stone in our development. England deserved to be ranked among the top four nations in the world. I apparently caused a stir in New Zealand by saying they ranked among the top three. Which one of the giants had they tipped out to get there – New Zealand, perhaps? I actually fielded numerous calls from the New Zealand media who were paranoid about my statement. Who cares? It was just an opinion.

As for Wembley on 11 April, what a game! What a finish! What an unbelievable feeling for a coach! People started hugging me when Neil Jenkins converted Scott Gibbs' try to put Wales ahead 32- 31 and I think I shouted, "Settle down, there's still three minutes to play!" It would have been sickening to have had victory snatched from us in those final, desperate moments and there was a chance of that as Mike Catt launched into a drop-kick, but to my intense relief – and the relief of an entire nation, I'm sure – he sliced it wide, and we'd won. We'd beaten England, beaten the guns, defied the odds, defied the critics, defied everything really. It was time to go and celebrate!

Two essential parts of our match strategy were to maintain discipline throughout – no matter what the provocation – and to keep England away from our end of the field as much as possible. Video evidence had revealed Clive Woodward's men were lethal, through their awesome pack, when allowed to launch attacks from inside or close to the opposition 22. One of their favourite ploys was to drive through to the goalline from lineouts. So we strove to keep them downfield as much as possible, which meant kicking more than we normally would have.

Where they did catch us by surprise, which demonstrated that Woodward is intelligent and innovative as a coach, was in using flyhalf Catt to run, as we'd done with Jenkins against France. In previous matches Catt had been used as a link, England preferring to launch its attacks from wider out. His running caught us by surprise.

The Welsh team came of age in this game. There's no question that England effectively won the game but we finished ahead on the scoreboard, and that was a tribute to our players' tenacity and character. Earlier Welsh teams would probably have capitulated. Hadn't the 1998 side conceded 60 points after scoring two early tries?

England probably played its best game of the Five Nations, certainly its most expansive, and busted us several times but we managed to stay within touch, thanks to our courageous (if often scrambling) defence and the pinpoint goalkicking accuracy of Jenkins. Asked afterwards how Neil compared with other goalkickers with whom I had been associated, I gave him top ranking. And considering I worked closely with, and am a close personal friend of, Grant Fox, that's rich praise.

At Wembley, Neil was phenomenal. A couple of those booming goals from the right-hand side of the field before halftime were almost freakish. He was so deadly accurate that if the goalposts had been only two metres apart, he would still have put the ball right down the middle. And, no, I didn't have any doubts that he would slot the conversion – from a challenging angle – to Gibbs' try to put us ahead.

The occasion reminded me very much of the 1998 Super 12 final at Eden Park when the Auckland Blues, after seeming to have the match in the bag, had victory wrenched away by the Canterbury Crusaders through a last-minute try. I remember coming away thinking, "How the hell did we lose that?" I'm sure that's exactly how Clive Woodward felt after this game.

The real plus for us was the tenacity and courage the players demonstrated on the several occasions England seemed likely to put a stranglehold on the game. The guys hung in doggedly, stayed within reach and when the winning opportunity came, they took it spectacularly. The English midfield defence had stifled us all afternoon and there didn't seem any way through, but Scott produced a touch of brilliance at the death. They reckon he evaded five defenders – I had the feeling he was looking for a few more to beat. Certainly, I was relieved when he finally grounded the ball!

We scored two tries to none in the second half, Neil Jenkins creating the first when he lobbed a beautiful ball across the noses of the English defence for Shane Howarth to cross wide out. That score was critical after we'd trailed 15-25 at halftime.

I said at the press conference that England did not respect us as a team. Undoubtedly, they respected certain individuals but not Wales as an opponent. If you've smashed a team by 60 points the previous year, it's hard to cleanse the sensation of superiority from your subconscious. I guess that's one advantage we won't be able to fall back on next year.

Besides the discipline, the character and Neil Jenkins' ability to do the business and keep us in the game, the most encouraging aspect of our performance was the huge progress made by the pack, which shows Lyn Howells' ability as a forward coach. England at forward is as good as any team in the world and would normally be expected to score at least one try from an attacking lineout. We not only denied them that, we secured all our own lineout possession – thanks to the magnificent leaping of Chris Wyatt – and probably achieved a slight advantage in the scrum. Considering the way we'd been buffeted in the lineouts and scrums by Scotland and Ireland, that represented a massive improvement in a comparatively short space of time.

It was frustrating that we didn't get the ball wide more often, considering the amount of quality possession we secured. We over-committed ourselves with the ball in hand and should have recycled it more often. Still, it was part of the learning experience.

CHRIS HEWITT
The Independent
The Welsh have been enjoying the green, green grass of someone else's home for two long years now and yesterday afternoon their English landlords marched into Wembley to reclaim the title deeds. They left empty-handed.

Scott Gibbs, the sort of squatter no police force would even contemplate trying to shift without three different court orders and a riot squad in support, broke the red rose defence – and its heart – clean asunder in injury time to deny the overwhelming favourites a fourth Grand Slam in nine years and a first under the joint stewardship of Clive Woodward and Lawrence Dallaglio.

As a finale, it was no more than a classic Anglo-Welsh contest deserved. Gibbs' try was a mind-boggling combination of the rapier and the broadsword as he busted and sidestepped English tacklers by the half-dozen.

Wales was a point adrift even then, but there was not the remotest possibility of Neil Jenkins missing a do-or-die conversion. Old Jug Ears would have slotted it home had it been from his own 22, let alone England's.

Dallaglio, certainly England's stand-out performer, was left to contemplate the Celtic double whammy to end them all: defeat by Wales and Scotland in the same afternoon. The triumph of the Red Dragonhood presented the Five Nations championship to Scotland.

Perversely, Wales will never again play in the shadow of the twin towers; their own Millennium Stadium will soon be ready to receive them. Still, they will be tempted to rip up the Wembley greensward by its roots and cart it down the M4. Having been left for dead by a confident England during the first 40 minutes, they drew so much physical and spiritual sustenance from the halftime break that they proceeded to cover the finest playing surface in world rugby like a red shroud.

DAVID HANDS
The Times

They were calling Graham Henry the great redeemer before this international season began. Maybe the age of miracles is still here after Wales, against all but their own expectations, concluded their temporary tenancy of Wembley with a victory so dramatic that few could have believed it, even though they were among the 79,000 to witness it.

Henry, not quite walking on water as he fought his way through the hordes, has turned Wales into a superbly competitive team with a furious belief in themselves. Even when they conceded a series of scrums through knock-ons and turnovers, they never faltered in the pursuit of Henry's game plan – to play at pace, to pull England about the field and try to crack the defensive white wall.

Whatever Henry said at halftime, Wales should bottle for export.

STUART BARNES
Daily Telegraph

Scotland are the champions and the only Grand Slam is the personal set of tries claimed by Gregor Townsend. The final weekend of the tournament might just rate among the greatest in its history.

The instinct of the Englishmen remains conservative to the point of being craven. England produces huge packs, of which this one, with Dallaglio, Johnson and Rodber to the fore, is as good as any. Sadly, we are incapable of seeing beyond the awesome power and physical courage of this unit.

We suffocate and squash, like a big bully, but lack the deeper bravery to make a decision, to make the big play and gun for glory. The courage I am writing about is the type which enables Neil Jenkins to take the risk and fire a miss-pass and cross the entire England blindside defence to put Shane Howarth in for a try. England does not take such risks.

It is no disaster losing to Wales. Clive Woodward has the platform on which to build a challenge for a World Cup but he has to discover the courage which epitomised the regimes of Jim Telfer and Graham Henry.

SOUTH WALES ARGUS
Front page, 12 April

Wales is talking about nothing else this morning. Yesterday's last-gasp rugby victory over England at Wembley has restored pride in our national game.

And now for the World Cup.

It was quite simply an unbelievable day, producing a victory over the old enemy in the last-ever Five Nations game. Can there have been a better day in recent Welsh sporting history? Now Wales heads into this year's World Cup with renewed hope.

SOUTH WALES ECHO
News story

Forget the usual Monday morning blues – there was joy in the Welsh air today. As the nation went back to work after yesterday's celebrations, commuters seemed to have more of a spring in their step than usual.

It was a wet and windy morning but the people of south Wales were having a little smile to themselves. Even the thousands with hangovers were feeling unusually lightheaded – who needs aspirin when you have just beaten the English at rugby?

As tonics go for the start of the week, this one will take some beating. The tills in South Wales' pubs and clubs started ringing at lunchtime, and did not stop all day. Outside the City Arms in Quay Street, Cardiff, they were dancing on the pavements. Landlady Marina Means said: "When they scored that last try, every red shirt ran out into the street. It was quite superb. They didn't stop singing all day. They raised the roof."

ANDY HOWELL
Western Mail
Wales was the laughing stock of world rugby stuck in the last-chance saloon when Graham Henry took over on 28 August. Eight months on he is being hailed as a saviour, the man who saved Welsh rugby from the depths of despair. Henry has turned around the fortunes to such an extent that Wales nearly beat world champion South Africa, then beat Northern Hemisphere powerhouses France and England. Its odds on winning the World Cup have shortened from 100 to 1 to 25 to 1.

And the odds on Graham Henry becoming a member of the Gorsedd of bards, the body of people honoured for achievement in Wales and who included sportsmen such as Robert Croft, shortened from 8 to 1 to 5 to 2.

Henry didn't come cheap at £1.25 million over five years. It was a massive high-risk investment but already looks like money well spent.

WESTERN MAIL
Front page, 13 April
Eminently sensible BBC and radio presenter Lisa Barsi is considering naming her new baby – if it's a boy (due in July) – after Graham Henry.

"I was in the pub watching the game and people realised I was pregnant," she said. "When Wales won, they were all shouting, 'You'll have to name him Graham Henry.' Those names are on my list – it's that or Scott Gibbs."

The Welsh Rugby union fielded more calls than normal from people wanting to buy everything from official Welsh rugby shirts to team posters.

I described the Paris experience, after we'd beaten France, as the highlight of my coaching career. Well, I'd have to put the

Wembley defeat of England right up there alongside it. We didn't get a share of the Five Nations championship but, against all the odds, we managed to outpoint Europe's two superpowers, doing so in style.

Ten days before the English international, Raewyn and I visited St David's, a delightful little town on the Irish Sea coast, about as far west as you can travel in Wales, famous for its cathedral which houses the tomb of St David, the patron saint of Wales.

The purpose of the visit was to fly the rugby flag at a prizegiving at the local school, after which a group of us were taken on a conducted tour of the cathedral. While the others were taking in a spiel on the historical significance of the church, I slipped quietly into the chapel and on to my knees. Not being a regular worshipper, I was self-conscious but I was the only person in the chapel at the time. I asked St David for assistance. I told him the Welsh people had experienced difficult times and needed his help. There would be no better opportunity for him to provide this assistance than on the occasion of the English international at Wembley.

Ten days later, as we entered the final moments of an epic contest with Wales six points in arrears, I looked up and said, "Well, St David, if you're going to come through, now's the time." Not 30 seconds later, Colin Charvis was the victim of a controversial late charge which gave us penalty from which we set up the lineout, from which Scott Gibbs scored his try, allowing Neil Jenkins to slot the winning conversion.

Neither religion nor superstition played any part in my life before I came to Wales but it's funny how happenings can influence you. As an example, the editor of the *Wales on Sunday* newspaper sent me a pair of red underpants, featuring the Welsh crest, as a promotional gimmick. I forgot about them for a few weeks but happened to be wearing them in Paris when we defeated France. I wore them again in Treviso where we scored handsomely. Deciding they were definitely lucky for me, I had them on at Wembley on the occasion of our famous last-gasp victory. Obviously, they're lucky underpants and now I'm terrified to attend a Welsh game without them on!

A Welsh couple sent me a miniature coalminer's lamp and a piece of coal as good luck charms. After the victory in Paris, the Welsh team flew directly to Cardiff where there were some 500

My assistant John Graham awaits his turn while I issue a few halftime instructions to Auckland during an NPC game in 1993.

The closest I came to coaching the All Blacks. Frank Oliver and I share a drink as assistant coach and coach of New Zealand A in 1998.

The Auckland Blues needed a bit of revving at halftime when they played Waikato Chiefs at Albany in 1997. We managed to get home with 10 points to spare.

Press conference before the Blues' game against Western Province at Eden Park in 1996. From left, manager Rex Davy, captain Zinzan Brooke, coach GH, Auckland CEO Peter Scutts and a couple of South Africans.

One of the delights of possessing the Ranfurly Shield was taking it on tour. Manager Rex Davy and I seem pretty relaxed before the East Coast challenge at Ruatoria in 1997. We got home 115-6.

One of the pleasant aspects of Super 12 rugby is that matches are staged in summer. Sharing the warmth with me at Eden Park are manager Rex Davy and assistant coach Mac McCallion.

Grant Fox… we go back a long way. I was always pleased to have him on my side.

My wife Raewyn was alongside me when I announced to the media in mid-1998 that I was flying off to the UK to become the national coach of Wales.

Huw Evans Picture Agency (all pictures)

The men who help make it happen with Wales – top left, assistant coach Lyn Howells; top right, selector Alun Lewis; bottom left, trainer (and spiritual adviser) Steve Black; bottom right, administrative manager Trevor James.

Alan Bateman

Scott Gibbs

Chris Wyatt

Scott Quinnell

fans to welcome us. I was making my way through the crowd when a couple approached me, offered their congratulations and introduced themselves as the pair who had sent me the good luck charms. To their delight, I reached into my pocket and produced the coalminer's lamp and the piece of coal. You see, there's a lot more to coaching in Wales than simply having an appreciation of onfield strategies!

We celebrated worthily at our London hotel after the England game before heading back to Cardiff on the Monday morning where, as you can imagine, the people were still celebrating. We were besieged by autograph hunters and the press conference set up at the Copthorne Hotel ran on for almost two and a half hours. There was no question that the victory had given the whole country a huge boost.

Not unnaturally, the media wanted me to say we were now brilliantly on target for the World Cup. I was more conservative than that, telling them not to get too carried away, that we still had a long way to go. I consider we need to improve by 20 to 30 per cent to be competitive against the top-ranking southern hemisphere nations at the World Cup. Having said that, I am confident that we will continue to improve. And we will certainly be competitive, against any opponent. We made major steps up the ladder in our last three tests. We wanted to play the season with pride, passion and character and to make the nation proud and I think we did that.

We've got five matches, including two internationals, in Argentina in June followed by tests at the new Millennium Stadium against South Africa, France and Canada, which should prepare us nicely for the big event which kicks off (with us playing Argentina again) on 1 October.

The problem with important matches is that, as a coach, I take about 72 hours to wind down. I slept for no more than two hours on the Monday evening and perhaps four hours the next night. I wonder if I would ever have regained my normal sleeping pattern if Thomas Castaignede had slotted that late penalty in Paris and Neil Jenkins had missed his conversion at Wembley. Some things don't bear thinking about!

Huw Evans Picture Agency

Chapter 10

Finding the winning edge

If you haven't got passion, you've got nothing.
Graham Henry

A SUCCESSFUL COACH IS ONE who prepares his team to deal with all eventualities. No factor affecting success is more important than preparation, something I came to appreciate early in my sporting career and which I have sought to refine as I've gone along. Not only must your players be fully briefed on the game plan and understand their individual requirements but you must familiarise them with the particular strengths and weaknesses of the opposition. I occasionally hear a coach say, "Well, we don't concern ourselves with the opposition – we just go out and do our own thing." Unless you are preparing a team of such awesome strength that no opponent is going to stand in your way, that's a pretty naive attitude. My coaching philosophy takes me to the other extreme. For example, I would have spent probably 30 hours studying videos of England's play before Wales went to Wembley in April.

I don't know how my preparations for a major contest compare with other rugby coaches, but I know what works for me.

I've had to vary my approach somewhat with Wales because

the Five Nations matches are spaced a fortnight apart and the players return to their homes every second week. So I don't have them under my jurisdiction for three months at a time, as with Auckland and the Auckland Blues.

The Welsh players – at least, those not seriously damaged in club action, which was always my greatest fear – would assemble on a Sunday evening, a week out from each international. We'd then conduct the post mortem on the previous game, an exercise which might spill over to the Monday morning. I would have spent several hours analysing our performance, going through it minute by minute. To inflict a replay of the entire contest on the players would be tedious and unnecessary, so I condense the video to about 30 minutes of relevant action. This is a critical part of the team's tactical development – identifying weaknesses so we can improve on them and also strengths so we can reinforce them. I always try and blend in an element of humour as we revisit the action.

Monday is a physical, set-piece day, a day when we set a lot of scrums and work diligently on ball retention. We spend a lot of time perfecting what we are trying to achieve on match day. We do all the hard work early in the week, which was always my approach with the Auckland Blues. Initially, I involved the players in two sessions a day but Blackie (Steve Black, our trainer) pushed for one and eventually I relented. It's important to have a full tank at the weekend and to ensure this the coaches need to be intelligent in their approach during the week. More doesn't necessarily equal better. Some coaches obviously come under pressure from the existence of the employing body, the eyes from afar, and feel they need to justify the wage bill. But the team must come first. What is best for the team is paramount – and, generally, less is better. It's all about knowing what you are doing and what is best, and implementing that. I guess it is about confidence and not being affected by outside influences. Less training, of high quality, is the best formula.

Tuesday morning we're back into the video room to assess the opposition. We're fortunate in Wales to have people who can help me piece the information together expertly. The product the players see – pinpointing strengths and weaknesses in the team they are about to engage – seldom runs for more than 10 minutes. But anything up to 30 hours of video analysis by myself will have gone into its preparation. Once I've identified the relevant aspects of the other team's play, I pass the videos – and there could be anything from two or three to nine or ten matches involved – on to Alun Carter at the Welsh Rugby Union. He's a video whizz and an ex-international, with a feel for what I'm wanting to achieve, and he extracts the essential action, piecing it together in a video that doesn't usually run beyond about 10 minutes. Back in Auckland, Grant Aickin had likewise been of enormous support to me with Auckland and the Blues.

What I'm looking for in these videos is, say, the numbers involved by the opposition in particular situations in different parts of the field. When do they use a six-man lineout as opposed to a three-man lineout? Who do they throw to in defensive situations? Who do they drive off in a five-man lineout? That sort of thing. If a pattern emerges, I record it.

Then I'll focus on the scrum and see whether they're trying to promote one side or the other, whether the No 8 prefers to run left or right, whether he's got limitations passing one way or the other. You're basically trying to build a pattern of what the opposition will do.

It's the same with kick-offs – what is their preference? Do they indulge in tricky little variations? The English surprised us at Wembley by splitting their forwards and kicking away from where we were grouped. That shows intelligence on their part and was a reminder that no matter how much homework you do, you've always got to be prepared for something different.

Generally speaking, video analysis of opponents is a huge part of coaching, provided you take the information culled on board and use it appropriately. Probably the best examples of such analysis paying huge dividends were Auckland's Ranfurly Shield victory, by 35 points to nil, against Canterbury in 1995 and the Auckland Blues' win over Natal in 1996. On both occasions, we identified established patterns among the opposition we were sure they would not deviate from. And they didn't. When I told Robin Brooke and the other lineout men they weren't going to jump on Natal's throw at Durban, they reacted as if I'd taken away their Easter eggs!

Video analysis is a bloody tedious exercise – you're continually stopping and rewinding. But it's essential and the reward for such tedium can be extremely satisfying tactical victories. Some teams are easier to analyse than others. Canterbury and Natal, on those celebrated occasions, fell into the easy category but a sophisticated team like the ACT Brumbies – who worked seemingly dozens of moves around David Knox at flyhalf – were far more challenging. England presented problems too for the 1999 Five Nations climax at Wembley because of the many lineout variations it operated, using anything from three to seven players in the lineout. Teams with lots of options are naturally harder to plot tactics against. The 30 hours I spent viewing England in action, involving eight games, would be the longest I've committed to any one team. I guess, in light of the final score at Wembley, we could say it was worth it although on the day England uncorked pieces of originality, which speaks volumes for coaches Clive Woodward and John Mitchell. I'm sure Clive and John would have spent a heap of time studying our methods.

My video analysis of England revealed that it had scored a lot of tries driving the ball through from attacking lineouts, so obviously we devised tactics to nullify that. It was actually something Lyn Howells and I had worked on before the Springbok game back in the autumn. To refine our operation, we used live opposition – summoning members of the A team to assist – but couldn't get our plan to work. So we changed and through trial and error came up with a method that was effective, as the English would testify, I'm sure. They obviously rated themselves from attacking lineouts. Why else would Lawrence Dallaglio instruct his kicker to go for touch from 38 metres out when they held a six-point advantage inside the final 10 minutes?

Because England had several times scored tries from wipers kicks (the probing, diagonal kick in behind the opposition backline), we spent 40 minutes – which is a long time in rugby training – organising our defence against this tactic. Guess what? The English didn't use it once! However, it could possibly be argued that that was because we controlled their field position.

The theory you extract from video study doesn't always translate itself into onfield effectiveness. That's where the intelligent, experienced players in your side come into their own. I recall the strategies we devised on the drawing board for our clash with the ACT Brumbies back in 1997, involving the loosies dealing with the Brumbies' inside back trio. They didn't work out

England.
✓ Scotland lineouts

① 4:30   10m Defence
5 man
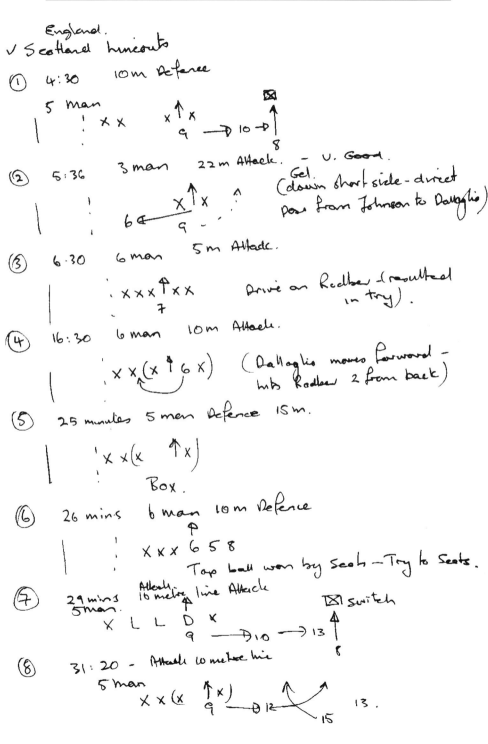
! x x   x ↑ x   ⊠
.   q → 10 →
                    8

② 5:36   3 man   22m Attack. - U. Good.
                              Gel.
!   (down short side - direct
!   6⟵ x ↑ x   ^   Pass from Johnson to Dallaglio)
                q - ·

③ 6·30   6 man   5m Attack.
.   Drive on Redber (resulted
: x x x ↑ x x   in try).
        7

④ 16:30   6 man   10m Attack.
.   (Dallaglio moves forward -
: x x (x ↑ 6 x)   hits Redber 2 from back)

⑤ 25 minutes 5 men Defence 15m.
'x x (x ↑ x)
      Box.

⑥ 26 mins   6 man 10m Defence
                ↑
! x x x 6 5 8
!   Tap ball won by Scots — Try to Scots.

⑦ 29 mins Attack 10 metre line Attack ⊠ switch
    5man.   ↑
x L L D x
        q ⟶ ⟶10 ⟶ 13 ↑
                        8

⑧ 31:20 - Attack 10 metre line
    5 man
x x (x ↑ x) ⟶ 12 ⟵ ↑ ↗   13.
        q   15

183

England Lineouts -

Full

1) Drive on 2   Johnson
2) Drive on 4   Rodber   30 metres
3) Drive on 5   Dallaglio.   from goalline

    P J P R D H B.
    1 4 3 5 8 2 6
                  7

6 man.   More often 6 man Drive
              rather than full lineouts

1) Drive on 2   Johnson
2) Drive on 4   Rodber
3) Drive on 5   Dallaglio
         Back
    ! P J P R D H
9   ! 1 4 3 5 8 6
                 7.
                      2 1 0.

(P↑J↑P) (P↑R↑D) (R↑D H↑)
  1 4 3   3 5 8   3 5   6
                                  7

Moves - Full.   [box] Must get inside the Blocks
                             epart from S.Q. on D

9 ———→ 10
9 ———→ 10   11
             14

184

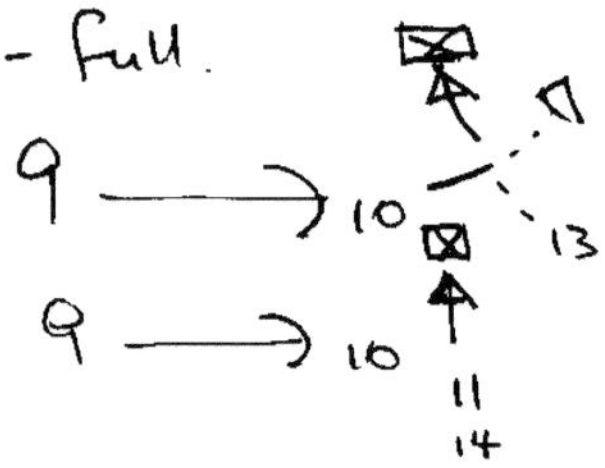

England Serums
Left Side

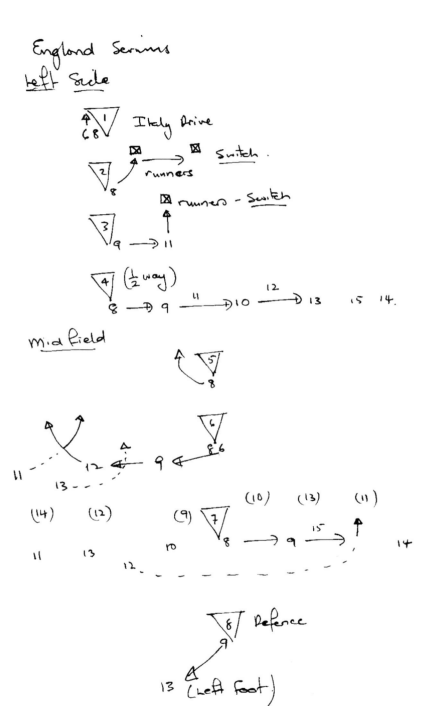

Italy Drive

runners Switch

runners - Switch

(½ way)

Midfield

Defence

13 (Left foot)

when we tried them on the training field. So the "brains trust", Zinzan Brooke, Michael Jones and Mark Carter, came up with an alternative plan which worked brilliantly on the day. Theory is worthless if you don't have the players wanting to make it work. And often theory on the drawing board looks the answer until you try and put it into action on the training field – flexibility until you determine the final strategy is essential.

Your team must always be flexible enough to adjust to innovative ploys from the opposition. And, of course, you always like to equip your own team with something original. I recall that when the Auckland Blues were hitting The Zone in 1996 and 1997 they'd often improvise, introducing fresh ideas as late as the Saturday morning. "We'll try this today" or "What about such-and-such a move – we haven't done that for a long time". It's refreshing to see originality occasionally, as long as it doesn't detract from the basic game plan. Remember, we suddenly stationed Jonah Lomu in the lineout against Natal in the 1996 Super 12 final, a piece of inventiveness that must have had their forwards wondering, especially as we scored from that lineout! That was something formulated on the Saturday morning.

How much information can a team handle? I must say, I'm a saturation man; in fact, it's become a joke among the Welsh players now. How about a couple of new moves, Graham?

I wouldn't begin to count the number of moves I have access to. Somewhere in the hundreds but many are simply variations on a theme. Some of the moves date back to my earliest days coaching with the Auckland Grammar School first fifteen. You wouldn't burden a team with 50 moves coming into a game, you'd concentrate on 12 or 15, say. Next game you might introduce another four, maybe even another eight as alternatives to those used in the previous game. The moves you call on should be appropriate to the upcoming opponent, also to the ability of the players in your side. There are obvious advantages in maintaining a consistency of selection where the players become familiar with each other and with the full range of tactical options.

As a coach, I couldn't have wished for a better leader to implement my ideas than Zinzan Brooke, who was forever devising fresh moves himself. It was a particular strength of the Auckland and Blues teams of Zinny's era that often when we created a set piece close to the opposition goalline, we scored.

I'm forever learning. Every time I watch a team play, there will be something happening that I'll note down and think, that's not a bad idea. We're all learning from each other all the time.

Defensive strategies are just as important as attacking ploys because defence provides the backbone of your whole game. Basically, the defensive screen you organise is the same game in, game out with a bit of fine tuning. In certain situations, you will scheme to neutralise a dangerous individual, although even with the most meticulous planning you can still be found out. The French, for example, paid the penalty in Paris for underestimating Neil Jenkins as a runner. At Wembley, we thought the English would attack outside Mike Catt at flyhalf but they attacked through him. It was only desperate, scrambling defence that saved tries after he'd split us a couple of times. So there's a session on defence each Tuesday.

On Wednesday morning, we concentrate on our game, going through our drills, practising what we intend to implement on match day. Then – and this is something new, and probably uncommon among international sides – we disperse. The players head home for a night. We have an advantage in Wales in that the guys are geographically all close to Cardiff – the furtherest any one player would have to drive is perhaps three hours to Manchester. It's probably not something you could do with the All Blacks, given the distance from, say, Dunedin to Auckland. But it works well in Wales and the players appreciate the opportunity to relax in a domestic environment midweek. It assists us because to try and maintain intensity right through the week would be impossible.

The guys reconvene on Thursday morning after which we travel to the match venue. With Cardiff Arms Park being rebuilt, it meant we didn't have any home matches last season – apart from the Pumas international, which was played at Llanelli – so travel was involved most times, to Edinburgh, Treviso, Paris and London (for the three games at Wembley). Once we arrive at the destination, we always have a light workout, nothing too strenuous.

Friday is something of a ritual (presuming the match we're building towards is a Saturday game; obviously everything goes back 24 hours for Sunday fixtures), with a visit to the match venue for a session of "spotting", going over the basic elements. It's essentially a walk and talk time with perhaps a little bit of fine tuning. Usually the only individual who works hard is the goalkicker. Neil Jenkins reminds me of Grant Fox – totally dedicated, religious in his preparation and not satisfied until he is striking the ball sweetly.

Friday evening, another ritual, is the captain's meeting. I usually show my face and walk out, leaving them to it. The Auckland and Welsh captains' meetings are very similar, with Zinny, when he was with Auckland and the Blues, and Rob Howley, with Wales, empowering players to accept greater responsibility. The balance of the evening is pretty relaxed – a quiet meal, card games in the players' room or a video (Hollywood style, not rugby!) and never late to bed.

Match day routine varies according to the kick-off time, but for the traditional mid-afternoon start, there's always a session involving lineout drills for the forwards while the backs usually run gently through their moves. Often it's in the car park or, as in London where we are always quartered at the Royal Garden Hotel in Kensington, it's next door in Hyde Park.

Approximately 15 minutes before the bus departs for the match venue, the coach delivers his team talk. Well… that's how I do it. It took me a while to appreciate that the requirements of the players in Wales are different from those back in New Zealand. I delivered something like 140 team talks to Auckland and the Blues. My biggest concern with them was that they would not be on the "edge". I was dealing with very talented individuals generally – many of them had played a lot of big-time rugby over a number of years. I had to work on the desire because attitude was everything. If the attitude was right we would generally play to a high standard and win.

Look at 1996 and the Super 12 matches in South Africa. Against Transvaal, our attitude was appalling and we got stuffed. Hell, I was wild after that game. Transvaal was bottom of the league and we were totally unprofessional with over-confidence and misplaced arrogance. But at the end of the day it's the coach's responsibility. I had not got it right… so more self-analysis, more team analysis.

A few days later we took on Natal, which was top of the league. This time the attitude was enormous – electric, in fact. The coach (with assistance from others, including Transvaal) had got it right. That was the greatest victory by the Blues in the three seasons I was involved. It was an unbelievable night at King's Park, Durban

– that's what coaches coach for.

Initially, I approached the Welsh guys with the same philosophy. I got it wrong, badly wrong. The Welsh rugby culture involves huge physical commitment and desire; in fact, it is often counter-productive. What was missing was the ability to think, to be composed and disciplined and focused mentally and to put the practised game plan into reality. With Auckland the team talk generally was focused on desire and being on the edge. In Wales, where I think I've now got it right, it's getting the top three inches working effectively.

The effective thinking process under pressure is a problem in Welsh rugby but thankfully not unsolvable. This has manifested itself through inadequate coaching and competitions and far too many matches for the young Welsh rugby player. There is a lack of high-intensity competitions at the tier below international level. Oh, for a Super 12 type competition in the northern hemisphere.

Philosophically, the next game is always the most important for a coach operating at international level and that was certainly the case as Wales prepared for its Five Nations clash with France in Paris in March. Although the French had been extremely fortunate to escape with a one-point victory against Ireland in Dublin, their record in front of their own raucous fans was daunting. The record books revealed they hadn't lost a championship match in Paris since 1996 and Wales hadn't succeeded there for an incredible 24 years.

I emphasised six points in my team talk in Paris. The first was the need to start well because in the two previous games (against Scotland and Ireland) we hadn't done that, we had not implemented the game plan. We'd run around like headless chooks against Ireland, undisciplined and sacrificing field position. Our intention was to blitz the French in the opening 20 minutes.

Point two: Be bold. We had to be bold to win, we had to take the French on with ball in hand and express ourselves. If you're not bold, I stressed, you can't win. It was my fault the game plan hadn't been implemented at Edinburgh and against Ireland at Wembley because the guys were apprehensive about executing a style of game with which they were unfamiliar.

Point three: Ruthless discipline. Perhaps a contradiction in words but it was important to concede few penalties and ideally none through indiscipline. The players needed to have crystal clear minds for 80 minutes. At stoppages, the guys were to come together and assess their progress and identify any problem zones. Certain individuals were responsible for particular aspects of play – Shane Howarth for the back three, Scott Gibbs for the defensive pattern, Neil Jenkins as the general for calling the shots in the backline, Rob Howley as the captain responsible for overall strategy, Scott Quinnell for the lineout calls, Colin Charvis for the forward defence from set pieces and Garin Jenkins, who was in charge of the scrum. At the stoppages, if any aspect was causing concern, the players responsible would be expected to make the necessary adjustments. All the other players were empowered to chip in if they identified some area of the game that required attention.

Point four: Don't let the French play. If you stop the opposition functioning, the game's half won and, in the case of the French, you've put a huge dent in their psyche. The guys needed to talk up their defensive patterns throughout the game.

Point five: An extra 20 per cent from everyone. I expected the guys to return to the dressing room after the final whistle with their tanks empty.

Point six: Re-establish credibility as a team on the world rugby stage which we would do by becoming the first Welsh team in 24 years to win in Paris.

At halftime, we led 28-18 after a sensational session of rugby. The guys had performed almost beyond my expectations. Apart from a couple of defensive lapses, they produced a near-perfect 40 minutes of rugby. The challenge now was to maintain the impetus to the finish. It was an emotional dressing room at halftime and I hastened to remind of them that we'd been in a similar situation against the Springboks and blown it. I appealed to the players to maintain composure, discipline and work rate, to continue being bold and to not allow the French to seize the initiative.

It's history now that although our tryscoring dried up in the second half, we clung to our lead and came away with a pulsating 34-33 victory, thanks to Thomas Castaignede missing with his injury-time penalty attempt. We simply ran out of steam in the final quarter. We weren't getting to the breakdowns and because our condition was giving out, we failed to maintain skill levels. We actually played poorly for much of the second half, but through sheer tenacity we hung in for the victory. And what an occasion it was, one of the most emotional experiences of my entire sporting career.

Although there were great celebrations throughout Wales at what was an historic victory, we couldn't afford to sit back for long and bask in the glory. We soon had to deal with Italy in Treviso and, far more significantly, take on the Five Nations favourite and front runner England.

I was accused of talking up England's prospects to an exaggerated degree. While there may have been an element of gamesmanship in what I said, an understanding of the facts certainly supported my observations. The England tight five boasted 191 caps. Compare that with our lot. Garin Jenkins might have been making his 42nd test appearance but the other four could claim only 24 caps among them. Clive Woodward's team ranked as one of the game's superpowers – there was no question that in their quest for Grand Slam glory, they rated far higher than us, a viewpoint confirmed by all the London-based critics in their match previews.

My team talk for Wembley was quite different from what I'd prepared in Paris. This time there were five points I emphasised.

Point one: England doesn't respect us as a rugby team. I told our players I would say that at the press conference (which I did). It wasn't just something I plucked out of the clouds – I knew it to be true. They'd hammered Wales by 60 points the previous season. How can you respect a team you can defeat so easily? My point in raising it was to create an edge with my players.

Point two: England's game plan is based on our lack of discipline, lack of intelligence and lack of mental hardness. They think we are soft, I told our guys. They expect to grind us down, after which we will fall to pieces. But – and it's an important but, I reminded our players – England is now under huge pressure because it's in a must-win situation and could panic. Our job was to apply pressure and increase it so that Clive Woodward's team would lose discipline, intelligence and composure.

Point three: The keys to England's game are the scrum, with Dallaglio breaking strongly from No 8, attacking lineouts from which they drive consistently, usually with Neil Back deputising at halfback, the high ball directed at the opposition fullback and wingers, the winger coming in outside the flyhalf and the five-man lineout with a target in midfield.

Point four: Talking up our defence. England is regarded as the No 1 defensive side in the world. Why can't we organise ourselves so efficiently, we become the best defensive side?

Point five: It was imperative we adhered to our attacking game plan, retaining the boldness we showed in Paris, by running at the English defence. The best way to break them down was by playing our game and stretching them. We had to take advantage of the stoppages, as we did in Paris, to ensure we were implementing our game plan as accurately as possible. Discipline was paramount, discipline and control. If anyone gave away a penalty for indiscipline, I'd personally shoot them! Field position was critical because the whole England game was based on maintaining pressure on the opposition. Finally, I said, England doesn't respect us – what are we going to do about that?

England led 25-18 at halftime but the boys entered the dressing room in good shape mentally. Though they were in the game, which is obviously important, it is vital to walk the talk rather than talk the walk – we had to make it happen. We had the wind advantage to follow and field position, especially against England, was critical. So we decided to kick more, to try and maintain field position. We had to be bold – we were a little negative in the first half. We had to take them on once field position was established. And being seven points in arrears, we had to score first. If they had scored first, we were history. Continued discipline and composure was essential. Defence was also highlighted. We had a problem there and it was only our ability to scramble that kept us in the game.

Team talks vary from game to game. I've always been a little sceptical of their true worth. Probably, in the early stages of a coaching appointment, they have merit and I guess where a maximum of seven or eight international matches are involved, they can be effective. However, when you're dealing with the same group of players through a programme of 25 matches or more in a season – as I was with Auckland – they can become tedious. In that situation, a coach is probably better selecting the more important games and concentrating his efforts on those.

In any circumstance, team talks should be confined to a maximum of 10 minutes. Any longer and you run the danger of losing the players' attention. The purpose of the talk is essentially to refresh their memories as regards the game plan you've been developing throughout the week and to give them a handful of key points to focus on.

After the team talk, the players file on to the bus for the journey to the ground. From that point, I personally say very little, leaving it to the assistant coaches to offer a few words of encouragement. Mac McCallion, my deputy at the Auckland Blues, would usually offer a few pertinent, colourful observations to the forwards in the dressing room while Lyn Howells, the Welsh forward coach, prefers to do his thing earlier on Saturday morning.

Once the Welsh players arrive at the match venue, they're in the hands of the conditioning coach Steve Black who is in charge of their final preparation. He gets them warmed up physically and spiritually out on the field. Some work hard, others do very little. It's a very personal time before a game and there is no hard and fast rule for how an individual should cap off his preparation for the game. With Jim Blair, everyone basically did the same thing whereas Blackie leaves it to the individual to decide.

The coach's job during the first 40 minutes is to understand why things are happening and how he can best improve his team's performance. He should be as constructive as possible during the halftime break, offering advice on how to enhance what hopefully has already been an encouraging display while identifying ways to stop the enemy. There's a bit of motivation involved but it's mainly a tactical assessment at halftime.

In the second half, the coach has to decide when to effect substitutions. Rugby is no longer a 15-man game, it's a 22-man game and intelligent use of replacements can have a major bearing on the outcome of a game. For the England game, we selected four props and at about the 65-minute mark substituted David Young and Andrew Lewis for Peter Rogers and Ben Evans, who'd done us proud. It gave us fresh oomph and allowed us to maintain the little bit of control we'd established over England in the scrum. We reasoned that if we were going to defeat England, we needed to achieve an advantage in the scrum, to help nullify the effectiveness of Dallaglio bursting off the back. Considering the embarrassments we'd suffered at scrum time against Argentina five months earlier, the achievement of our pack at Wembley was extremely satisfying (and a great credit to Lyn Howells). So was the final score!

Photosport

Chapter 11

Anatomy of a rugby team

To be independent of public opinion is the first condition of achieving anything great.

G.W.F. Hegel

THERE ARE MANY COMPONENTS to a rugby team, obviously. Down the grades it doesn't matter too much if an overweight, leaden-footed forward has to fill in at second-five or a 40-year-old club stalwart who holds the resident record for downing a yard of beer is summoned in desperation to make up the numbers in the front row.

But at representative and international level, it's essential that each player is a specialist in his position. To the layman a flanker is a flanker, a midfielder is a midfielder, a winger is a winger. However, once you become intimately involved in coaching, you recognise that there are essential qualities required for each position.

The blindside flanker's role is as different from the openside flanker's as halfback is from fullback. And the subtle skills you look for in a second-five are vastly different from the more aggressive qualities you seek in a centre.

Some coaches place different interpretations on certain positions, which obviously relates to the style of game they want to play. For the purpose of this exercise, however, let's assume we are concentrating on the expansive, high-energy, 15-man game cultivated by Auckland over the past 15 or so years and now adopted by Wales.

While tackling and defensive patterns are just as important as the attacking moves that will produce tries, we are not concerning ourselves with negativity. Our players will be selected for their bold, some may say daring, approach. We want to play rugby that will entertain and excite the fans and startle the enemy. Basically, what we are trying to achieve here is high-speed, high-intensity, ball-in-hand rugby. Stability at set pieces is critical, so that the ball can be carried over the advantage line, recycled quickly at the tackle with a number of options at that point to outnumber and outmanoeuvre the defence.

A **fullback**, first and foremost, has got to be able to catch and tackle. If he can perform these basics, then he is assessed on his ability to attack from set pieces because the fullback has more opportunity to attack than any other guy on the field and, indeed, is now the most important attacker in the game. The fullback is a perpetual motion performer because he's joining the backline virtually every time his team wins the ball. Forty years ago – when Don Clarke was entering the scene – fullbacks were condemned if they left their station. They were the Last Line and their primary roles were to field high kicks, kick accurately to touch and effect trysaving tackles. I wonder what Don Clarke and company would have thought if the fullback's game in the nineties had been outlined to them. With the change in the lineout laws and teams not wanting to kick out, it's vitally important now to have a fullback who is pacy and strong on the counter-attack.

Shane Howarth, the No 15 for Wales, is playing better rugby now than when he was an All Black. The professional scene – experienced initially with league – helped him because he used it to draw the best out of himself. Amazingly, his pace increased from the age of 25 to 30. He's a true professional, an excellent communicator, an individual who exudes confidence, which is great for the team. I went out on a limb for him when I discovered his Welsh ancestry and there would have been a negative reaction if he hadn't produced the goods. But he did, fitting in well. He's a thoroughly nice guy who was quickly accepted as one of the team.

He wasn't selected on reputation. When I attended the Sale v Cardiff match, he was the best player on the field.

All Black Christian Cullen is a super athlete and a brilliant individual who needs to attack more with the team. Individually, he has no peer. He can be frightening when you're coaching against him – he scores tries no one else can.

Matt Burke, the Wallaby who busted his shoulder scoring the match-winning try against the All Blacks at Sydney last August, is probably the best all-round fullback in the game. He's a reliable goalkicker who possesses an Aussie Rules ability to go high after the ball. He's phenomenal off the ground and a sure defender who attacks well. The Aussies will be so much more dangerous at the World Cup with him in the No 15 jersey. Springbok Percy Montgomery possesses a lot of Cullen's qualities but he also has some deficiencies, lacking consistency under the high ball, particularly.

There are a lot of exciting, running fullbacks around, guys like Glenn Metcalfe (Scotland), Matt Perry (England), Conor O'Shea (Ireland) and Emile Ntamack (France), Ntamack being a huge natural talent. It's what the game's come to – if you haven't got a fullback with counter-attacking skills, you're behind the eight ball, to start with.

Wingers are finishers. They need other skills – in fact, the requirements to operate at fullback essentially apply to wingers – but above all, their main role is to score tries once given a sniff of the goalline. Wingers need to be able to work both sides of the field, which means they should be able to kick with both feet. New Zealand was blessed with quality wingers when I pulled out in 1998; in fact, there were probably 10 of world class. Unfortunately, there aren't a lot of champion finishers in Wales. We've got guys better suited to midfield who lack the gas to finish. In that international against South Africa last November there were times when we put players into space who couldn't finish. Jeff Wilson or Joeli Vidiri would have taken the five pointers but we didn't. So we've got to work on our pace.

Jeff Wilson is the ultimate winger, the best in his position in the world. He's got it all, as he demonstrates at fullback – pace and skill and that deft ability to chip ahead and regather. He maintains a high work rate and is as effective on the left wing as on the right.

He's a bit ahead of all the other wingers, although Australia's Ben Tune isn't far behind. I've got a lot of time for Wilson and there's no doubt that the revival of Otago rugby is closely linked to his presence. Tune is innovative and highly competitive. He's quick with a good feel for the game.

South Africa's Pieter Rossouw, who claims experience at fullback with Western Province, is an individual with extra skills. He possesses that freakish capacity to score tries from unlikely situations, beating people along the way. His coaches must love him because he keeps plucking those critical five-pointers out of the hat, like that matchwinner against the All Blacks at Athletic Park in 1998.

No analysis of wingers would be complete without reference to Jonah Lomu, who I was fortunate enough to have in my Auckland Blues backline in 1996 and 1998. He's the ultimate game breaker, a player of immense talent. If it hadn't been for medical problems, he would have continued to dazzle the rugby world as he did at the last World Cup. His Blues partner, Joeli Vidiri, is inconsistent but when on song, there's no more awesome sight. How he's not a regular international performer, I don't know. I'd mortgage my house to have his talent in Wales. Unfortunately, I don't think there are any Thomases, Joneses or Jenkinses in his lineage!

Although there are a couple of useful youngsters around, the northern hemisphere doesn't claim the same degree of talent in the position. Englishman Steve Hanley, an imposing 16-stoner who made his test debut against Wales in April, is going to be good, but we're thin on quality wingers in Wales. Daffyd James, a centre most of his career, will develop into a competitive winger while Gareth Thomas is talented but inconsistent.

Centre is a demanding position, the effectiveness of which relates to the alignment of the backline. There's a bit of depth at centre in Welsh rugby which is pleasing and getting Allan Bateman back from league was a huge bonus. He's a world-class performer, talented and mature, although he has been sidelined in 1999 with injury. He's 33 but looks 25 and, like Frank Bunce, can go on and on.

Outside centre is a position which demands maturity because it's the hardest position to play in the entire backline. The best outside centres are hard runners, strong tacklers and decision makers… tough individuals who thrive on the eyeball-to-eyeball situations that exist there. It's a position where players of weak character can be psyched out by hard-nosed individuals.

Look at Joe Stanley and Frank Bunce, who dominated the No 13 jersey for the All Blacks for a full decade from 1986 to 1997. When I talk of the need for maturity, Joe operated there from the age of 29 to 35 and Frank from 30 to 36, which is extraordinary really. Circumstances – and the whim of the selectors – were responsible for their belated entries on to the international scene but their experience was invaluable when they got there.

When Frank finished after the 1997 season, his logical replacement was Eroni Clarke, who'd been a key member of two championship winning Super 12 teams and a host of trophy winning NPC sides. Year in, year out, Eroni was voted Auckland (and the Blues') most valuable performer, yet John Hart and his panel ignored him until they were forced to select him when their injury list reached alarming proportions. He immediately proved his worth. I feel sorry for Eroni. Apart from me pushing him, I think the players appreciated he was an integral part of the Blues jigsaw puzzle and that he could do the job for the All Blacks as well.

Inside centre (or **second-five** as it's tagged in New Zealand) requires players with good distribution skills, a strong boot and, ideally, the ability to probe gaps. Three players I can think of who have all these qualities are Tim Horan, Lee Stensness and Scott Gibbs.

Gibbs was the difference in the second half of our match against Argentina at Llanelli last November. He cut them up and freed the ball for the outsides to finish, a performance that lifted the team when the Pumas' powerhouse scrum was threatening to take control of the game. He's another with a ton of experience. He's only 26 and can look forward to two World Cups. He's intelligent and strong and has business interests outside rugby which helps bring out the best in a person. In empowering players to produce their best, he's a key. Scott's try at Wembley to defeat England in April represented a touch of brilliance. He was also our man of the match in Paris, six times claiming turnover ball for us.

Less Stensness, who could operate equally effectively at first-five, was an enigma. He was the most talented second-five in New Zealand in my time. Occasionally he was found wanting defensively and that cost him. He didn't enjoy the high-pressure environment of the All Blacks, being a player who preferred a relaxed setting. More consistently than any other second-five, however, he had the ability to create, for he was very talented. If he'd "grown up" in the All Blacks, he would have become a world-class operator, but he was mucked around which did a lot of damage to his psyche. He often became a scapegoat when he didn't deserve to be.

Jeremy Guscott has been a class act for years, consistently the best centre in the Five Nations championship and much under-rated defensively. A rival for him would be Allan Bateman, once he gets over his frustrating run of injuries. Another Welshman, Mark Taylor, has been one of the finds of the 1998-99 season. Strong with an excellent temperament, he will develop into a quality international.

The French, so well served by Philippe Sella for so long, struggled in midfield this year but an Italian player who impressed me was Cristian Stoica. Only 22, he's big and strong and can bust tackles.

The South Africans are well served in midfield. Pieter Muller and Andre Snyman were rock-solid throughout the 1998 Tri-series, while somewhere in the background is Japie Mulder, a player I rate. Likewise, the Aussies are well served through Tim Horan, Daniel Herbert and Jason Little.

Indeed, the only major rugby power short on midfield backs is New Zealand! It had a champion, but let him get away – John Leslie. He was nothing short of phenomenal in the 1999 Five Nations championship. He's changed from a tucker (operating with the ball under his arm) to carrying the ball in two hands. He was outstanding for Otago in the NPC and he's just got better and better. He operates flat and creates endless opportunities for those around him. You'll probably find he had a hand in 12 of the 16 tries Scotland scored this year. He obviously didn't impress the All Black selectors last year; ironically, if he'd played for the New Zealand A team I coached (Jason O'Halloran was our second-five), John would have been ineligible to turn out for another country. Scotland would have missed out on his genius.

At **first-five** in the modern game you must have a player who can function under pressure. Probably the finest example is Springbok Henry Honiball, who has added another dimension to the position.

If the **first-five** (or **flyhalf** as they are known in most countries outside New Zealand) can operate flat – which is absolutely crucial – he takes the loosies out of the game. I've been absolutely delighted with how Neil Jenkins has adjusted to what has been a completely different role for him. He's turned in a series of quality performances for Wales since I arrived, stunning the French with his electrifying breaks and emerging as a hero against England. He's the most experienced player in the side, having made 64 test appearances at 27, and has a lot of years left in him yet. Although he possesses capable hands, kicks well and is an extremely accurate goalkicker – I daringly described him as a better goalkicker than Grant Fox after his performance against England – he has not always been Wales' first-choice flyhalf. In his upbringing, he's not been required to do a lot of tackling, so that's an adjustment he's having to make. Neil has used Foxy as a role model. A dedicated professional, he goes through the same rituals as Foxy to develop his personal skills.

The Welsh have got a thing about flyhalves. Down the years their rugby factory has produced a series of dazzling individuals, players like Cliff Morgan, Barry John, Phil Bennett and Jonathan Davies. Neil's not out of that mould and therefore the Welsh people, and particularly the media, have criticised him a lot, which has got to him. Neil's the sort of stoical character who's tended to confront the critics head on, which hasn't always been in his best interests. So I'm delighted that he derived so much enjoyment from his Five Nations performances this year.

Wales has another quality flyhalf in Arwell Thomas, a player of immense skill. He needs to work on his consistency but he's in the equation and performed outstandingly for Wales A in 1999.

The All Blacks possess two of the most gifted first-fives in the game, Andrew Mehrtens and Carlos Spencer, but the chopping and changing that went on throughout 1997 and 1998 hasn't helped the backline function effectively. Mehrts was the outstanding player in the Super 12 last year, while Carlos possesses so much ability it's unbelievable. He does stuff others only dream about and he can kill an opponent. New Zealand is extremely fortunate to have the choice of two such talented individuals, but their best won't be seen at test level until the current management decides precisely what game it wants the All Blacks to play.

I enjoyed working with Carlos. We first encountered him when Auckland took the Ranfurly Shield on tour and played Horowhenua at Levin Domain. Then just a schoolboy of 17, Carlos scored a cracking try – stepping past Shane Howarth, our fullback, to do so – and banged over a long-range penalty goal. The Ponsonby boys instantly recognised his potential and brought him to Auckland, which was timely because Grant Fox's remarkable career was fast coming to a finish.

I consider I was privileged (and fortunate) to have Foxy at first-five in so many of my teams. Although he operated at a time when rugby was quite different to what it is now, he was an amazing player, a major reason why the Auckland and All Black teams of the late eighties and early nineties enjoyed such a phenomenal sequence of successes. There was never a better organiser of a backline or of a team's strategic plan.

Thomas Castaignede, the French pivot, has had a difficult year because he was not right physically, but when France won the Grand Slam last season, he was the key. He can electrify a backline, but he didn't have the same opportunities this year because his forwards failed to achieve domination up front.

A player who's got everything is Scotland's Gregor Townsend. He's a gifted attacker who has benefited from playing with Brive in the French competition. It's obviously been good for him. He's always been classy but the players around him have not always understood what he was doing. He built a telling association with John Leslie this year and they both played superbly.

Although he operated mostly at centre in the Five Nations, England's Jonny Wilkinson is also a quality first-five, at 20 a player of the future. England has a cluster of exciting young backs coming through and he's the pick of them.

When you're assessing **halfbacks**, the pass is all important. The player with the best pass in the world is Ofisa "Junior" Tonu'u, yet he's made only five test appearances for New Zealand, three of them as a replacement. The length and speed of his pass creates an extra metre of space for the centres. I believe Junior is a colossus but he has been probably his own worst enemy. Injuries and attitude have probably counted against him at the highest level, along with the presence of Justin Marshall.

Having said that, one of the big mistakes the New Zealand selectors made in 1998 was bringing Marshall back too soon. The Springboks and the Wallabies realised he wasn't a threat because he couldn't run, which thrust pressure on to the other backs. If Junior had been given a regular slot through '98, I'm certain he would have cemented his place in the team. Personally, I thought the All Black backline performance improved dramatically when he came on as a replacement for Marshall during the second half of the Springbok test at Athletic Park. His career was interrupted at an important stage with a stress fracture in his foot. As a consequence, he couldn't do a lot of running and put on a considerable amount of weight, which was obviously seen as a negative and counted against him. A shame, because he's a hell of a capable player with the best pass, bar none.

With the Auckland Blues, we developed a lethal ploy for transforming defence into attack, using Vidiri to chase Tonu'u's beautifully-judged lobbed kicks over scrums and rucks from inside our own 22. Many an opposition winger has panicked and spilled the ball with Vidiri – a fearsome sight at the best of times – bearing down on him!

Wales is fortunate to have Rob Howley, who is hugely competitive and has a great desire to see Welsh rugby realise its potential. He's got it all – he can kick, run and pass and has vision. As the captain, he's taken on the ownership of the team.

I learnt about taking ownership of a team from Sean Fitzpatrick, who was the All Black captain although he operated under Zinzan Brooke with Auckland and the Blues. He struggled with the captaincy initially but when Harty took over, he urged the senior pros to take responsibility for the team and give as much support as possible to the captain. It's something I've introduced to the Welsh team with great effect. It's the key to ensuring the captain develops with confidence.

Probably the two most influential halfbacks in recent seasons have been George Gregan and Joost van der Westhuizen. Gregan is intelligent, a competent passer, incisive runner and fearless tackler whose only shortcoming is perhaps the tactical kick, while van der Westhuizen is the most dangerous running halfback in the world.

The Springboks will be praying he recovers from his knee injury to direct operations at the World Cup.

Of the European halfbacks, I'm a great admirer of the Scottish captain, Gary Armstrong. He's enormously competitive, a true professional.

In discussing **No 8s**, I'm heavily prejudiced, having developed a close relationship with Zinny. He was a player of immense vision who could do things no others could. With the All Blacks at Carisbrook, he fielded a restart from the Wallabies in his own 22 and flung a giant pass out to Christian Cullen who scored at the other end of the field. Against Counties-Manukau in the final of the NPC in 1996, with the scores close, and a penalty awarded in our 22, I'm thinking security. But Zinny takes a tap... and Adrian Cashmore scores under the bar! Seven points, which was the starting point that enabled Auckland to get into The Zone and play some brilliant rugby. As I say, Zinny was a player of remarkable vision who ranks with Grant Fox and Matthew Ridge as the most competitive individual I've ever met. Everything was a competition with Zinny. He couldn't just go to the urinal for a leak – he'd have to pee higher than anyone else!

Leadership enshrouds some individuals but Zinny thrived on the role. As a captain, he lost his inhibitions and let it all hang out. There's never been anyone who led more by example. He possessed a big defence, could run with the backs, scored an astonishing number of tries, organised everyone else and, if all else failed, he could drop-kick a goal! He was at the peak of his powers through 1996 and early 1997 when the Blues were winning the Super 12 and Auckland the NPC.

He had the common touch which worked magically with Auckland, a side with a multicultural mix. There was a huge variation in interests and beliefs, with Samoans, Tongans, Fijians, Maori, Europeans... even a couple of Eskimos, I think... in the side. Some were social characters, others weren't; some were extrovert, others timid, some were religious, others atheist, but Zinny related to them all.

There are a couple of special qualities a No 8 must have these days. He needs a halfback's ability to pass left or right and a low centre of gravity so he can get his body and the ball over the advantage line. The rangy backrowers of old, guys like Mervyn

Davies and Brian Lochore, would be employed as blindside flankers or locks now. It's imperative to have the right build. Taine Randell is the right height but doesn't have the necessary bulk while Gary Teichmann is a bit tall. The Aussie, Toutai Kefu, and the new All Black, Isitolo Maka, are pretty close to the ideal build. Zinny was the ultimate and also possessed the ability to create opportunities for those around him. He engendered amazing confidence in his teams, which is understandable. If a winger gets the ball 10 times in a game, he is going to be more enthusiastic and a greatly improved player than if he only receives it 10 times in 10 games. That tended to happen in Zinny's teams.

Wales' Scott Quinnell, who was outstanding against the Springboks, is a player with all the bits and pieces who could be up with the best. It's up to him, really. He's a true professional, having played league for Wigan. He's another who's sharing in the leadership of the team.

While No 8 is obviously a worry for the All Blacks, there are several backrowers of outstanding quality operating in the UK. England captain Lawrence Dallaglio, besides being an inspiring leader, is an accomplished lineout operator and is potent with the ball in hand. Ireland's Vic Costello is an under-rated player with great strength. Until a broken kneecap sidelined him, Scotland's Martin Peters was also playing great rugby.

Samoan captain Pat Lam is a world-class performer, deservedly named club player of the year in England in 1998. He's an absolute inspiration for Samoa, an astute individual who's getting better with age. He was unlucky to have Zinny in front of him when he was emerging as an international. If he was available to the New Zealand selectors now, I'm sure they would snap him up.

Springbok Bobby Skinstad operated in 1998 as a flanker but the Stormers have used him exclusively as a No 8 this year, with spectacular results. He's a fabulous player who's got it all – a modern day Michael Jones. He's obviously a natural leader too. He could become one of the most influential players in the game over the next few years.

Flankers come in two varieties – the opensider, who operates off the back of the lineout, and is essentially destructive, and the blindsider, who is a support player and ideally a quality lineout jumper.

Josh Kronfeld has been setting the standard for opensiders. He makes tackles and turns the ball over for his side, a real jack-in-the-box. He's destructive and constructive all in the one operation. And he's such a pleasant guy with it.

Michael Jones used to be the consummate openside flanker but the constant pounding his body took forced him to review his part in the scheme of things. Such is the man's remarkable talent, he became equally effective as a blindsider, but only after he'd changed his body shape to meet the physical demands of this different position.

Angus Gardiner from Canterbury was a flanker who never gained the recognition he deserved. The selectors seemed to regard him as too small, but I thought for a couple of years he was decidedly the most skilful player in New Zealand around the tackle zone. It's a demanding area in which to operate because you can get smashed, with players coming in from all directions. It demands courage.

I thought Mark Carter was a quality performer who had some outstanding games for Auckland and the Blues. I could not understand why his obvious talents were not used more extensively by the All Blacks.

Although the South Africans seem to prefer larger, more physical flankers – players like Andre Venter, Johan Erasmus and Bobby Skinstad – there's a trend back towards smaller opensiders as the game continues to evolve.

Neil Back couldn't get a look in originally alongside England's giant loosies but he was one of the standout performers in this year's Five Nations.

There's a young fellow of promise in Wales, Martin Williams, from Pontypridd. At 22, he's swift and intelligent and helps provide that essential continuity good teams need, although he lost his position to the New Zealander Brett Sinkinson, who, with his NPC background, brought a harder edge to the position and a greater presence defensively.

The ideal blindside specialist is an accomplished lineout jumper, strong defender and able support player. He needs reliable hands and should have good anticipation. Good examples currently featuring on the international scene are Tim Rodber (recently converted to lock), Johan Erasmus and Taine Randell. The best in the world at the time of the first World Cup was Alan Whetton. He not only dominated the rear of the lineout, nothing got past him down the blindside of the scrum and near the goalline, he was virtually unstoppable. Michael Jones, now probably past his best, was the ultimate specialist because of his amazing instincts and with his capacity to be in the right place at the right time. As an attacker and defender, he consistently did the damage.

Colin Charvis has been impressive for Wales. He's strong with a ruthless streak and, along with Gibbs, is the surest defender in the team. He's powerful as he demonstrated in forcing his way across for two tries against Argentina. He just needs to develop his lineout proficiency and consistency from game to game.

Lock is a position which has evolved interestingly during the past decade. Just when it seemed the gargantuans, great hulks measuring up to 6ft 10in, were about to take over, rugby speeded up and suddenly the demand was for lighter, more mobile players. Then the IRB approved lifting (or is supporting the proper term?) and the requirements for guys wearing the Nos 4 and 5 jerseys altered again. That's made the task of the jumpers easier as they soar to great heights to collect their hookers' throws. Many of the specialist lineout jumpers these days have played basketball.

For most international teams, the fellow who jumps at the front of the lineout is a big, strong individual who smacks into rucks and mauls and who might only be required to pull in three or four throws in an entire match. His colleague who operates in the middle of the lineout must be an accomplished jumper with soft hands – a John Eales or an Ian Jones – who will unfailingly gather the 12 or 15 balls thrown to him.

Given the tempo at which modern internationals are played, both locks must be mobile, athletic and be able to give and take a pass.

I had the good fortune to have Robin Brooke in my pack throughout my time with Auckland and the Blues. He's an outstanding footballer and one of the most knowledgeable lineout players in the world. He ran the lineout for us and I've have to concede I learned a lot from Robin. He's a thinker, an innovator. For instance, he'll order a quick throw-in to thwart the opposition and not allow them time to arrange a competitive, defensive jump. He enjoyed the academic side of the lineout and came up with some great ploys. Obviously, he had a major input when we were scheming a way to neutralise Natal's lineout strength in the Super 12 game at Durban in 1996.

Robin Brooke and John Eales would be the best all-round locks in the world. They can scrummage, run and pass, operate at two or five in the lineout and maintain a physical edge. If that's not enough, Eales also operates as a captain and kicks goals as well. The right environment brings out the best in top players, and John Eales and Robin Brooke are two who always deliver when they're most needed. Rod Macqueen will be praying that Eales recovers from shoulder surgery in time for the World Cup.

Chris Wyatt, who we've introduced into the Welsh team, is an exciting prospect. Previously a No 8, he's a natural jumper. He's got to learn to do the donkey work at the scrum and at the tackle, but he shows great promise and his performance against England at Wembley was memorable. He was acknowledged as one of the players of the Five Nations championship. Craig Quinnell equally came on as his partner and possesses real athletic ability. With total fitness, he could be a world-class performer.

There are any number of quality locks operating in Europe. Ireland has a beauty in Malcolm O'Kelly, a superb physical specimen with limitless potential, while Scotland's Scott Murray was arguably the most improved forward in the Five Nations. Ireland also has Jeremy Davidson, a world-class performer on the comeback trail after injury. England's pair, Martin Johnson and Tim Rodber, are the equal of any international combination and will take the side a long way in the World Cup. Many in the UK believe Johnson is the No 1 lock in the world. We will see at the World Cup.

In the same way that lock has gone through a transition, so has **prop**, although not to the same, extreme extent. Instead of stacking front rows with men-mountains capable of scrummaging opponents into the dust, most international teams now are sacrificing brute strength at scrum time for individuals who are mobile and possess good ball skills. If you're wanting to compete against the leading nations of the world, who are all now developing the all-action, high-intensity game, you don't really have much choice. The plodders get left behind.

Of course, the All Blacks have been using highly mobile props for many years now – guys like Olo Brown, Craig Dowd and Bull Allen. In this respect, Auckland and New Zealand teams have been blessed with talent. Olo, unfortunately sidelined with a prolapsed disc as the fourth World Cup approaches, has been tagged for some years as the best tighthead prop in the world. A superb physical specimen, he's another businessman who plays rugby, someone who's achieved an ideal balance in his life. He was close to being dux of Mt Albert Grammar School and worked for a leading firm of accountants while an amateur. He's continued with his business interests since rugby went professional, which is great. There are too many paid rugby players now with time on their hands, whose only outlet away from rugby action seems to be on the golf course.

Craig Dowd is a guy who's continued to develop and, along with Olo, took on his share of the Auckland leadership. He was a pleasure to have in the side, a great role model.

The new-age guys in New Zealand are obviously the Otago pair of Carl Hoeft, who has looked uncommonly good in his test outings to date, and Kees Meeuws, who I've followed with particular interest since he was a fourth former at Kelston Boys' High School. It's hard to believe now, but he was always in the final of the 100m sprint! He's a player who, sadly for Auckland, had to go elsewhere to get regular representative play. Auckland had the New Zealand front row for a long time – now it's Otago's turn.

With Olo and Craig so dominant for so long, guys like Meeuws and Kevin Nepia had to select a different union. In hindsight, they probably should have moved earlier, particularly Kevin.

Around the globe, there's been a move away from domination through scrummaging power, except with Argentina which can claim the best scrum in the world. They see things differently – obviously the macho image is important in South America – but all the major rugby nations now realise if you can achieve parity in the scrums and are efficient around the field, you're a more rounded team.

Among the most impressive front rowers in the UK are the Lions pair of Tom Smith (Scotland) and Paul Wallace (Ireland), who are effective around the field while Christian Califano, the Frenchman, was one of the stars of the 1998 Five Nations and is an individual with a huge reputation.

The scrum was a bit of a concern for Wales at the end of '98, but the emergence of Peter Rogers, who played for Transvaal and who specialises at loosehead, and Ben Evans, an extrovert 19-stoner, fixed that. Evans is unlike any prop I've ever encountered – he's always talking and laughing. Initially, I thought no prop could be like that and still play rugby but he's the exception. Wales can also call on David Young, an experienced customer who is coming back from serious injuries.

The **hooker** has to be the team's best lineout player. If he cannot throw accurately to ensure his jumpers win possession at the lineout, he's got nothing. Without that, everything else for a hooker is a waste of time.

I had the ultimate professional as my hooker – Sean Fitzpatrick. Our association goes right back to 1982 when, as a young whippersnapper fresh out of the Sacred Heart College, he fronted up at a University club training in Auckland, putting himself forward as a prop. I assessed his physical qualities and said I didn't think he was going to be a dominant player as a prop and that he should try hooker. He wasn't that keen initially but he accepted the wisdom of the inscrutable University senior coach and made the switch.

For a start, he was a hopeless thrower to the lineout. He was nothing if not enthusiastic and talked the position through with Kevin Boyle, who was the Auckland hooker at the time. I know Kevin initially didn't take him seriously. In fact, I think if you'd suggested to Kevin at the time this fresh-faced fellow would play more than 90 tests for the All Blacks in the position, he would have split his sides with laughter.

It's well documented that Fitzy missed a game or two on Auckland's overseas tour in 1984 because he couldn't throw accurately – and there was no greater sin when Andy Haden was the jumper – but such was his dedication he became one of the best throwers-in the game has ever seen. It's incredible to think that in the seven years I coached Auckland, I really only had one hooker. No wonder poor Ross Nesdale decided to try his luck with Ireland!

The way Auckland previously and Wales now play the game, with perpetual movement, it's crucial the thrower hits the button every time, because so many attacking movements have their origin at the lineout.

Ireland's Keith Wood is undoubtedly the best in the world at the moment. He's an extremely good athlete who gives his team the edge. He scored a try against Wales from about 25 metres out by sidestepping the backs. He's got a great attitude.

New Zealand's Anton Oliver, who was young when he hit the international scene, is a player with a big future. He could be world class, especially as he seems to possess his dad's attitude.

Garin Jenkins finished up in the Welsh No 2 jersey, a player I initially misread. I wondered whether he was equipped to play the modern game. Not only can he handle every assignment you offer him, he possesses marvellous leadership qualities and brings out the best in those around him. In addition to Jenkins, there is Jonathon Humphreys, a quality specialist. He had an outstanding game against South Africa but unfortunately injury curtailed his international season.

South Africa's James Dalton is a great competitor but has discipline problems while Australia's Phil Kearns, the best in the world at the time of the 1991 World Cup, is probably now past his peak although still extremely competitive.

No matter how gifted your players may be, they are going to need a **coach** to organise them. And what a coach needs to be above all else is a good organiser. Initially, he needs to organise a strong management team around him, then to organise his players. Players need direction. Training sessions must be high intensity and must flow because the way a team trains correlates to the way it plays.

I plan every minute at training, from the first to the 60th (or the 90th if it's an extended session). All those involved must respect the players, because if there is no respect, you've got nothing. The buck stops with the coach. It's no good blaming the doctor or the physio or the manager or your assistant. If there's a problem on the field, it's the coach's problem – there's no way you can dissipate that. Every time a team I am responsible for performs poorly, I look at myself and ask why we stuffed up, knowing that I'm responsible.

The coach needs people around him all working in the same direction, all totally loyal. If you have one individual waiting for you to fail, that is a recipe for disaster. I must say I've been fortunate, with Auckland and now Wales, to have the right people around me.

I can't speak highly enough of John Graham, who was my assistant when I first took over the Auckland team in 1991. I hadn't played rugby to representative or international level, but he had, which gave him credibility. We were coaching guys who were seasoned All Blacks and so his hard-nosed attitude was crucial. It wasn't that I didn't think I could do the job, but he made it so much easier.

Mac McCallion, who assisted me with the Auckland Blues, was another great supporter of the cause. A straight-up-and-down character, he was hellishly loyal, backing me 100 per cent of the way. I sometimes wondered if our roles had been reversed whether I would have been as good as Mac and I think it unlikely.

As a coach himself, he did extremely well at Counties-Manukau with limited talent. Year in, year out, he had his side competitive. It was sad he didn't win the Blues appointment after I moved to Wales. He deserved the job but the NZRFU allowed its bias for the corporate image to influence it in making the appointment. Mac, in their eyes, obviously didn't come from the right side of the tracks. It was a wrong decision.

New Zealand has a rich base of coaching talent which the NPC and Super 12 championships have helped promote. Robbie Deans, who put it over Auckland in the 1997 NPC final, is one with a future, I believe. He has a good balance in his approach and relates well to provincial and international players alike. Wayne Smith and Steve Hansen, who are now in charge of the Canterbury Crusaders, are an effective twosome. They obviously do their homework and have their team playing attractive, attacking rugby.

Tony Gilbert emerged in 1998 as I was preparing to move on. He did amazingly well to bring the Highlanders from last to fourth, then confirmed his talent as a coach by taking out the NPC with Otago. It was great to see the southern men finally in the winner's circle because through most of my time with Auckland, Otago, while always competitive and attractive to watch, never managed to pull off the big one. The great thing about Otago – which is a tribute to its earlier coach Gordon Hunter – is that it was never overawed. Hunter's team beat the Springboks in 1994 and played some marvellous rugby without, as I say, hitting the jackpot.

Remarkably, Gilbert did the job at his first attempt. Although 50-something is late to enter the representative coaching scene, Gilbert obviously possesses special qualities as a coach and it wouldn't be surprising to see him going higher. He's already picked up the New Zealand Colts.

I always enjoyed Frank Oliver's company because Frank was Frank, totally upfront with no hidden agendas. A genuine rugby person, he's there for the game. It's obvious people enjoy working and playing for him.

John Boe is a successful provincial coach who put Waikato back on the map and then did the job with the New Zealand under-19 team at the world championship. He deserves an opportunity to demonstrate his skills at a higher level.

On the international scene, I've been enormously impressed with Nick Mallett and Rod Macqueen. Mallett is a balanced person who can speak three languages. He went out of his way to chat after the South Africa-Wales game last November. His record since he took over the Boks in 1997 speaks for itself. Rod and I developed an excellent relationship when he was coaching the ACT Brumbies. He took over a rag-tag assortment of players and organised them into Australia's most potent Super 12 side and, if that wasn't impressive enough, in 1998 he claimed three straight test victories over the All Blacks.

Scotland's Jim Telfer, who seems to have been in the job forever and who is an unashamed fan of New Zealand methods, is going out with a bang. After his team scored that thrilling win over France in Paris, we conspired to get it the Five Nations title by defeating England. Jim has mellowed over the years and become more successful because of it. He obviously realised that relationships with your players are as important as tactics. To be successful as a coach you need the total package.

I enjoyed Pierre Villepreux's company before and after Wales' game in Paris. A legend as a player, he's into quality 15-man rugby. Somehow, the French team he and Jean-Claude Skrela prepare managed to lose its way in 1998, but they have enough quality players available to remedy that pretty quickly.

Warren Gatland does not have a lot of experience in coaching but has been doing an excellent job with Ireland. One of his problems is that so few of the Irish national squad actually play their rugby in Ireland. The greater percentage of them are involved each weekend across the water in England. Quite a few of the Welsh boys are contracted to English clubs too, but we're only a couple of hours drive away. I hate to think how many times a season the leading Irish players have to fly across the Irish Sea.

Since he took over, Clive Woodward has done an excellent job with England. It's not an easy job he's got, with all the media hype, but he and John Mitchell (it's astonishing how many Kiwis are involved in important coaching positions around the world now) have moulded a powerful side which will take all sorts of beating at the World Cup.

Bryan Williams has been achieving wonders for a number of years with Samoa which, when it gathers its best players together from the four corners of the globe, ranks right up among the best cluster of teams in the world. Beegee and I have got on okay in recent times – I think he eventually forgave me for criticising him and Maurice Trapp when they were coaching Auckland back in 1991.

Chapter 12

And so to the World Cup

Complacency is the last hurdle any winner, any team must overcome before attaining potential greatness. Complacency is the Success Disease: it takes root when you're feeling good about who you are and what you've achieved.

Pat Riley, basketball coach, The Winner Within

NOTHING ANNOYS A COACH – particularly this coach – more than when a player witlessly concedes a free kick or penalty, or, worse still, gets sent to the sin bin for undisciplined play. To me, it's unforgivable. One moment of indiscipline by a thoughtless player can cost his side victory.

We had a transparent attitude regarding onfield behaviour when I was associated with Auckland and the Blues. It was something I reminded the players of every week and I became very, very angry when anyone transgressed.

In the old days, before video surveillance at rugby fields, players could sometimes get away with merry hell. There was a certain rough justice about it all and offenders were often dealt with summarily on the field – they didn't have to attend judicial committee meetings to learn their fate! Unfortunately, there were always a few rogues about who wanted to get their retaliation in first and others who didn't consider their weekend of rugby complete without smacking one of the opposition.

Those days, thank goodness, are now in the past. The lawmakers have done a great job in cleaning up the game, which is so important for rugby's image. Hundreds of thousands of people, probably millions actually, watch every Super 12 and international game and the last thing you want them to see is skullduggery going unchecked. You still get the occasional incident, but nothing like the thuggish behaviour that marred the 1994 NPC final between Auckland and North Harbour.

I remind the players of any team I'm responsible for of the need for discipline, no matter how severely they might be provoked. For the 1999 Super 12, the referees determined that punching of any kind would incur a yellow card, which meant 10 minutes in the sin bin. That means you'd have to be an absolute clod to throw a punch in any circumstance, because of the dire consequences. Yet every week there was someone being given 10 minutes on the sideline for punching. Games were being won and lost while thoughtless players were off the field.

In Wales' game against South Africa at Wembley, with the scores locked at 20-all, the South Africans were handed the opportunity to rescue the game through a moment of hotheadedness by one of our players. We'd been awarded a penalty and Neil Jenkins was coming forward to kick for goal, a critical moment in the game. Suddenly a scuffle broke out and a Welsh player lost his cool. Next thing, the referee reversed the penalty. The relieved Springboks kicked themselves onto attack and set up the lineout from which they scored the winning try.

Although there was a lot to admire about the Welsh performance that afternoon, that particular incident irritated me. It's a process of maturity which seems to have been lacking from Welsh play in recent times. Players have allowed themselves to be provoked and seem to think it's acceptable to whack an opponent. It's something I've noticed is prevalent in club rugby in Wales and it has been permitted to carry over to the national team. I reckon I saw more fights in my first two months in Wales than in 10 years back in New Zealand. You can't win at top level if you allow yourself to get dragged into that sort of crap.

If you watch the Tri-series teams, New Zealand, Australia and South Africa – who on performances in recent years rank one, two and three in the world (not necessarily in that order) – you appreciate that they are all extremely well controlled. You'd be lucky to see one punch thrown, or a serious scuffle, in the entire series. That's where the modern game is going, although it's not fully appreciated by every club in Wales just yet.

We have a code of conduct in the UK which only goes part of the way towards keeping the game clean. I'd like to see the introduction of a system with more teeth, perhaps where players, who are all contracted and on generous incomes now, are fined if they transgress. Nothing hurts a rugby player more than raiding his pocket.

If players discipline themselves, that's one less factor with which the poor coach has to concern himself. Then basically all he's got to worry about are the enemy and the referees, whose sometimes original interpretations of the laws can frustrate players and have an influence on the result.

If rugby coaches had a collective wish, it would be that all referees were perfect. They in turn would seek to have all players and coaches operate entirely within the law, which is an equally impossible dream.

Games are won and lost on refereeing decisions. Unfortunately, sometimes those decisions are patently wrong. But you accept that – it's the rub of the green. With my first two games as coach of Wales, I experienced the two extremes. Against South Africa, several critical decisions went against us and we lost. Against Argentina, the decisions went our way and we won.

I guess as a coach, all you can ask for is neutrality, honesty and consistency. Like the players (and coaches too), referees will inevitably make mistakes. Although from my experience, the best referees make fewer mistakes.

Cricket has embraced the electronic age, with third umpires utilising television replays to make judgments on run outs, stumpings, catches and whether the ball has crossed the boundary. I'm often asked whether I believe rugby should make greater use of video replays and, generally speaking, I have to say no. While there might be an argument for having a camera focussed on the deadball line, it would be to the detriment of the game to repeatedly halt play while a "fourth umpire" ruled on every questionable decision. It would quickly become tedious. No, the game at top level now has three highly-qualified officials in charge who collectively are capable of making all the decisions that have to be made. Inevitably, the human factor means there will be mistakes but you have to accept that. You just hope that any monumental blunders don't go against your side. For example, in a Super 12 match at Durban in March, the Otago Highlanders' No 12 was despatched to the sin bin for 10 minutes on the ruling of a touch judge when television replays clearly indicated the guilty party was No 13. At least, the right team was involved, but it showed how even the best officials can get basic things wrong. The No 13 was subsequently cited and received a three-week suspension, so the hapless Highlanders were penalised twice for the one offence!

There are some extremely competent people refereeing at the top level, although there are huge demands on them these days. Their often hectic schedules mean they can be physically and mentally drained at times, and they don't have the camaraderie of a team situation to fall back on. At best they travel in pairs and hope their colleague is a good mate. Quite often, their appointments are in foreign-speaking countries which only adds to the challenge. I spoke to a couple of New Zealand's top-ranking referees who told me how taxing it was to fly around the world to the UK or South Africa and strive to shrug off tiredness and jetlag and be at the peak of their powers for the 80 minutes of the international with which they had been entrusted. If administrators want referees to operate to their potential, they've got to look after them.

The ideal referee is a fellow who controls play effectively and efficiently but remains No 31. Regrettably, with the adjustments to law interpretations that have hit in during 1999, too many of the game's arbitrators have been featuring as No 1. Down Under, I know it's been a source of great concern with coaches, media and public all outraged.

Personally, I believe the ball-carrying side should have the advantage, but I know there are administrators in the UK who felt the laws were seriously stacked against the side without the ball. Which is why referees are now interpreting the tackle ball situation differently, giving the tackled player and tackler no rights. All the advantage is now with the arriving players, provided they stay on their feet. In theory, it's workable, but in practice it's becoming a nightmare because not every referee is ruling on this aspect of play the same way. The lineout used to be the major source of penalties but now probably 50 per cent of rugby's penalties are coming from tackle ball situations. It's something that needs to be sorted out before the showpiece of the sport, the fourth Rugby World Cup, unfolds in October and November. Devotees of other sports are hardly likely to be won over to rugby if they see a penalty awarded every time a player is tackled.

It's easy to coach stationary set-piece situations, where every player has a role, but it's a huge challenge right now to prime players on how to deal with the tackle situation with defensive and offensive players coming in from all angles. Until a ruck forms, there is no off-side, so it's open slather, or mayhem, or whatever you want to call it, and players are having to make assessments and decisions at speed.

Previously, the team in possession didn't have tacklers interfering with the ball presentation, which naturally allowed them to free it up again and achieve continuity. This inevitably led to tries being scored. But tries from such situations are drying up because the ball is being contested by both sides and defences are now better organised. It's rare for a team to commit more than three or four forwards to a ruck, the residue now taking up station in midfield to reinforce the backline defence.

The amended lineout and scrum laws of recent years had a major influence on how the game was played, for the better. Essentially, it meant if you were in possession, you couldn't afford to give the ball away. If you kicked it out, you weren't going to get it back. So if you did kick, it had to be planned and designed to pressure the opposition.

Counter-attack became an art form because teams weren't prepared to put the ball into touch. So did offensive defence, because teams realised the only way they could regain possession was through a turnover following a tackle. The stronger the tackle, the more likely the opposition was to yield the ball.

Over the past year or so defence has become the most developed area of the game. If you look at the trends in the Super 12, there were, on average, six tries a game in 1997 and 1998 but this year it's down to an average of less than three tries a game. These things go in cycles. Now coaches are looking at ploys to break these strong defences and chip kicks are coming back into vogue.

We got the scrums and lineouts right a couple of years back and this in turn encouraged consistently spectacular (ball in hand) running rugby. Now the game is being slowed up because it is defence dominated. If the tackle ball area could be tidied up, it would help the flow of the game again.

The referees held a meeting in Vancouver early in 1999 in which they determined that in the year of the World Cup they would referee strictly according to the charter. This was a northern hemisphere-driven incentive, one of the reasons being they considered that in the Super 12 and Tri-nations competitions the players were being allowed to hold possession too long when tackled. The law actually states that the tackled player should place or release the ball "immediately" and southern hemisphere referees were, in the interests of a freer-flowing game, applying a more generous interpretation of the term.

As a consequence of the charter being applied so rigidly, penalties came in bucketloads at the start of this year's Super 12 competition and I know players and coaches were perplexed. Penalty counts increased dramatically while games became more static and tryscoring dried up. In two of the Auckland Blues games (against the Queensland Reds and the Sharks) there were no tries scored at all. When you consider the average number of points per game in Auckland Blues Super 12 matches in 1997, when I was involved, was 60, that's a pretty dramatic meltdown.

Because the leading referees are understandably seeking World Cup appointments, they began diligently applying the directive which came out of the Vancouver summit. The referees were obviously concerned that if they were seen applying a looser interpretation of the post-tackle law, they would be downgraded. As a result, they went overboard. The coaches, not being silly, would have quickly identified the tackle area as a turnover zone and would have trained their players to be first on the spot to secure the ball. So the post-tackle area started producing either turnovers or penalties. At the end of the day, the referees' uncompromising interpretation has produced a shambles and the game has suffered as a spectacle.

At the time I moved from New Zealand to Wales, I considered southern hemisphere referees attack-friendly and their northern hemisphere counterparts defence-friendly. Because of this, when nations from the two hemispheres opposed each other, the northern countries were disadvantaged because they were unfamiliar with the greater tempo at which the game was being played. A classic example (disregarding the absence of a substantial number of leading individuals which obviously affected the outcome) was England's 76-0 thrashing by Australia at Brisbane in 1998. The

English players were in the game until 10 minutes before halftime, then collapsed with exhaustion.

What we're trying to get to in rugby, hopefully soon, is a universal consistency in the interpretation of the post-tackle area. I was involved with the laws committee in New Zealand and one of the options we considered was the establishment of an offside line at the tackle. I believe it has merit but I also believe we need to have some games of an experimental nature to determine whether it would be a positive law. It could revolutionise the game, make it more attacker-friendly. Then again, it may become impossible to achieve turnovers – which are an important element in the game – if that offside line is introduced. Until we experiment, it's hard to say what the effect would be. Maybe we're better off with the current law – once players and coaches become more efficient at it.

Rugby is a lot more physical in the UK, I've discovered, definitely more macho. I think this attitude is possibly waning, which would be a good thing. Fortunately, Scotland came through to win the Five Nations championship with a refreshingly different approach, because in recent years the competition has been dominated by teams with powerhouse forwards and accurate goalkickers. Scotland blew that concept out the water, succeeding by keeping the ball available for long periods. And I'd like to think that Wales' attacking game also enhanced the competition in 1999. The Scots probably mirrored Otago, which had taken out New Zealand's NPC with a similar ball-in-hand approach. Coach Jim Telfer deserves a pat on the back for his enterprise and, in the context of the Five Nations championship, I guess you'd have to say daring. I wonder what effect John Leslie had by taking the Otago concepts to Scotland.

The general playing conditions in the UK are not conducive to running rugby, except at the international stadiums, which is why the more physical game has flourished. There's a push in Wales, thank goodness, to develop better playing surfaces up to international standard, which is long overdue. It's almost as if there's been a time warp, the terrible muddy surfaces clubs are expected to play on being reminiscent of what New Zealanders used to put up with in the 1950s and 1960s.

You can't play an attacking, ball-in-hand style of rugby when underfoot conditions are atrocious. Even in England, clubs have to contend with some diabolical surfaces. I attended a game between premier clubs Northampton and London Irish, which quickly degenerated into a mud scramble. I had no hope of assessing any of the outside backs on display.

Conversely, of course, the major stadiums in the UK are magnificent and the gem of them all will be Wales' new headquarters, the Millennium Stadium, a brave £126 million project which, not without some anxiety (construction has being going on around the clock for the past year to meet the deadline) will be completed in time for the Rugby World Cup launch at the beginning of October. The state-of-the-art stadium will even have a retractable roof – a famous first for a rugby ground – ensuring that Wales will never have to play another home game in other than perfect conditions. Yet within 10 miles of the Millennium Stadium, club rugby players can be floundering around on appalling surfaces with mud up to their ankles.

When you come from the opposite side of the world, you know you will be amazed by certain aspects of life and living in your new country. As a rugby coach, nothing surprised me more than discovering the significance of the Five Nations tournament. I should have been more aware of its status because it has been running since 1910, whereas the Tri-nations championship, which kicked off in 1996, is still very much in its infancy. I've been blown away with the whole thing – the massive public and media interest, the rivalry between the neighbouring nations and the tension generated. You can't learn about the Five Nations until you've experienced it. Once I cottoned on to what it meant to everyone, I think it helped my coaching. The Five Nations is so important to the players it affects their psyche, so we had to try to change that.

When I was familiarising myself with the Welsh players soon after taking up residence in the northern hemisphere, I asked what the Five Nations meant to them. The responses were extraordinary. One said success correlated to the wellbeing of the nation, another described it as the equal of war. Apparently, it was not unusual following serious losses for players to remain hidden in their homes till the following Wednesday or Thursday, unprepared to face the public. The performances of the Welsh team certainly have a major bearing on the mood of the nation. When Wales win, the percentage of people who go to work increases significantly and newspaper sales go up. There's an incredible story about a fellow who sold the slate off his roof so he could buy a ticket to a Five Nations match.

WESTERN MAIL

Leader, 13 April (following Wales' 32-31 win over England)

Does anyone still doubt the effect that the game of rugby can have on the mood of the population of Wales? Since Sunday there has been a smile on the face of every Welsh fan who watched in glee as Messrs Gibbs and Jenkins snatched a famous victory from under the noses of England in the grandest of finals.

There are men and women across Wales who have had previous little to cheer of late: factory workers who have seen their jobs disappear, farmers who have watched their livelihoods wither away, ex-miners who have had to wait in pain for compensation for industrial injuries.

The fortunes of the Welsh rugby team may seem trifling in comparison but successive victories in Paris, Treviso and at Wembley have done wonders to lift the morale.

With both the National Assembly and the Rugby World Cup looming and with Welsh rock bands still calling the tune, this certainly can be a great year for Wales.

It's no wonder a perplexed coach has to reach for a cigarette every now and then. Do I smoke? Yes, but not in public, only socially. And not during the summer. It's stupid, but I only resume smoking when the rugby season kicks off which probably says something about the anxieties rugby coaches have to endure!

I never smoke during a game. Not because I don't want to, but because I consider it important young people should not see me puffing away. I'll wait till I get home before I light up. There's a strong link between rugby and cigarettes with me, which I'm not pleased about.

How do I relax away from rugby? Well, Raewyn will tell you there haven't been a lot of holidays on the Riviera, or even at Auckland's surf beach Piha, which in a way is why it's so nice to be based in the UK for five years, with the continent so accessible. We see it all as a great adventure, giving us the opportunity to meet people and visit new places.

For more years than I care to admit to, I was always impossibly busy, as a teacher, then a headmaster and a rugby coach. There wasn't time for much else, especially as Raewyn and I were raising a family of three. I worked long hours during the day and topped up at home in the evenings.

During those years, I never bothered with what you would call a personal life. Relaxation, I guess, was talking rugby with colleagues over a few beers at the Barbarians club. Otherwise, all my energies went into my family, my job and my sport... and not always in that order. I was so lucky to have a positive family life. It's only in recent years, with some good professional advice, that I've even thought about my future. I had enough problems keeping my own backyard in order without bothering about other places, but I was convinced I should invest in real estate and as a consequence bought a couple of properties in Auckland... a bit of insurance for our old age.

The relationship between Raewyn and I has been pretty unique, I would think. While I've been committed to rugby and cricket, she's always been involved in netball and basketball. We were enthusiastic participants before we both became coaches. I guess it was a special achievement in 1997 when Raewyn was appointed coach of the Auckland netball team while I was coach of the Auckland rugby team. There wouldn't be too many husband-wife partnerships both coaching at top representative level.

We met at Otago University where we were both pursuing physical education degrees and right from the start we always had sport as a powerful common interest. I doubt our marriage would have survived had Raewyn not been as besotted with sport as I was. It's important to have a partner who understands where you're coming from and what you're striving to achieve. More than that, she has a good eye for talent and has often spotted a player of exceptional skill before I have. She's come up with the odd suggestion regarding tactics too which has been most helpful.

Raewyn is a thoroughly pleasant person, balanced and with a positive outlook on life. She always got on well with the Auckland boys. They understood each other, which was bloody marvellous because at times our home was a cross between the Auckland team's dressing room at Eden Park and Grand Central Railway Station, with all sorts of people coming and going.

Raewyn was supportive over the move to Wales. If I'm totally honest, I'd have to say I entered into negotiations without knowing whether she was interested in uprooting herself from Auckland and moving to another country. She's sacrificed her own interests to come to Cardiff which is a huge thing. How can you thank someone for doing that?

Apart from joining me for a time when I was researching Blackheath on behalf of Auckland the previous year, Raewyn had never been to Europe, so now that it's all happening, we see the five years in Wales as an exciting challenge. I'm determined to give the job 12 out of 10. When you coach Auckland, there's a huge expectation to win, because for almost two decades Auckland has been a winning side. Wales, however, is a different, stimulating, challenge. I'm taking over a team which has been underachieving for a long time, in a country where the people are passionate about the game and desperate for success. Despite their intensity and enthusiasm, the expectation is not to win every game. Well, that's not my philosophy. I do expect any team I am responsible for to win every game – that's always been my attitude. The day I say I expect my team to lose is the day I announce my retirement from coaching.

Kiwis who call on us at the Coach House invariably ask Raewyn and I whether we are missing Auckland. If I'm dead honest, I'd have to say yes. There are lots of things I miss – walking our dog through Cornwall Park in the morning, the beaches around Auckland and on the Coromandel Peninsula, Auckland's restaurants, the warmer climate, all our friends and family, mates calling in, following the fortunes of the New Zealand cricket team, backyard barbecues. Actually, the climate being what it is in Wales, I can't see me hosting too many barbecues at the Coach House!

Over a period of 10 years or so, Raewyn and I had renovated our Epsom house, developing it into the perfect family home – open plan, the sort of house family and visitors alike could relax in regardless of who was doing what. And usually Raewyn and I were involving ourselves in the happenings of our respective sports teams in some form or other.

However, while I do miss those things, I'm finding our new existence in Wales stimulating. Obviously the rugby is a massive challenge and with a tour of Argentina coming up in June and the World Cup tournament fast approaching, it's consuming nearly all my time. After seven years with Auckland, I needed a change and there was no greater, more exciting, challenge on offer than the Welsh national team. For me, it's been a total immersion in Welsh rugby. I don't consider my involvement starts and finishes with the national team – I'd quickly get bored if that was the extent of my brief. I'm also involving myself with the second tier of players and helping to establish an infrastructure that hopefully will guarantee continuing success for Welsh rugby long after Graham Henry has departed the scene. I've made a commitment to Welsh rugby (until the year 2003) and I'm happy with that.

ROB HOWLEY
Welsh captain
Graham Henry has turned around Welsh rugby by himself. I didn't believe anyone had the vision, ability and understanding to do that. It takes a hell of a man to leave the position he held back in Auckland to take on Wales, given the situation we were in. Since his arrival he's transformed the game over here.

He's given confidence to players like Neil Jenkins, Craig Quinnell and Chris Wyatt. I don't know anyone else who could have achieved what he has in such a short time.

There have been two defining moments in his time with Wales. The first was when we reassembled following the Springbok game. I think most people in Wales were happy with the performance considering the results that had gone before. But Graham was obviously disappointed we had lost. He stressed to us that we'd been in a position to beat South Africa and hadn't. Most other coaches would have been satisfied, I'm sure. Graham wasn't.

Then after the Irish loss, he reminded us of the attacking game he wanted us to play. It took a strong coach to stick with the declared policy. It would have been easier, after two losses, to have thrown the whole lot out the window. But Graham had a vision of how he wanted us to play. His tactical plan would manifest itself magnificently in Paris.

I would still like to coach the All Blacks – I wouldn't be a Kiwi if that wasn't my ambition. However, that's impossible with the present constitution forbidding individuals who have taken up coaching appointments with other countries from ever being associated with New Zealand's national team. I believe the union will have to re-examine its constitution because I think it will be impossible to sustain. In the corporate business world, appointments go to individuals who can claim overseas experience. But the NZRFU is penalising coaches who go overseas. A coach couldn't have a better grounding than what I'm doing, preparing a national team to compete in the Five Nations championship and at the World Cup. New Zealand's attitude defies logic.

When you're living in New Zealand, it's a major mission to travel overseas, unless you're popping across to Australia or up to Fiji. You're confined to an aircraft for more than 24 hours to get to Europe, South Africa or South America. Which is one reason it's such a blessing to be based in the UK. We're only a stone's throw from Europe, as Raewyn appreciated when she went on a walking tour of Tuscany with some friends. I will be diverting to Portugal and Spain at some point to arrange a summer training camp. And with Raewyn and I being wine buffs, I would image we'll probably check out an assortment of the superior wine-growing regions of France during the summer. They're scarcely an hour's flight from Heathrow.

It's taking a while to adjust to the full-on attitude of the Welsh to rugby. Everybody, and I mean everybody, is interested in rugby. The game has been referred to as a religion in New Zealand. Well, in Wales it's more like an infectious disease that has ravaged the entire population confined to that comparatively small area bordered by the Bristol Channel, the Irish Sea and, to the east, the English border. The people are friendly and open and want to be part of the scene, which is great. However, it can be overpowering at times.

I understand a controversial issue back in New Zealand is whether players operating overseas – in Japan, France and the UK, for example – should be eligible for All Black selection, which at the moment they're not. In this instance, I agree with the NZRFU. To qualify for All Black selection, you should be resident within New Zealand.

You can see the problems they have with the New Zealand league team – it's impractical. You would be herding players together from all over the globe. Overseas clubs, reluctant to release individuals, would give them the minimum amount of time off, so they'd be jetlagged to hell preparing for tests. It would be difficult for the selectors, too. How do you compare a centre playing in France with one performing in the Super 12? The Super 12 is the ultimate trial ground for All Black selection. You would open a rare old can of worms if you introduced an open selection policy.

The fourth Rugby World Cup is going to be a marvellous

occasion for the Principality of Wales. The opening match, the grand final, one quarter-final and a fair number of pool matches will all be staged in the new Millennium Stadium, a centrepiece right in the heart of Cardiff. Apart from a rugby field, the new complex will feature restaurants, bars and shops, conference facilities and a riverwalk alongside the Taff. It will be absolutely fabulous and will be the focal point of a major redevelopment of Cardiff.

From a playing viewpoint, the stadium will give a major boost to Wales which has had no significant home games for two years while the stadium has been under construction. When you think of the atmosphere created at Wembley, Wales' makeshift home, you can imagine what it's going to be like in the Millennium Stadium when 75,000 fans cram in. The atmosphere will be electric – I just hope as a team we can do justice to it.

You can't help but admire the Welsh Rugby Union for having the balls to push ahead with the project. Glanmore Griffiths, the WRU chairman, had a vision and has been the driving force behind it. I'm sure he was elated when Wales defeated the Big Two, France and England, because at the time the decision was taken to replace Cardiff Arms Park, Welsh rugby certainly had its share of problem, not least its humble standing on the international stage. Bass Breweries, a corporate giant, has been granted pouring rights for the new stadium. Perhaps the wins in Paris and at Wembley helped clinch the deal.

At the beginning of 1999 it was popularly believed the major southern hemisphere nations, South Africa, Australia and New Zealand, would again dominate the World Cup, but I fancy there has been a shortening of the gap in playing strength between the two hemispheres. It's hard to say, for sure. When the UK teams toured Down Under in 1998, they were all ludicrously under-strength, while the Springboks and the Wallabies appeared jaded when they played in Europe. So we won't know for sure what's happening until all the nations, hopefully at the peak of their powers, come together in October.

Prior to the '99 Five Nations, you'd have said England and France would be Europe's best hopes of taking down the Big Three and that Samoa, Argentina, Scotland, Wales and perhaps Ireland would be competitive. But what we saw in the Five Nations championship has probably caused many to take a re-assessment and that includes the bookies who shortened Wales' odds from 100 to 1 to 25 to 1! Scotland came from rank outsiders to win the Five Nations championship and did so with such effectiveness – scoring a startling 16 tries in the process – that no team can be looking forward to tangling with the rejuvenated Scots (kilted Kiwis and all) on Murrayfield.

The Springboks have drawn the same pool as Scotland, so they know they'll be in for a torrid battle. Likewise, the All Blacks who are drawn to play England at Twickenham. They'll find that a hell of a lot different from playing England (a depleted England at that) at Carisbrook and Eden Park. That in itself is going to make the fourth World Cup the most competitive yet.

I guess the Springboks, who until they stumbled at Twickenham late in 1998 – when they were plainly suffering from an excess of rugby – were patently the most accomplished team in the world, would have to start favourites. Under Nick Mallett's guidance, they seem to be a bit ahead of their rivals. Apart from their awesome record, they have got their whole act together. They have an inspiring captain in Gary Teichmann (and another dynamic leader coming through in Bobby Skinstad), a good nucleus of international players, a settled team and a selection of gamebreakers (individuals like Skinstad, Joost van der Westhuizen, Henry Honiball and Pieter Rossouw). They'd won 17 tests in a row before losing at Twickenham, which emphasises their effectiveness. Mallett is such an astute person, he may well experiment during the Tri-nations series, knowing that the ultimate prize for any rugby nation in 1999 is the Webb Ellis Trophy.

The next group would comprise Australia, New Zealand and England and, until they derailed themselves during the Five Nations, should also have featured France. The French are in turmoil at the moment, bedevilled with injuries to leading players and obviously confused as to the game plan they should be pursuing. Hopefully for them, they'll unravel some of those problems on their mid-year tour of New Zealand.

We probably did the English an enormous favour, defeating them in the Five Nations decider at Wembley. Clive Woodward and his players would have been gutted by the result which will only serve to steel them for the World Cup challenge. It will really sharpen them up. They are an impressive team and they'll dissect what happened at Wembley, I'm sure, and be the stronger for it.

As I told a journalist back in April, they'll be on the edge of the edge, a frame of mind essential to beat my old mates from New Zealand.

The English possess as powerful a pack as exists in world rugby right now while the management and leadership and quality of players puts them up with the best. They possess arguably the best back five in the world and their defensive organisation is colossal. As a team, they've been together for a long time now and have a settled combination. The loss to Wales might be just the lesson they needed to help them become the first northern hemisphere nation to win the World Cup.

Unquestionably, England's clash with New Zealand in pool play is going to be one of the most critical encounters of the entire tournament because the loser will face a horrendous route to the final, starting with a quarter-final against the Springboks in Paris (presuming the Boks have survived their Murrayfield ordeal against the Scots).

Australia's prospects will depend hugely on the rate of recovery of three of its superstars – John Eales, Matt Burke and Stephen Larkham – who in mid-year were all sidelined, recovering from major injuries. Eales is crucial to the Aussie campaign, as a lineout specialist, captain and, quite remarkably for a hard-toiling forward, as a goalkicker. There would be a huge question mark over Australia if these three didn't front up.

The Wallabies have responded well to Rod Macqueen's coaching and he'll have them mentally attuned for the World Cup. There's a composure and intelligence about his teams which, to a degree, reflects where they come from. Rugby is essentially a private schools game in Australia; thus those who play it are equipped to compete at the top. They're one of the more intelligent teams in the world. If you compare the numbers playing rugby in Australia with New Zealand, their success rate over the last 15 years is phenomenal.

New Zealand had problems leading into the first World Cup back in 1987 yet bounced back spectacularly to triumph. The nation will be hoping history repeats itself in 1999. New Zealand sportsmen always respond when they're under pressure, particularly the All Blacks, and after the shock of losing five tests in a row last year, the management and players will be grimly determined to turn things around. It's in New Zealand's favour that the wheels fell off in 1998. If it had happened this year, there wouldn't be time to correct the situation.

If they can seal over some of the cracks that appeared last year, the All Blacks are well capable of winning the tournament again because in Jeff Wilson, Jonah Lomu, Christian Cullen (if he recaptures his best), Robin Brooke and Josh Kronfeld they possess a set of dynamic gamebreakers.

The selectors took steps in '98 to correct the downward slide by introducing fresh players like Carl Hoeft, Royce Willis and Kees Meeuws. There are a hell of a lot of quality players in New Zealand and it might require the introduction of a few more talented young stars before the rejuvenation process is complete. Obvious areas of concern last year were the midfield and No 8. With seven tests to play before the World Cup, I'm sure John Hart and his assistants will remedy those problems.

Scotland was a revelation in the Five Nations and there's no reason why Jim Telfer's team shouldn't carry that winning form through into the World Cup. They have stability up front, quality lineout jumpers – with Scott Murray among the most improved tight forwards on the international scene – a dependable halfback and highly competitive captain in Gary Armstrong, quality five-eighths and determined finishers out wide. Every opponent is going to have to take special precautions to keep Gregor Townsend and John Leslie under control. The Scots could be the dark horses and their clash with the Springboks in pool play is going to be extremely interesting.

Ireland has made solid progress under Warren Gatland and will have to be respected at Lansdowne Road. Its pool includes Australia, who will be only too mindful of what happened there in 1991. And I'm sure the French will come right. They haven't won two Grand Slams without quality players. They just seem to have lost their way a bit tactically but with the home advantage, I'm sure they will be among the top five or six teams.

Samoa and Argentina are two nations to be respected. The Samoans possess outstanding leadership with Bryan Williams, Pat Lam and Inga Tuigamala calling the shots. They also boast an abundance of international experience and having qualified for the quarter-finals at the two previous World Cups will be primed to go at least that far again. Argentina is one of the fast developing rugby nations of the world. If it can develop attacking back play to complement its awesome scrum, it will make an impact. The pool featuring Samoa, Argentina and Wales is one of the most competitive, with Wales determined to avenge its shock loss in the 1991 tournament.

And what of Wales? We're in the infancy of our development and although we've had a couple of good results, realistically we'll be stronger contenders in 2003. We're going to give it our best shot and the home advantage has to be worth something. But our tight five's full of rookies and we don't have great depth. Nor do we have gamebreakers like Jeff Wilson or Bobby Skinstad. But we do have tenacity and a bit of steel which counts when you're playing at that level. Our first challenge is to get past Argentina and Samoa in what is an extremely challenging pool.

So my tip for 6 November, the day of the final? If I was a betting man, and thank goodness I'm not, I'd probably go for a South Africa-England quinella.

Graham Henry's
Coaching Record

	Played	Won	Lost	Drew	% Success
Auckand Grammar School	102	95	7	-	93.14
Auckland University	98	79	17	2	81.63
NZ secondary schools	19	17	2	-	89.47
Auckland Colts	40	39	1	-	97.50
Auckland B	9	6	2	1	72.22
Auckland	102	80	22	-	78.43
Auckland Blues	39	32	6	1	83.33
Wales	7	4	3	-	57.14
Totals	**416**	**352**	**60**	**4**	**85.10**